SLAVERY AND THE EVOLUTION
OF CHEROKEE SOCIETY

SLAVERY AND THE EVOLUTION OF CHEROKEE SOCIETY 1540–1866

Theda Perdue

THE UNIVERSITY OF TENNESSEE PRESS
KNOXVILLE

MANUFACTURED IN THE UNITED STATES OF AMERICA.
FIRST EDITION.

Clothbound editions of
University of Tennessee Press
books are printed on paper designed for an effective life
of at least 300 years, and binding materials are chosen
for strength and durability.

Library of Congress Cataloging in Publication Data

Perdue, Theda, 1949–
Slavery and the evolution of Cherokee society, 1540–
1866.

Bibliography: p.
Includes index.
1. Cherokee Indians—Slaves, Ownership of.
2. Indians of North America—Slaves, Ownership of.
3. Afro-Americans—Relations with Indians. 4. Slavery
in the United States. I. Title.
E99.C5P394 301.45'19'7073 78-16284
ISBN 0-87049-259-4

FOR MY PARENTS

Howard and Ouida Perdue

Contents

	Acknowledgments	*page ix*
	Prologue	*xi*
1	Aboriginal Cherokee Bondage	*3*
2	Cherokees and the Indian Slave Trade	*19*
3	Red-Black Contact	*36*
4	The Development of Plantation Slavery	*50*
5	Post-Removal Chaos	*70*
6	Masters and Slaves	*96*
7	Civil War in the Cherokee Nation	*119*
	Epilogue	*141*
	Notes	*146*
	Bibliographical Essay	*174*
	Bibliography	*183*
	Index	*199*

MAPS

1	Major Indian Groups and European Positions in the Colonial Southeast	*page 10*
2	Participants in the South Carolina Indian Slave Trade	*24*
3	The Cherokee Trade	*27*
4	Land Cession and Removal	*86*
5	The American Civil War in Indian Territory	*133*

Acknowledgments

In the course of my research and writing, I incurred a number of debts to both individuals and institutions. F.N. Boney, Constance Head, Alf Heggoy, Aubrey C. Land, William G. McLoughlin, Ronald N. Satz, and Max Williams carefully read either all or part of this work and made many helpful criticisms and suggestions. In addition to evaluating the manuscript, Mary E. Young generously shared pertinent information from her own research. James M. Gifford directed me to material on the African colonization movement, and Gary White drew the maps which illustrate the text. Laura King provided Cherokee words, and Duane King located eighteenth-century villages. My department head, Ellerd Hulbert, and my colleagues at Western Carolina University offered support and encouragement, and the students who have worked in the history department over the last three years, particularly Lynda Morgan, assisted me in many ways. Terry Nienhuis tackled stylistic problems, and Jeanne Nienhuis typed countless drafts and buoyed my flagging spirits.

I completed this work with the aid of a research grant from the Graduate School of Western Carolina University, a summer stipend from the National Endowment for the Humanities, a fellowship from the Newberry Library Center for the History of the American Indian, and financial assistance from the office of Western Carolina University Vice-Chancellor Robert E. Stoltz.

Some of the ideas and material contained in this study appeared previously in "People Without a Place: Aboriginal Cherokee Bondage" (*Indian Historian*, July 1976) and in "Cherokee Planters: The Development of Plantation Slavery before Removal" (*The Cherokee Indian Nation: A Troubled History*, edited by Duane King, University of Tennessee Press, 1979).

Finally, my greatest intellectual debts are to Charles Hudson, who taught me that social, political, and economic institutions reflect fundamental values and beliefs, and to Charles Crowe, who made me aware that even the most objective historical study reflects the values of the historian.

Prologue

Cherokee bondage evolved in a general context of European imperialism and New World slavery.[1] Spurred by the ideals of the Renaissance and the values of the commercial revolution, Europeans began to seek new sources of wealth and to dominate and exploit the lands and peoples they found. Among the European colonizers of the Western Hemisphere, the Cherokees had contact with the Spanish, the French, and particularly the English. At least from the beginning of the eighteenth century, the tribe's relationship with the latter was a major concern for the Cherokees, but the English considered Cherokee relations to be only a small cog in the elaborate machinery involved in empire building. The English had embarked for the New World, not to establish diplomatic alliances with Indian nations, but to discover precious metals and stones. By 1620 many Englishmen realized that the wealth the New World offered the mother country was not gold but land. The introduction of tobacco culture in Virginia pointed the way, and soon profits from the sale of tobacco —and rice, indigo, naval stores, and sugar—began to fill English coffers. All these commodities commanded a sizable European market and promised handsome returns on capital invested in their production. Since land was relatively abundant and inexpensive, profit and production hinged primarily on an adequate supply of labor. The production and cultivation of staples demanded a larger labor force than could be provided by indentured servants and hired hands, so the English as well as other European powers resorted to the enslavement of Africans and Indians for use on their New World plantations.

Slavery became an integral part of European expansion and

the hallmark of European presence in the Americas. Even in those areas such as New England where slave labor was not needed, free workers in mills, factories, shipyards, and distilleries processed raw materials from southern or West Indian plantations and produced goods that found markets in those same regions. New England merchants actively participated in the African slave trade and their ships plied the seas with cargoes produced by slave labor. Furthermore, the impact of slavery extended beyond the colonial empires to continental Europe and particularly to the British Isles, and the institution dramatically altered the European economic scene. The profits from plantations and the African slave trade provided capital for the Industrial Revolution, and New World cotton, which became the major staple crop of the nineteenth century, supplied the textile mills of Europe. Slavery, therefore, should not be viewed narrowly as a minor episode in European colonization but as the institution which made colonies in the Western Hemisphere profitable and fostered the growth of modern capitalism.[2]

Since slavery was so widespread, some slight differences did exist in the status and condition of the slave owing to variations in climate, staple, population distribution, and European empire. Nevertheless, similarities far outweigh differences.[3] Everywhere the slave was chattel property, and his person, his labor, and the product of his labor belonged to his master. The demands of the economic system and of staple production regulated his life. In all fully developed commercial agricultural economies in the New World, custom, religion, or law rarely restrained a slave's master from exercising whatever control or coercion seemed necessary to increase production and to maximize profits.[4] The plantation system, the institution of slavery, and the economic values of these European planters and colonizers were truly alien to the aboriginal Cherokees who lived at the subsistence level and sought harmony with each other and balance with the natural world. The tribe, however, came under the domination of these Europeans whose empires rested on plantation slavery and had to adjust to the new colonial situation.

Native inhabitants of European colonial empires, such as the Cherokees, often react similarly to exploitation and domination.

In *The Colonizer and the Colonized,* Tunisian philosopher Albert Memmi has suggested that the oppressed man initially attempts to divorce himself from his own culture and tries to forge a new identity apart from his own experiences. For this man, according to Memmi, "There is a tempting model very close at hand—the colonizer. The latter suffers none of his deficiencies, has all rights, enjoys every possession and benefits from every prestige. . . . The first ambition of the colonized is to become equal to that splendid model and to resemble him to the point of disappearing in him."[5] However, the colonizer will never accept the colonized as his equal. With the discovery that his imitation of the oppressor has been in vain, the colonized reacts by resurrecting his long-abandoned heritage. "He has been haughtily shown that he could never assimilate with others; he has been scornfully thrown back toward what is in him which could not be assimilated by others. Very well, then! He is, he shall be, that man. The same passion which made him absorb Europe shall make him assert his differences; since those differences, after all, are within him and correctly constitute his true self."[6] The reactions which Memmi has described occur at a social as well as an individual level and may drive one segment of a society toward the values and life-style of the colonizer while leading a second group in the rejection of the colonizer's model and the reaffirmation of traditional relationships and behavior. The usual result is a deep and unresolvable friction between the two groups.

From initial contact with whites to the American Civil War, the Cherokees gradually developed a severe case of this same social schizophrenia. Confronted with the specter of European exploitation and domination, the Cherokees displayed the expected dual reaction and either actively participated in the economic system of Europeans and began to emulate their colonizers or clung to values which sanctioned their aboriginal way of life. The first step for those Cherokees who had made the Europeans their mentors was the acceptance of capitalistic values. The institution of slavery among the Cherokees changed to accommodate this new value system and to support the life-style which developed. As a result the Cherokees altered their social organization, political structure, and economic system. These transformations, of course, did not occur in a vacuum but in response to and as a part of European colonization. Therefore, a study of slavery and the evolution of Cherokee society is merely a chapter in the broader story of the expansion of Western Europe and the impact of capitalistic values and institutions on human societies.

SLAVERY AND THE EVOLUTION OF CHEROKEE SOCIETY

1

Aboriginal Cherokee Bondage

Early Europeans who came into contact with the Cherokees described an indigenous institution they called "slavery." In 1540, for example, the chroniclers of Hernando de Soto's expedition reported the presence of "masters" and "slaves" among the natives they encountered on their trek across what is now the southeastern United States. Their narratives include a particularly detailed account of the Lady of Cofitachequi, apparently a "slaveholder" of great wealth and power whom the invading Spaniards captured along with several of her female attendants. These prisoners finally managed to escape, but other Indians did not have such good fortune. De Soto depended on natives to serve as burdeners in transporting his expedition's supplies and he usually seized the laborers he needed by force, placing them in chains with iron collars around their necks. Occasionally, however, chiefs gave the conquistadors their "slaves" for use by the Spaniards as burdeners. Although de Soto's technique in dealing with the Indians of the Southeast suggests that these "gifts" may have been acquired through duress, his experience indicates that some chiefs did have in their possession individuals whom they could hand over to the Spaniards.[1]

Early European observers of the Cherokees, such as de Soto's chroniclers, assumed that these unfree people occupied a subservient social position and performed a distinct and essential economic function in aboriginal Cherokee society. Europeans were well acquainted with the enslavement of both red and black men to satisfy the persistent demand for labor in their own mercantilist economies, and blinded by their own ethnocentrism, they expected to find an identical economy, demand, and bondage among the native inhabitants of North America. Had these observers managed to overcome their preconceived notions about aboriginal Cherokee society, they would have discovered an egalitarian social system, a sexual division of labor, and a subsistence economy which defied any explanation for bondsmen comprehensible to them. In fact, Cherokee bondsmen bear so little resemblance to European slaves that the term "slave" can perhaps only be used inaccurately. The Cherokees called these unfree people *atsi nahsa'i,* or "one who is owned," and the role they played in aboriginal society can only be discovered within the context of the subsistence economy, the social and political organization, and the values and beliefs which were so alien to early Europeans.

The aboriginal Cherokees obtained their "slaves" or *atsi nahsa'i* almost entirely through the warfare in which they frequently engaged. Europeans commented on the Cherokees' bellicose nature by describing them as "being always at war" and placing "their chief happiness in military glory." In response to calls for peace with the Tuscaroras the Cherokees reportedly replied, "We cannot live without war. Should we make peace with the Tuscaroras, with whom we are at war, we must immediately look for some other, with whom we can be engaged in our beloved occupation." The capture of slaves was a normal practice in aboriginal warfare, and the eighteenth-century British officer Lieutenant Henry Timberlake noted that the Cherokees regarded "slave-catcher" as a military rank, albeit a low one.[2]

Until extensive contact with Europeans and the development of a market for war captives, however, slaves remained only a by-product of conflicts waged primarily for vengeance. Occasionally a peaceful solution could be found for an aggressive act by another tribe, but usually the wronged party responded that "crying blood is quenched with equal blood" and sounded the war signal. Since the object of warfare was to avenge "crying blood," Cherokees placed no premium on the capture of enemy warriors. The victors usually killed the wounded in the field and scalped or dismembered them so that the warriors would have trophies with which to demonstrate their valor. The warriors' aim was never to leave the battlefield until the number of enemy killed equalled the number of tribesmen lost in earlier struggles. The enemy's death was more important by far than his capture, and most prisoners ultimately died from torture. James Adair, an eighteenth-century trader among the Cherokees, observed that "those captives who are pretty far advanced in life as well as in war gradations, always atone for the blood they spilt, by the tortures of fire."[3]

Upon their return from battle, Cherokee warriors delivered a captive intended for torture to their women who first stripped the prisoner and placed wet clay on his head to protect the precious scalp from the flames. Next the women beat the condemned captive with bundles of dry cane as they led him to the stake. After tying the prisoner to a pole with a long vine which allowed freedom of movement within a fifteen foot circle, the women stood within the circle and taunted their unfortunate victim with flaming torches. In defiance of pain, the captive warrior sang war songs about his heroic deeds. The prisoner, when severely burned but not quite dead, received a brief respite so that he could recover enough to offer additional sport to his captors. Finally the victors took the prized scalp of their enemy.[4]

Europeans commonly pointed to incessant intertribal warfare and the practice of torture as proof of the savagery and barbarity of native Americans. Although Cherokees did wage war and torture prisoners in order to terrorize their enemies, the primary motivation was vengeance. Whites did not realize that vengeance was a duty and that Cherokees could not allow the death of a fellow tribesman and particularly a kinsman to go unavenged. The threat of reprisal represented the only legal protection available to Cherokees and those who failed to exact retribution forfeited this source of protection.[5]

In the Cherokee myths collected by the late nineteenth-century anthropologist James Mooney, the bears are represented as having originally been human beings, but they had chosen to live in the woods and consequently acquired fur, claws, and other physical features of bears. Human hunters began to seek bears as game, and when the bears foolishly neglected to avenge the deaths of their own kind, hunters became free to kill them with impunity.[6] In order to avoid the fate of the bears, humans were bound to avenge wrongs committed against them.

The victims of this demand for vengeance attributed their misfortune to "forfeiting the protection of the divine power, by some impurity or other." Cherokees did not view capture as an unavoidable accident, and each individual was responsible for pursuing a course of action designed to preserve his freedom as well as his life. Before embarking on a raid, warriors assembled in the town house for a period of fasting and for purification ceremonies. When the war party left the village, the members obeyed strict rules of behavior in order to avoid any sort of pollution which might jeopardize the venture. The warriors were extremely wary of bad omens, and if a sign indicated divine displeasure, either the entire party or particular individuals returned home to the plaudits of the people for being so sensible. Adair commented that "the more virtuous they are, they reckon the greater will be their success against the enemy."[7] If the raid proved a failure, Cherokees assumed that the participants had abandoned their state of purity and perhaps deserved to be captured. If the prisoners happened to be released, they underwent purification in the village council house upon their return home. Colonel George Chicken, the South Carolina Indian commissioner, observed one such ceremony in 1725 and reported "that when any of these people (who are taken) return back to their own Nation . . . they are kept four days and nights in the Town house and . . . the people of the Town dance all the time."[8]

Generally the Cherokees spared female captives and young prisoners from the torture inflicted upon adult males. An early history of North Carolina insisted that the Indians of that region treated kindly the prisoners who escaped torture and that "in all their wars they never destroy women or children, but carefully preserve them." The warriors supposedly respected the virtue of the women and had never been known "to violate or even attempt the chastity of female captives."[9] This celibacy probably resulted from the widespread practice among southeastern Indians of abstaining from sexual intercourse for several days before, during, and after their return from war and not from an inactive libido or any particular regard for their female prisoners. James Adair, who accompanied a war party in the mid-eighteenth century, noted with assurance that after the period of abstinence "some of them forced their captives, notwithstanding their pressing entreaties and tears."[10]

Southeastern Indians sometimes held their prisoners of war briefly for use as a diplomatic tool. On one occasion in 1725 when the Creeks were trying to encourage the Cherokees to join them in their opposition to the English, they offered to free all enslaved Cherokees in exchange for an alliance. The Creeks sent a delegation to the Cherokees to discuss the matter and a captive Cherokee known as Slave Woman went along as interpreter. Slave Woman also functioned as an ambassador and maybe as a spy, for when her captors departed, they left Slave Woman behind with instructions to convince the Cherokees to accept a truce.[11]

European captives in particular often found themselves in a position to further the interests of their own people as well. French John, a slave of the chief Old Hop, helped to bring the overhill Cherokees under French domination during the mid-eighteenth century. The English probably first became aware of the Frenchman's presence among the Cherokees in February 1757 when Mankiller, who favored the English, reported to Captain Raymond Demere at Fort Loudoun, which was west of the Appalachians, that French John and a group of Cherokees had gone to New Orleans and that the overhill Cherokees anticipated a visit by one hundred gift-bearing Frenchmen upon their return. When questioned about the impending visit, Mankiller replied by expressing his belief that "no Presents nor the French would come, that it was too far off for them. But he thought that French John would come back with their People because he is a Slave to Old Hop, and he went upon those Conditions to return." Captain Demere immediately began formulating a plan to rid the Cherokees (and the English) of French John whom he accused of being a "crafty, cunning, dangerous fellow." The captain failed in his attempt to purchase French John from Old Hop who looked upon the captive "as his own Child and keeps him there upon that account." Next Demere tried to discredit this Frenchman who threatened English hegemony among the Cherokees but finally admitted to Governor William Henry Lyttleton of South Carolina, "I am at a Loss to know what steps I must take to French John." Demere hesitated to kill French John outright because as "French John was a Property and under Old Hop's Protection, I could not have killed him, it would have been the same as if I had killed one of them." While the captain had few qualms about offering presents to Mankiller for murdering French John, the Cherokees seemed to be reluctant to interfere with Old Hop and his slave. At last French John solved Demere's problem by journeying to New Orleans, where he "had a great many Presents given him to purchase his Freedom of his Master, Old Hop." The Frenchman apparently succeeded in emancipating himself and returned to New Orleans.[12]

A captive who was not ransomed but managed to avoid torture and death faced two possible fates: he was either adopted by a Cherokee clan and fully incorporated into the tribe or he maintained a precarious position within Cherokee society but outside the kinship system until such time as a clan elected to adopt him or he died. If the warrior who took a captive in battle had no use for him, he generally offered to give or tried to sell the prisoner to the kinsmen of fallen warriors since they probably would be the most interested in obtaining him. Woolenwaugh, the Great Warrior of Tennessee, said that when a Cherokee "took a slave and carried him to the next relative of any person who had been killed by those to whom such a slave belonged they had 200 and sometimes 300 weight of leather for such a slave."[13]

Clans frequently adopted prisoners of war to supplement their own numbers and to replace kinsmen who had died or been killed. The Cherokee warrior who captured the Frenchman Antoine Bonnefoy in December 1741 sold his prisoner while the war party was still on the way back to its town. The buyer promised certain merchandise in exchange for the captive and provided Bonnefoy with bedding, shirts, and mittens. Bonnefoy recorded in his journal that from this point he was treated not as a slave but as an adopted brother. When the war party returned to the village the warrior collected merchandise from his family and presented it to Bonnefoy's original owner. The clan then formally adopted Bonnefoy in a ceremony which included the painting of his body, feasting, singing, and burying a lock of the newly adopted brother's hair. Although he was free, Bonnefoy stayed with the Cherokees for two months during which time he dressed like his kinsmen, participated in the same activities as they did, and received the same treatment.[14]

A clan was not obligated, however, to adopt a captive who had been purchased by one of its warriors. David Menzies, an English physician whom the Cherokees captured, recounted the experience of being offered to and rejected by a clan:

> In proceeding to the town I understood that these Cherokees had in this expedition lost one of their head warriors, in a skirmish with some of our rangers; and that I was destined to be presented to that chief's mother and family in his room: At which I was overjoyed, as knowing that I thereby stood a chance of not only being secured from death and exempted from torture, but even of good usage and carresses. I perceived that I had overrated much my matter of consolation. . . . The mother fixed first her haggard bloodshot eyes upon me, then riveting them to the ground, gargled out my rejection and destruction.

Although the mother's refusal to accept Menzies as a replacement for her son condemned him to torture, he survived the ordeal and later secured his freedom.[15]

The role of the mother in Menzies's account is in accord with what we know about the Cherokees' matrilineal kinship system, a feature of their social organization which baffled whites until modern anthropologists made sense of it. In this kinship system, a person belonged to his mother's clan and his only kinsmen were those who could be traced through her—mother's mother, mother's sisters, the children of mother's sisters, and the most important and powerful man in a child's life, mother's brother. The primary responsibility for discipline and instruction in the arts of hunting and warfare rested not with a child's father but with his maternal uncle. Not even the continued presence of the father in the home was assured because Cherokee women owned the dwellings and usually practiced serial monogamy. An ousted

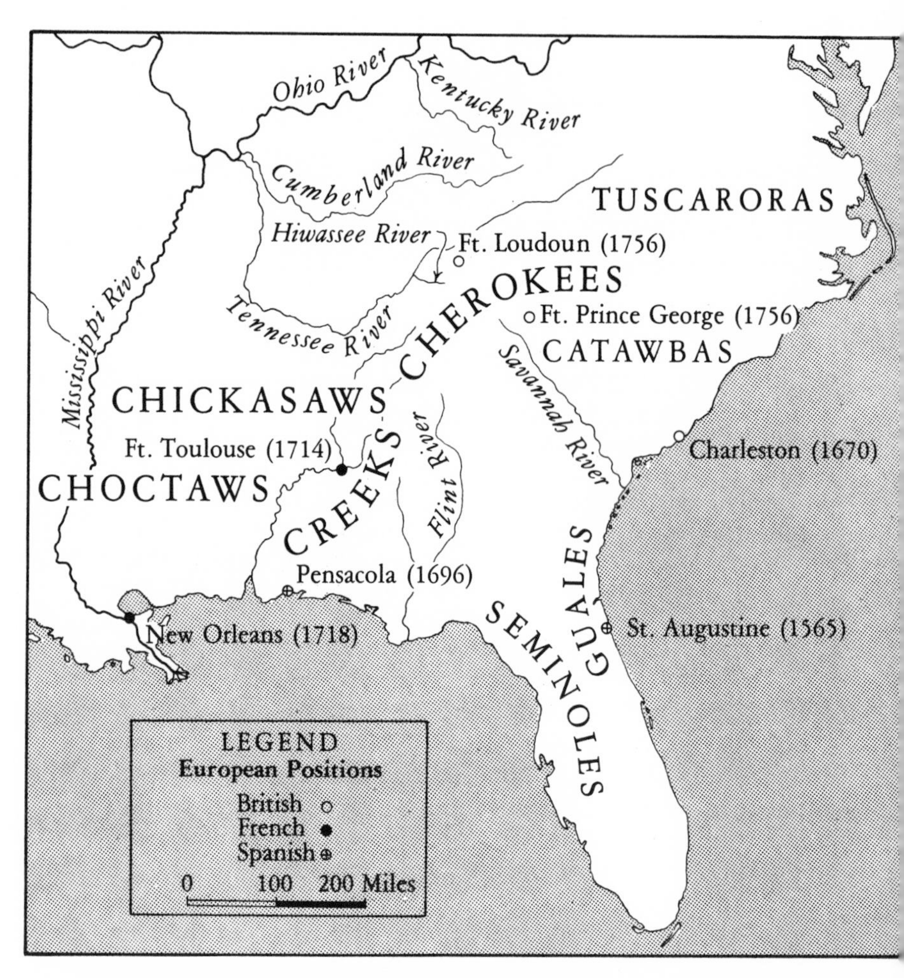

Map 1. Major Indian Groups and European Positions in the Colonial Southeast

husband simply returned to the residence of his lineage until he married again and his children remained with their mother and kinsmen. John Lawson, who wrote an early eighteenth-century history of Carolina, expressed amazement that "two Indians that have liv'd together, as Man and Wife, in which time they have had several Children; if they part, and another man possess her, all the Children go along with the Mother and none with the Father." Accustomed to a strongly patriarchal society in which mothers had absolutely no claim to their children in the event of separation, Europeans could not conceive of a system of kinship in which children were not blood relatives of their fathers. Since kinship was matrilineal, Cherokee women probably decided the matter of adoption and often had the power to determine the fate of captives. The highly honored War Women, or Beloved Women, apparently could pardon a captive who had already been condemned to torture and death. The Beloved Woman Nancy Ward, for example, saved the life of Mrs. William Bean in 1776 by granting her a reprieve just as the Cherokees were about to burn her at the stake.[16]

The Cherokees accorded the same privileges to war prisoners who had married or were adopted into the tribe as they did to those whose membership derived from birth, and adopted captives often were reluctant to leave the Cherokees. Mary Hughes, a trader's widow who was captured about 1760, told Lieutenant Timberlake that the Cherokees at first had treated her harshly and had deprived her of sufficient clothing. Later, however, she married her husband's murderer and declined to leave him after the English ransomed her. Similarly twenty boys who had been captured during the French and Indian War were unwilling to leave the Cherokees. They cried and refused to eat when they were returned to their families.[17]

Clan membership was essential to one's existence as a human being within Cherokee society because of the pervasiveness of the kinship system. Since clans were divided into white or peace clans and red or war clans, a Cherokee's clan determined his political alignment and his role in society. Kinship governed social relationships, dictated possible marriage partners, designated friends and enemies and regulated comportment by indicating through terminology which kinsmen had to be respected and with which kinsmen one could be intimate. A Cherokee derived his rights from membership in a clan, and the clan protected those rights by promptly avenging any offense committed against a kinsman. If the actual perpetrator of a crime could not be apprehended, the clan of the wronged party retaliated against the offender's clan. The clan which adopted a captive became liable for his misdeeds as well as responsible for avenging wrongs done to him. To be without a clan in Cherokee society was to be without any rights, even the right to live.

Some of the captives were never adopted into a clan. These people remained within Cherokee society but existed outside the kinship system. Captives without clans were the *atsi nahsa'i,* and the Cherokees sharply distinguished between them and the adopted members of a clan. An adopted brother had all the privileges of tribal membership while the *atsi nahsa'i* had no rights at all, and the owner of an *atsi nahsa'i* had absolute power over his property. When a Shawnee captive refused to accompany his Cherokee master Black Dog, he was killed immediately with a tomahawk.[18] Black Dog did not act out of wanton cruelty but rather from the fact that his slave did not possess the right to live. The captive who was not adopted, the *atsi nahsa'i,* simply existed outside the kinship system from which one's personal and legal rights stemmed. Consequently the *atsi nahsa'i* faced a painfully uncertain future with his continued existence depending solely on his master's protection and good will.

The exact purpose served by the *atsi nahsa'i* and the functions they performed are not completely known, but one thing appears to be fairly certain. The Cherokees did not keep the *atsi nahsa'i* for economic reasons. The aboriginal Cherokee economy did not require a large labor force, and the absence of a profit motive combined with the Cherokees' disregard for material wealth indicate that they did not expect the *atsi nahsa'i* to increase or even contribute to economic productivity. An early historian remarked that "tho' their grounds be fertile and able to produce much more than they do; yet they are contented to live upon a little," and Adair noted that the Cherokees desired nothing more than "a bare support of life." The Cherokees had no need for the surplus which was so important to budding European capitalism, and the Cherokees considered the white man foolish for hoarding things that he could not use. An Indian related the following story to Adair:

> They say, they have often seen a panther in the woods, with a brace of large fat bucks at once, near a cool stream: but that they had more sense than to value the beast, on account of his large possessions: on the contrary, they hated his bad principles, because he would needlessly destroy, and covetously engross, the good things he could not use himself, nor would allow any other creature to share of, though ever so much pinched with hunger.

The greedy panther, according to the story teller, was like the white man.[19]

In the subsistence-based Cherokee economy, anything that the *atsi nahsa'i* produced over and above what he himself could consume was useless to his master and to the economy. Furthermore, any excess that the owner of an *atsi nahsa'i* managed to accumulate through the labor of his bondsman was disposed of at the Green Corn Ceremony, a festival commemorating the harvest and marking the end of the old year and the beginning of the new in personal relationships and material possessions. Early traders marveled at this demonstration of the Cherokees' disregard for material wealth, but James Adair did note that the destruction of all their old provisions "helped greatly to promote a spirit of hospitality among the Indians."[20] Furthermore, the Cherokees did not attempt to acquire fortunes which they could bequeath to their heirs since they destroyed the personal property of the deceased or interred it with them. The absence of a profit motive in Cherokee society and their disregard for wealth meant that the Cherokees declined to work any longer or harder than was absolutely necessary, and the Cherokees therefore required only a minimum of labor from the *atsi nahsa'i.* John Lawson reported that "they have no Sabbath, or Day of Rest. Their Slaves are not over-burden'd with work, and so not driven by severity to seek that relief."[21]

Cherokees exhibited considerable disdain for material wealth because as Lawson pointed out, "Riches . . . are as often in the possession of a Fool as a Wise-man." Personal accomplishments rather than the acquisition and accumulation of wealth brought prestige and community esteem. The brave warrior, expert hunter, and wise medicine man were the most highly regarded members of Cherokee society. Wealth did not give rise to political power either, for Cherokee government did not progress to the point of delegated power until the late eighteenth century. Before this development, Cherokee leaders governed strictly by concensus and lacked any sort of coercive power.[22] Thus the owners of *atsi nahsa'i* probably did not expect to use their bondsmen to amass fortunes or power.

Any benefit derived from the employment of unfree labor accrued primarily to the town as a whole and not to the individual owner. Although improved fields and houses probably belonged to a lineage composed of a mother, her daughters, their husbands and children, and any unmarried sons, much of the labor seems to have been communal. Adair reported that the Cherokees "obliged every town to work in one body, in sowing or planting their crops; though their fields are divided by proper marks and their harvest is gathered separately." Furthermore, Cherokees had no need to seek individual wealth, for according to the naturalist William Bartram, the economic system of southeastern Indians was redistributive:

> Previous to their carrying off their crops from the field, there is a large crib or granary erected in the plantation, which is called the king's crib; and to this each family carries and deposits a certain quantity, according to his inclination, or none at all if he so chooses: this in appearance seems to be a tribute or revenue to the mico [or chief]; but in fact is designed for another purpose i.e., that of a public treasury supplied by a few and voluntary contributions and to which every citizen has the right of free and equal access.

The Cherokees' communal labor and redistributive economy no doubt contributed to the generosity that greatly impressed Europeans. John Lawson described a ceremony that the Indians held whenever a tribesman suffered a loss through fire, war, or some other catastrophe. The unfortunate victim invited all the people of the town to a feast to which they brought food. Following a speech by one of the leaders of the town, everyone presented gifts to the host "which very often amounts to treble the Loss he has suffer'd." The Cherokees criticized whites for not showing similar unselfishness: "They say we are covetous, because we do not give our poor relations such a share of our possessions as would keep them from want."[23]

Since the division of labor in Cherokee society was fundamentally sexual, unfree laborers worked alongside their masters in the performance of many of the same tasks. *Atsi nahsa'i* accompanied the men when they left the villages in the winter to hunt and were "employ'd to carry Burdens, to get bark for the Cabins, and other Servile Work; also to go backward and forward to their Towns, to carry News to the old People, whom they leave behind them." Upon the hunting party's return, the *atsi nahsa'i* dressed the deer skins by first soaking them in water and scraping the hair off, then immersing them in deer brains dissolved in water and finally smoking the skins.[24] *Atsi nahsa'i* also helped the women in the various aspects of cultivation such as clearing the fields by girdling the trees and burning them when the dead wood was dry. The women and *atsi nahsa'i* never fertilized the fields except by "setting fire to the weeds, which makes very good manure," and they used an "instrument made of wood which was like a broad matock" to cultivate corn, gourds, melons, cucumbers, squash, cymlins, beans and a "red pease" that "makes them break Wind backwards, which the men frequently do and laugh heartily at it."[25]

Nevertheless the *atsi nahsa'i* were neither the primary agricultural workers nor hunters. For the Cherokees farming was women's work and hunting was men's work not only in practice but also in their conception of the dichotomous roles of the sexes.[26] Cherokees never would have employed unfree labor exclusively in the cultivation of the soil as antebellum planters came to do nor would they have relied on *atsi nahsa'i* to supply game because in their indigenous culture tasks affirmed sexual roles, social order, and cosmic balance.

Why then did the Cherokees maintain or even tolerate these people who existed on the fringe of society and contributed almost nothing socially, politically, or economically? Perhaps a clue lies in the term *atsi nahsa'i* which Cherokees applied not only to bondsmen but to any animate thing which was owned by a person. In the first decade of the eighteenth century John Lawson noted that the Indians he encountered employed the same appellation for human and nonhuman possessions and reported that their "Slave, and their Dogs, Cats, tame or domestic Beasts, and Birds are called by the Same Name: For the *Indian* word for Slave includes them all. So when an *Indian* tells you that he has got a Slave for you, it may . . . be a young Eagle, a Dog, Otter, or any other thing of that Nature, which is obsequiously to depend upon the Master for its Sustenance."[27] The Cherokee "slave" was relegated to the same position as animals because he lacked affiliation to a kinship group, wherein lay his claim to humanity. Since kinship determined political alignment and dictated personal relationships, the absence of kinship ties almost entirely excluded the *atsi nahsa'i* from participation in Cherokee society. Furthermore, the *atsi nahsa'i* had no legal rights or protection because these stemmed from kinship and the blood vengeance which clans practiced. Therefore, a person whom the Cherokees called *atsi nahsa'i* was an anomaly because he had a human form but could not lead a normal human existence, and the Cherokees probably tolerated the *atsi nahsa'i* simply because he was an anomaly.

The Cherokees' attitude toward things which deviated from a general rule can best be seen in their belief system and the way in which it categorized nature.[28] Instead of trying to obscure or to deny the existence of those things which could not be easily classified, the Cherokees paid special attention to them. For example, in Cherokee cosmology three categories of animate things occupied the world: human beings, plants, and animals. An anomaly to these categories is the bear, obviously a four-footed animal but one which frequently stands on two legs and uses its front paws to grasp, reach, climb or hold as human beings do. Cherokees did not ignore these human characteristics of the bear but magnified them, and the bear became a major figure in Cherokee myths. Not content with the irregularities which actually existed, the Cherokees also created mythical ones such as the dragon-like *Uktena* which had the body of a snake, the antlers of a deer, and the wings of a bird. The Cherokees did not view abnormalities as causes for fear but as subjects of profound interest, and by emphasizing the exceptions to their categories, they strengthened their system of classification. Such anomalies would have normally challenged the entire Cherokee belief system, but the Cherokees avoided this threat with their acceptance and accentuation of anything which defied exact categorization.

The *atsi nahsa'i* were anomalies because they had the physical appearance of human beings but could not live as such because they lacked membership in a clan. Rather than banish or kill these individuals, the Cherokees supported them in recognition of the fact that people did exist outside their kinship system. To ignore the existence of such people would have left the entire kinship system open to constant challenge. By maintaining *atsi nahsa'i* the Cherokees gave cognizance to these anomalies and also demonstrated daily through the operation of their kinship system why such individuals could not be considered complete human beings.

The *atsi nahsa'i* also functioned as deviants in Cherokee society. Deviance is a logical and necessary element in all societies because it confirms common values and group identity. The members of a society frequently establish their identity not by proclaiming what they are, or the norm, but by carefully defining what they are not, or deviance. The role of deviance in Cherokee society was perhaps particularly important because intense individualism and the absence of a centralized government hampered the development of a group identity. In this situation the kinship system far more than a common language and culture united the Cherokees. Each of the seven clans probably had representatives in every town, and a Cherokee always found a warm welcome among kinsmen even when he was far away from his own town and lineage. The local members of a clan were responsible for avenging any wrongs done to a visiting kinsman, although he might be a stranger, and they were liable for any wrongs he might commit. Thus the norm in Cherokee society was to have kinsmen. Being a Cherokee and identifying with that society did not mean giving allegiance to an omnipotent chief or council; it meant belonging to a Cherokee clan. A deviant in Cherokee society was not only one who disobeyed the law but one who was excluded from the kinship system. The presence of a deviant, an *atsi nahsa'i,* in Cherokee society reaffirmed the norm. By clearly demonstrating inconveniences and dangers of not being a member of a Cherokee clan, the *atsi nahsa'i* helped establish and strengthen group identity among the Cherokees.[29]

Thus Cherokee "slaves" did perform an essential function in their society although Cherokee bondage failed to conform to European preconceptions. The only liability, albeit a serious one, which the Cherokees imposed on the *atsi nahsa'i* was his exclusion from the kinship system. Bondsmen were not important in the Cherokees' subsistence economy, and the Cherokees' lack of regard for material wealth and the absence of a profit motive contrasted sharply with European economies. Overlooking these differences, Europeans continued to act on the assumption that Cherokee "slaves" had the same legal status and economic importance as their own bondsmen. Consequently in the eighteenth century when a tremendous demand for labor in the British colonies led white traders to bargain with the Indians for their "slaves," the Europeans did not foresee the drastic changes in Cherokee social, economic, and political institutions that would result.

2

Cherokees and the Indian Slave Trade

Although Europeans did not immediately foist the white man's version of slavery on the Cherokees, their economic system gradually undermined and transformed the indigenous institution of bondage. The traders, who inspired and directed much of this transformation, found a ready market for European goods which they exchanged for the Indians' deerskins and war captives. Of the two Indian commodities that commanded a market, deerskins had long been essential in the Cherokee economy while captives had contributed nothing economically. Suddenly the acute labor shortage in the British colonies which led white planters to employ unfree labor in the clearing of fields and the cultivating of crops made war captives a marketable commodity. Although the Cherokees continued to have no need for the labor of these captives they rapidly developed a dependence on European manufactured goods and needed captives to barter. Warfare, the only means of obtaining a constant supply of this human commodity, escalated, and the Cherokees came to view slavery in an entirely different way.[1]

Traders from Virginia as well as South Carolina did business with the Cherokees but the Carolinians maintained commercial hegemony throughout the colonial period. Although many of the early South Carolina planters came from the West Indies with the intention of continuing as sugar planters, some of them soon realized that the Indian trade provided an easier path to wealth. The Indian trade remained the foremost business in South Carolina until the advent of rice as a staple crop at the close of the seventeenth century, and it continued to be important to the economy even after the establishment of the plantation system.[2]

The Cherokees were geographically remote from the Charleston-based Indian trade, and other Europeans vied with the Carolinians for their business. Spanish goods probably preceded English traders in the Cherokee Nation, for when James Needham and Gabriel Arthur visited the Cherokees in 1673 to survey the commercial prospects for a Virginia firm, they reported the presence of sixty Spanish muskets. The Cherokees possibly obtained these from the Choctaws and Chickasaws who were supplied by the Spanish in Florida rather than directly from Spanish traders. The French also circulated among the Cherokees, particularly in the eighteenth century, and some towns were probably visited by traders from all three nations. However, the English traders from Carolina conducted their business over a wide territory ranging as far as one thousand miles into the continent, and by the end of Queen Anne's War in 1713 had led the Cherokees into the British sphere of influence. In 1730 Sir Alexander Cuming accompanied a delegation of seven Cherokees to London for the signing of a treaty which limited trade to the English and excluded other Europeans from settlement within the boundaries of their territory.[3]

Partly because of their distance and inaccessible location, but also because of the slowness of the English, the Cherokees were not important to the Carolina Indian trade until well into the eighteenth century. Furthermore, the Cherokees exhibited less talent than some other tribes in obtaining the deerskins and slaves which found a market in South Carolina. With the demise of the coastal tribes, however, interior nations became more important to the trade, and by the second quarter of the eighteenth century the Cherokees occupied so essential a place in the Carolina commercial system that trouble between the Cherokees and South Carolina from 1728 to 1730 caused an economic slump.[4]

Exactly when the first Carolina traders arrived among the Cherokees is not clear, but the fact that Dr. Henry Woodward, in 1674, correctly located the Cherokees upon the headwaters of the Savannah River indicates at least indirect contact by that year. In 1699 Colonel Cadwallader Jones, a Virginia Indian fighter and trader, encountered a number of Carolina traders among the Cherokees on the Tennessee River while he was searching for a path through the Blue Ridge Mountains to the west. The early traders, such as those whom Jones met, were itinerants visiting the Cherokees in the spring and summer and then returning to Charleston in the fall. Gradually the volume of trade with the Cherokees increased, and traders finally established permanent residences in the Nation about 1711.[5]

Although the South Carolina Indian trade originated in private initiative, the General Assembly in 1707 established Commissioners of the Indian Trade to supervise the commerce. The bill creating this regulatory board required a trader to purchase a license and give bond for his compliance with certain rules including prohibitions against the enslavement and sale of free Indians, the use of extortion to obtain furs, and the sale of ammunition to enemy Indians. In 1716 the assembly determined that "it has been found by Experience that the Indian Trade as formerly carried on by private Traders, has been prejudicial, and tended very much to the great Damage and Detriment of this Province." Consequently the Indian trade became a government monopoly "for the sole Use, Benefit and Behoof of the Publick of this Province." The colony proceeded to fix the prices and quality of goods, to stipulate the extent to which credit would be extended to Indian patrons, and to build trading factories at key villages which included the Cherokee towns of Tugaloo, Keowee, Tunesee, Savannah Town, Quanasse, Cowee, Tellico, and Congarees.[6]

At first the Cherokees bought only a few kinds of goods from the white traders. The Cherokees certainly did not require the tools of the white man to exist, for the Indians' knowledge of and ability to exploit their environment enabled them to live comfortably in a land where vast technological superiority did not permit the Europeans to escape a hard struggle for survival. James Adair noted the red man's remarkable adaptability:

> If an Indian were driven out into the extensive woods, with only a knife and a tomahawk, or even a small hatchet, it is not to be doubted he would fatten even where a wolf would starve. He could soon collect fire, by rubbing two dry pieces of wood together, make a bark hut, earthen vessels, and a bow and arrows;

> then kill wild game, fish, fresh water tortoises, gather plentiful variety of vegetables, and live in affluence.[7]

For the main part Indians wanted substitutes for their own products, knives and hatchets to replace stone tools, and guns to replace bows and arrows. John Brickell, who wrote a natural history of early eighteenth-century Carolina, described the process by which Indians adopted the white man's tools:

> At this early period, to the Indian a knife, a hatchet, or a hoe, was a useful and invaluable acquisition. He observed with what facility the strangers supplied their wants, which were many in comparison with his, by means of the various implements they used. The woods fell before the axe, the earth opened before the hoe or the spade, and the knife was useful on numerous occasions. Having obtained these in process of time, he found the tomahawk and musket equally useful.[8]

The fact that the metal implements far surpassed native tools led to the willing acceptance of European products. Manufactured goods had little direct impact, however, on the culture of the Cherokees because changing the instruments with which the Cherokees performed traditional tasks did little to alter or change fundamental values and beliefs.[9]

The ramifications of technological changes nonetheless proved to be far-reaching: "What was at first only convenient, as his wants increased, became absolutely necessary by which the original bond between Europeans was strengthened and confirmed."[10] In abandoning the production of necessities, the Cherokees made themselves dependent on the traders and subject to the dictates of the white man. Adair reported that Indian crafts had fallen into disuse. "The Indian, by reason of our supplying them so cheap with every sort of goods, have forgotten the chief part of their ancient mechanical skill, so as to be not well able now, at least for some years, to live independent of us."[11]

Cherokee dependence on European manufactured goods made it possible for the whites to employ economic coercion successfully in dealing with their Indian customers. In 1717, for example, the residents of Quanasse, Tellico, and Tunesee ceased supplying the white traders who lived among them with necessities and avoided helping the factors build and repair the trading houses. These Cherokees refused to carry skins down the river and constantly pilfered packs that arrived from Charleston. In an attempt to curb such activities and to encourage a more cooperative attitude, the South Carolina commissioners threatened "to recall those Factors which were abroad and decline trading or furnishing the Indians anymore with Goods or Ammunition, the Consequence whereof would render them poor and miserable." Rather than become easy prey for their enemies who would continue to be supplied, the headmen of the recalcitrant towns relented and promised to foster more friendly feelings toward the English among these people.[12]

The growing demand for European manufactures resulted in an artificial increase in hostilities among Indian tribes, and slaves became the objects of warfare rather than merely by-products. Often traders actually incited intertribal warfare in order to profit from the sale of captives. Adair observed that "the Indians are not fond of waging war with each other, unless prompted by some of the traders; when left to themselves, they consider with the greatest exactness and foresight, all the attending circumstances of war."[13] In 1714 the commissioners of the Indian trade in South Carolina found two of the Cherokee traders, Alexander Long and Eleazer Wiggen, guilty of encouraging the Cherokees to raid the Yuchi village of Chestowe. Several witnesses at the hearing testified that Long was partly motivated by a personal grudge. One witness stated that "two or three years ago there was a Difference between Mr. Long and one or two People of Chestowe about Debts," and another reported that he had heard Long swear that "he would never let the Cherokees rest till he had Satisfaction against the Euchees." A third witness suggested additional incentive in recalling that "Mr. Long and, as he thinks, Mr. Wiggen told him there would be a brave Parcel of Slaves if Chestowe were cut off." Furthermore, the Cherokees had become heavily indebted to the two traders who hoped to receive war captives in payment. The Cherokees hesitated to go against a peaceful town even to clear their debts without instructions from the governor, and so the traders deceived the Indians into believing that the orders for the attack came from Charles-

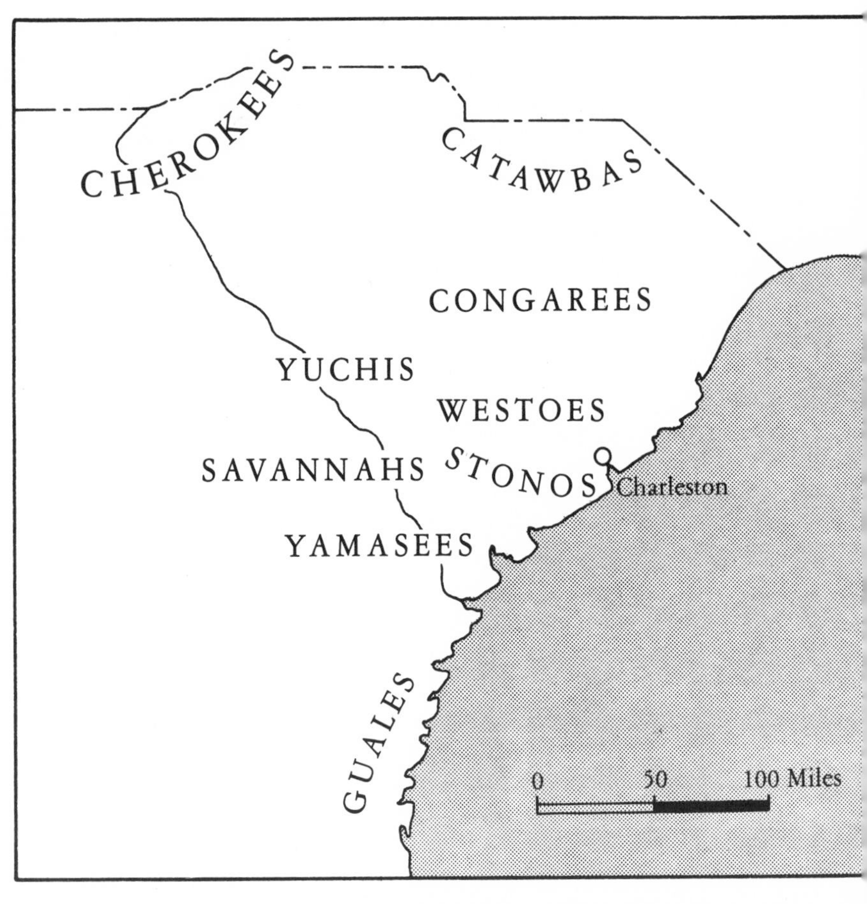

Map 2. Participants in the South Carolina Indian Slave Trade (From Chapman J. Milling, *Red Carolinians,* Chapel Hill, 1940)

ton. After attacking Chestowe, the Cherokees paid off their debts with slaves to the substantial profit of the traders. Although the commissioners frowned on such warmongering and revoked the licenses of Long and Wiggen, Wiggen ultimately regained his license and by 1717 he was the chief factor to the Catawbas.[14]

The group of English noblemen who held the charter to Carolina made several half-hearted attempts to curtail the enslavement of Indians because they feared that the resultant wars would give Carolina the reputation of being unsafe for prospective colonists. After the proprietors formed an exclusive trading alliance with a powerful coastal tribe, the Westoes, many colonists criticized the monopoly and decided to destroy the tribe by arming the Savannahs and offering them rewards for the defeat of the Westoes. Within three years only about fifty Westoes survived the killing, and the enslavement and the defeat of the tribe helped shatter the power of the proprietors.[15]

In contrast to the rather weak protestations of the metropolitan government, the colonial governments of Carolina actively encouraged the enslavement of Indians by offering bounties for captives. In 1674 during the Stono war, which Indian raids on white livestock had prompted, the South Carolina governor promised a reward for every Indian brought to Charleston, and the government subsequently sold the captives to slave traders in order to raise money for the defense of the colony. The assembly passed a law in 1702 establishing a committee to purchase captives for sale to meet the cost of expeditions against the Spanish.[16] The colonial governments recruited militiamen by pointing out that a "great advantage may be made of slaves," and in an effort to encourage citizens to volunteer for a campaign against the Cherokees in 1760, North Carolina passed an act providing "That each of the said Indians who shall be taken a Captive during the present War by any Person as aforesaid, shall, and is hereby declared to be a Slave, and the Absolute Right and Property of who shall be the Captor of such Indian."[17]

Public officials also frequently benefited from the sale of war captives. Governor James Moore of South Carolina, for example, decided to use his office, "not knowing how long his precarious power might last, for bettering his low and indigent circumstances." Moore quickly discovered that the traffic in Indian slaves presented the easiest way to make a fortune. He launched an operation against the Appalachee Indians in order to procure a large number of Indian slaves, "who he employed to cultivate his fields, or sold for his own profit and advantage." Thomas Pollock, president of the council in North Carolina, bought eight Indian captives at ten pounds each for shipment to the West Indies, where they brought him a handsome profit. In another instance, Colonel Thomas Broughton, the son-in-law and trading partner of South Carolina Governor Nathaniel Johnson, instigated a raid by Cherokees against a friendly Indian tribe and richly rewarded the aggressors when they delivered about 160 captives to the Charleston slave market.[18]

Thus the interests of the colonial governments and the Indian traders often coincided. Furthermore, Carolina politicians who usually participated personally in the Indian trade realized that Indian warfare was profitable politically as well as economically. The colonists clamored for land, and the decimation of the native population facilitated westward migration. The Indian trader in the colonial South, therefore, served as the chief instrument of expansion partly because he acted as scout, explorer, and diplomat but primarily because his policies led to the extermination of the Indians through white campaigns against the Indians and also through the incitement of intertribal conflicts.

As a large and powerful tribe, the Cherokees frequently participated in slave raids. The Cherokees joined forces with the Yuchis against the Guales in 1680, and over two hundred Cherokee warriors took part in the Tuscarora war in which they captured or killed nearly one thousand of the enemy. In 1715 a group of Cherokees met with Carolina troops on the Hiwassee River and demanded war with tribes that the whites were trying to pacify. They maintained that if they made peace with these tribes, they would have no means of obtaining slaves to exchange for English goods.[19]

The Board of Commissioners carefully regulated the trade in war captives. Their instruction to Theophilus Hastings, the

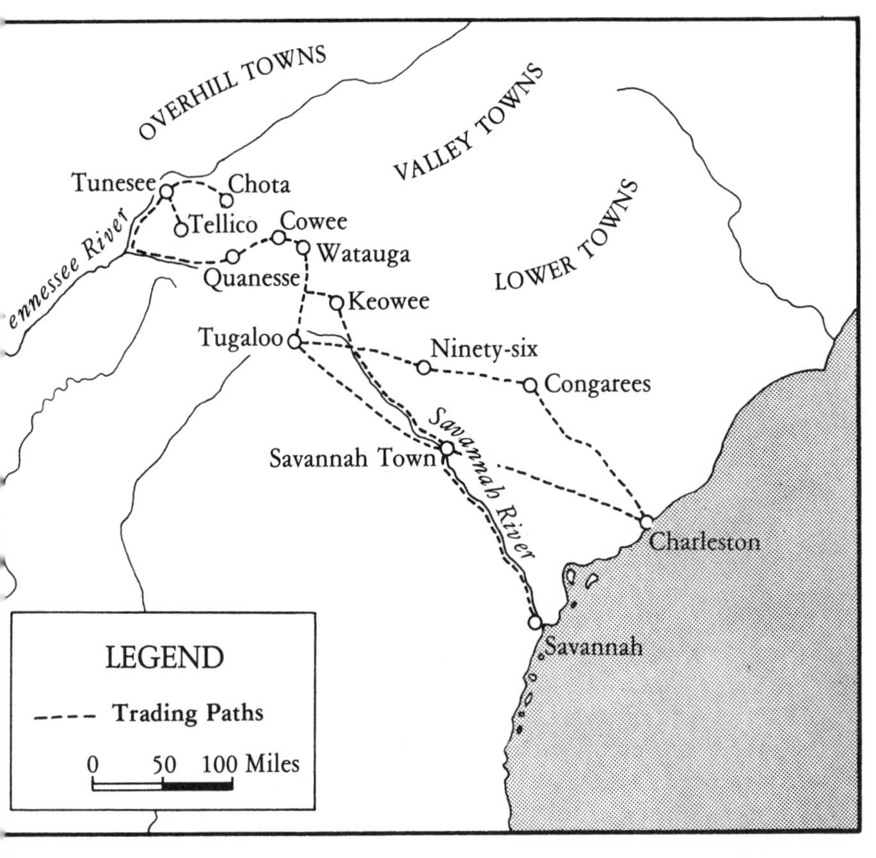

Map 3. The Cherokee Trade (From Verner W. Crane, *The Southern Frontier, 1670–1732,* Durham, N.C., 1928)

Cherokee factor, stipulated that he was "not to buy knowingly any free Indian for a Slave." Hastings's original instructions included slaves with skins and furs as commodities to be branded with the letters "C/H," but the provision relating to slaves was later remanded and the instructions altered to provide that slaves be marked "with Powder, or by some other usual Means, and not to inflict the Torture of a Brand in them." At first the commissioners forbade the trader to purchase any male slave over fourteen years of age but later amended the prohibition to apply to slaves over thirty. The commissioners insisted that Hastings supply the slaves with food and they appropriated goods for the Cherokees who had been hired to care for the captives. Hastings conducted the captives he had purchased at the Cherokee factory to Charleston, where the clerk of the Board of Commissioners advertised them two days prior to their sale. The Commissioners provided that "every slave be sold singly, unless a Woman with her Child," and demanded that the clerk keep and render an account to the Board.[20]

The purchasers of many of the Indian captives who had been brought to Charleston transported their chattels to the West Indies, New England, and New York. Occasionally the colonies exported Indian slaves directly to these markets, as in the instance of the Tuscarora war when the colony of North Carolina hired a sloop "to carry off what slaves the Indians have here." Other captives remained in the South to share along with black slaves the strenuous task involved in rice culture and the cultivation of other crops. In 1708 the population of the colony of South Carolina totaled 9,850, including 2,900 African slaves and 1,400 Indian slaves.[21]

In one instance an Indian captive was bought for the purpose of freeing him. Colonel John Barnwell, one of the commissioners, contracted to buy, educate, and free a "Mustee boy" who had been purchased at the Cherokee factory and brought to Charleston with a group of captives. Barnwell paid ten pounds for the boy for a term of nineteen years and posted a bond of five hundred pounds which would be forfeited unless he fulfilled the contract that provided "for setting free and discharging the said Boy, at the expiration of the said nineteen years; and that the said boy shall not be exported or carried off or shipped from this Province, during that Term; and further to educate the said Boy, Christian-like, and cause him to be instructed in a good Trade."[22] Barnwell's slave no doubt fared far better than most of the Indians captured in slave raids.

The Cherokees frequently became the victims in warfare prompted by the desire for slaves. The Cherokees sent a delegation to Charleston in 1693 to complain that the Catawbas, Congarees, and Savannahs had been preying on them and selling the captives to the English for slaves in violation of trading regulations. In reply to their demand that the captives be returned, the governor informed the Indians "that the prisoners were already gone, and could not be recalled." In 1716 a permit issued in Charleston provided for the exportation of several "Seraquii" slaves captured by the Savannah Indians. This group probably included both warriors and noncombatants because both were subject to enslavement. The warrior Cesar who later played a significant role in offensives against tribes hostile to the English served John Stephens as a slave for a while in the second decade of the eighteenth century. Cesar ran away and Stephens refused to relinquish some supplies belonging to certain Cherokees until the Nation surrendered Cesar. The commissioners intervened and recommended that Cesar be purchased by the Cherokee factor and freed since he "may prove serviceable on Occasion." The commissioners also ordered a Mr. St. Julian to appear in Charleston to account for his holding two Cherokee women as slaves. During the Cherokee war in 1760 "a considerable sum was voted for presents to such Creeks, Chickasaws and Catawbas as should join the province and go to war against the Cherokees." According to the treaty that concluded the war both sides agreed to return captives, but the North Carolinians reneged on this provision, and the Cherokees retaliated by taking two young girls they had captured to Pensacola where they demanded the release of their people before assuring the return of the girls. As late as the American Revolution whites enslaved Cherokee captives and either sold them at public auction in Charleston or transported them to the West Indies.[23]

European powers encouraged the Indians' "natural passion

for war" in their own imperialistic rivalries. The seizure of a European by an Indian promised a reward to the captor through sale to an enemy power or ransom by the captive's countrymen. The French, Spanish, and English each had their own Indian allies whom they employed against their enemies. For example, several years of gift-giving by the Spanish culminated in the Yamassee war. The Indian who captured an English woman during the war confided to his prisoner "that rewards were given to Indians for their prisoners, to encourage them to engage in such rapacious and murderous enterprises." In 1716 a Cherokee purchased a Frenchman from the warrior who had captured him for "a gun, a white duffield matchcoat, two broadcloth matchcoats, a cutlash and some powder and paint." He then gave the prisoner to his sister and she conducted him to Charleston where the British reimbursed her in strouds for the value of the goods her brother had paid and gave her a "suit of Calicoe Cloathes for herself and a suit of stuff and a hat for her son."[24]

White encouragement of intertribal conflicts and the necessity of waging war to acquire slaves as barter for European goods altered the whole concept of Indian warfare. Originally Cherokees went to war only to avenge a wrong committed against them by another tribe. The aggressors usually sent a delegation to offer retribution and, recognizing the seriousness of a military offensive, the Cherokees deliberated carefully over their enemy's proposal. If the compensation could not be accepted for the offense, the war chief assembled the warriors who chose to go to battle with him in the town house for three days of fasting and purification ceremonies and then embarked on the campaign.[25]

The size of Indian war parties varied, and sometimes only two or three warriors would conduct a raid to "strike their prey as panthers." Lieutenant Timberlake reported a party as large as 165, but generally the number ranged from twenty to forty and consisted primarily of the kinsmen of people killed by the enemy since these were men with a particular interest in revenge.[26] The relatively few participants in a military operation made it likely that a surprise attack could be carried out with limited casualties. The war party took extreme precautions to avoid detection and ambush and often traveled single file with each warrior stepping in the tracks of the one before him. At other times the warriors, communicating by mimicking animal sounds, attached bear paws or buffalo hoofs to their feet and followed the courses that these animals were likely to take. The route through enemy territory usually skirted a swamp in which the invaders could take refuge if attacked. When the war party sat down in the woods, they always did so in a triangle so as to avoid surprise. To lose warriors was a very serious matter, and if this happened, the Cherokees blamed the war leader and degraded him by taking his martial titles and reducing him to the status of a boy.[27]

Cherokees did not originally conceive of war as a continuing or long-range effort but rather as a retaliatory raid. The warriors fought one battle and promptly returned home. Even as late as 1750 one of the traders complained to Governor James Glen of South Carolina that "they are such thoughtless Creatures, they never reserve anything for Tomorrow. The Presents you sent, they soon made away with them, never expecting any more War."[28] Until the traders began exchanging goods for war captives, sufficient revenge appeased and pacified the warriors, but the value of the captives as saleable items meant that the frequency and extent of warfare increased. Cherokees needed to pursue war, not in reprisal but to obtain slaves to exchange for the European goods without which they could no longer manage. Revenge gradually became less important than the capture of slaves, and by the mid-eighteenth century the Cherokees had generally abandoned torture as the chief means of dealing with prisoners of war. During the French and Indian War, Lieutenant Timberlake observed that "this savage custom had so much mitigated of late."[29]

Before the advent of the Indian slave trade, warriors had little power in Cherokee political organization. Adair attributed this lack of power to the Cherokees' realization that "man was not born in a state of war."[30] Actually every male had an equal right to participation in aboriginal Cherokee government, and decisions resulted from consensus. John Lawson described the process by which they reached consensus. "After every Man has given his Opinion, that which has most Voices, or, in Summing up, is found the most reasonable, that they make use of without any Jars or Wrangling, and put it in Execution, the first Opportunity that Offers."[31] Even the leaders lacked coercive power and a central government to enforce their will. According to Adair, every town was independent and bound together only as a "friendly compact" and the ties of kinship, language, and customs. "The Indians, therefore, have no such titles or persons, as emperors, or kings; nor an appellative for such in any of their dialects. . . . They have no words to express despotic power, arbitrary kings, oppressed or obedient subjects."[32]

Europeans simply could not comprehend a political system as anarchical as the Cherokees' and generally acted on the assumption that the Cherokee government functioned after a fashion similar to that of European monarchies. The colonial governments identified certain men as "chiefs" and then held these men accountable for any crimes committed by their "subjects." This policy as applied toward the Cherokees originated in 1730 with Sir Alexander Cuming, an English emissary to the tribe who "nominated Moytoy commander and chief of the Cherokee Nation, and enjoined all the warriors of the different tribes to acknowledge him for their King, to whom they were to be responsible for their conduct." Subsequent Cherokee political history is the chronicle of the centralization of power in response to white pressure.[33] The men generally recognized as "chiefs" were warriors who previously had possessed little power in times of peace. One reason for the designation of warriors lies in the fact that these men had the ability to police Cherokee society and prevent depredations on whites.[34] Furthermore, Europeans equated wealth and power, and since warriors exhibited the first inequality of wealth within Cherokee society through the capture of slaves, Europeans assumed that warriors were "chiefs."

These warriors began to value their economic status because the traders demonstrated through their way of life the desirability of accumulating wealth. The blatant example of affluence the traders presented and the economic inequality their presence engendered undermined the Cherokees' subsistence economy. The white entrepreneurs possessed "a great deal of yellow and white stone, of black people, horses, cows, hogs, and everything else our hearts delight in" and constructed large houses and buildings "like towers in cities beyond the common size of those of the Indians."[35] The Indians also became quite aware of how the traders gained fortunes because the factors frequently sold the Indians inferior goods and gave inaccurate weights and measures. In 1763 an observer reported that "the Savages daily saw themselves cheated in Weight and Measure; their Women debauched and their Young Men corrupted" by traders who were a "Shame to Humanity, and the Disgrace of Christianity."[36] The Indians began to see the advantages of making a profit and hoarding rather than sharing, and the traders taught them by example exactly how one went about it.

For a few years a gross inequality of wealth was exhibited only between Indian and white, but the market for captives introduced an internal inequality as superior warriors avidly began supplying the market and reaping high returns for their products. The nature of the indigenous Cherokee property law, which distinguished between three kinds of property which belonged to either the tribe, the lineage, or the individual, allowed them to do this. According to an early history, ownership in the hunting grounds was communal:

> The boundaries of their hunting grounds being carefully fixed, each tribe was tenacious of its possessions, and fired with resentment at the least encroachment of them. Each individual looked upon himself as a proprietor of all the lands claimed by the whole tribe, and bound in honor to defend them. . . . No Indian, however great his influence and authority, could give away more than his own right to any tract of land, which, in proportion, is no more than one man to the whole tribe.[37]

Lineages seem to have owned the fields and houses, for one of the chroniclers of the de Soto expedition observed that "the maize is planted and picked in, each person having his own field" and Adair noted that each household had its own "corn-house, fowl-house, and hot-house."[38] The way in which Cherokees dealt with theft and debt suggests individual ownership of chattel property as well. Stealing was extremely rare, but when it occurred, the offender had to compensate the victim for the stolen goods. "It scarce ever happens that they rob one another of so much as an Ear of Corn, which if any is found to do, he is sentenced by the Elders to work and plant for him that was robb'd till he is recompensed for all the damages he has suffer'd."[39] A creditor had the right to seize the goods belonging to a delinquent debtor in satisfaction of the debt, and as later evidence indicates, individuals rather than lineages, clans, or the tribe owned horses and canoes as well as guns.[40]

Similarly, Cherokees owned slaves individually and not communally. Lieutenant Timberlake recorded that prisoners taken in war became the property of their captors. When Cherokees attacked the garrison evacuating Fort Loudoun in 1760 during the Cherokee war and captured Captain John Stuart, Attakullakulla, a pro-English chief who considered Stuart to be a particular friend, "hastened to the fort and purchased him from the Indian that took him, giving him his rifle, clothes, and all he could command." Demere failed to convince the Cherokee council to interfere with Old Hop and French John because the council considered the Frenchman to be the personal property of Old Hop rather than the joint possession of the tribe. Bonnefoy referred to the warrior who had seized him as "the savage to whom I belonged" and "my master," and when Bonnefoy's captor sold him, it was a transaction between individuals.[41] Thus the warrior who managed to capture slaves brought wealth to himself and not to the tribe or even to his clan.

Warriors also obtained wealth through bribes and gifts tendered by the colonial governments. The South Carolina Commissioners of the Indian Trade frequently sent friendly head men rum, guns, blankets, shirts, pipes, and other articles of value "as a Reward for particular Services, and to incourage them to assist the White Men." In 1717, for example, the board gave Charite Hagey (also known as Conjuror), Cesar, and Partridge each "a Gun, a Cutlash, and Belt, a Cag Rum, a Bagg Sugar, a Blanket, a Piece Calicoe and some strings of Beads" for conducting an expedition against the Spanish in St. Augustine. The chiefs arranged to leave their goods in Charleston until their return from Florida and provided that the payment be forwarded to their relatives in case of their deaths.[42]

Thus the economic changes brought about by the traders and colonial officials in the eighteenth century had an effect on the indigenous system of bondage among the Cherokees. With the advent of a market for war captives, "slavery" as Europeans knew it came into existence. Previously slaves had not been essential to the Cherokee economy, but with the introduction of European trade goods and the development of a market for war captives, slaves occupied an increasingly important position as a financial asset rather than a liability. The Cherokees still did not value slaves as laborers at this point because they continued to work communally and profit-making was limited to trade rather than to agriculture. Additional workers might possibly add to the wealth of the whole, but no particular benefit accrued to the individual who owned a slave unless he sold him. Therefore, as long as warfare continued and a market for captives existed, the Cherokees sold slaves instead of keeping them.

In time, however, several new factors ended the traffic in Indian slaves. Once the survival of the British colonies became a certainty, the English no longer found it necessary to incite one tribe against another in the interest of self-preservation. Furthermore, European rivalries on the North American continent declined after the Seven Years' War, and European nations no longer insisted that their Indian allies raid the cohorts of their enemy. In 1755 the British government transferred the administration of Indian affairs from colonial officials to agents appointed by the Crown, and began a concerted effort to pacify the Indian tribes. The Proclamation of 1763 which established a boundary line between the colonists and the Indians represented a codification of this new policy. Both the British government and the colonists, however, viewed the boundary line as only a temporary impediment to westward expansion. Indian land continued to whet white greed, but trickery and duplicity rather than force of arms promised greater success.[43] Finally, and perhaps most significantly, whites found African slaves to be a far more satisfactory labor supply than Indian war captives.

3

Red-Black Contact

The Cherokees encountered Africans at least as early as they did Europeans and may have seen blacks even before the conquistadors visited their towns. When the black slaves in Lucas Vázquez de Ayllón's ill-fated colony on the Pedee River revolted in 1526, some of the rebels fled to the Indians, and it is at least possible that the Cherokees saw these Africans or their offspring. Black slaves later accompanied Spanish expeditions to the Cherokees including those of Hernando de Soto in 1540 and Juan Pardo in 1567. When de Soto's prize prisoner, the Lady of Cofitachequi, escaped from the Spaniards, a black slave belonging to one of his officers accompanied her to Xuala, where they "lived together as man and wife." Although the initial reaction of Cherokees to Africans with their black skins is unknown, the cohabitation of the Lady of Cofitachequi and the Spaniard's black slave indicates that the Indians probably regarded Africans simply as other human beings who were either traversing or invading their territory. Since the concept of race did not exist among Indians and since the Cherokees nearly always encountered Africans in the company of Europeans, one supposes that at first Cherokees equated the two and failed to distinguish sharply between the races.[1] Soon after their first contact with Africans, however, the Cherokees no doubt realized that Europeans regarded blacks as inferiors and that they were in danger of receiving the same treatment.

In the years following their initial meeting, the enslavement of Indians and their employment alongside African slaves produced extensive contact between the two peoples. The English colonists purchased their first cargo of Africans at about the same time they began enslaving Indians.[2] The Indian slave trade in the South, however, reached its peak in the Yamassee war of 1715-17 and declined steadily thereafter until United States policy in the post-Revolutionary era formally ended a declining trade. Although early historians attributed the dwindling market for Indian captives and termination of the Indian slave trade to the racial and cultural unsuitability of Indians for forced labor,[3] contemporary accounts portrayed the Indian as a good worker. Brickell, for example, reported in his natural history that "some that are Slaves prove very industrious and laborious."[4] The demise of Indian bondage can probably be attributed to the fact that the African wrenched from his homeland with no opportunity to escape and return represented a better investment. Certainly the higher prices commanded by Africans reflect the planters' preference for them.[5]

Slave owners had special problems with Indians because the geographical proximity of their kinsmen and fellow tribesmen prompted many of them to escape, and advertisements for runaway Indian slaves frequently appeared in colonial newspapers. Revolts also seemed a troublesome possibility because the nearness of probable supporters increased the likelihood of successful resistance. The involvement of Indian slaves in one of the earliest suspected plots for an insurrection in South Carolina heightened the colonists' concern. In addition to the economic liabilities of Indian slavery, the pacification policy embarked upon by many colonial governments and ultimately adopted by the United States contributed to the demise of Indian bondage since the presence of Indian slaves made it difficult to establish rapport with other tribes. Colonists in early eighteenth-century Massachusetts, Pennsylvania, Connecticut, and Rhode Island cited the suspicion and hostility aroused among local Indians over seeing other Indians enslaved as a reason for passing laws forbidding the importation of Indian slaves.[6]

While Indian slavery and the resultant warfare existed, Cherokees became acquainted with blacks not only through the experience of common bondage but also as warriors capturing black bondsmen. Antoine Bonnefoy reported the existence of black captives among the Cherokees. "We found also a negro and a negress who formerly belonged to the widow Saussier, and having been sold in 1739 to a Canadian, deserted on the Quabache on their way to Canada, and were captured by a group of Cheraquis who brought them to the same village where I found them." Another account of the capture of blacks by Cherokees is that of David Menzies, whom the Cherokees seized along with the gang of slaves he was supervising, and in a similar episode Chief Bowl attacked a boat on the Tennessee River in 1794 and took twenty black slaves captive after having killed the thirteen whites on board.[7]

The Cherokees discovered that the capture of black slaves was particularly profitable, and by the American Revolution most Cherokees traded almost exclusively in black slaves. The Indians stole slaves from settlers in one location and sold them to planters living on another part of the frontier, rarely keeping black servants for their own use. The most commonly used tactic in the capture of slaves was that employed by a group of Cherokees who "took by Force a Negro Boy away out of John Geiger's House, when there were but two Women in it, whom they threatened to shoot as they offered Resistance." Acquiring them through duplicity was far less violent and seems to have been almost as successful as a South Carolinian's account of the theft of slaves in 1751 affirms:

> The half-Breed Fellow who came down from the Cherokee Nation in Company with James Maxwell, did seduce 6 of my Negroes to run away from me into the Cherokees, from whence they might depend on their Freedom. They proceeded on their way as far as Broad River, and there three of them receded from whom I have this Account. There is many Circumstances to coroborate the Truth. As he is a subtil Fellow, he may have the like Influence on many Slaves in South Carolina. It's necessary some Expedient should be fallen on to prevent a Practice of such dangerous consequences.[8]

Whether Cherokees abducted slaves or lured them away with the promise of freedom, the capture of Africans quickly replaced the capture of other Indians when the market for Indian slaves disappeared.

The most notorious Cherokee kidnapper of slaves was Chief

Benge, one of the Chickamaugan warriors who refused to make peace with the Americans until 1794. On his last raid into southwest Virginia, Benge captured Susanna and Elizabeth Livingston and three black slaves and attempted to transport them back to northwest Alabama where the Chickamaugans resided. While on the trail Benge queried Elizabeth about the slaveholders who lived on the North Holston River, particularly a General Shelby, and told the white woman that he would "Pay him a visit during the ensuing summer and take away all of his Negroes." On the third day after the raid, the Virginia militia attacked the abductors and killed Benge and most of his comrades. Colonel Arthur Campbell, the military officer of the area, wrote Governor Henry Lee of Virginia: "I send the scalp of Captain Benge, that noted murderer, . . . to your excellency . . . as proof that he is no more." The death of Benge marked the end of such brash slave raids.[9]

Some Africans who came into the possession of the Indians were not captured but had instead sought refuge among the Cherokees whose mountainous territory discouraged all except the most avid slave catchers. The treaty signed between the British and Cherokees in London in 1730 contained a provision for the return of these fugitives. "If any negroes shall run away into the woods from their English masters, the Cherokees shall endeavor to apprehend them and bring them to the plantation from which they run away, or to the Governor, and for every slave so apprehended and brought back, the Indian that brings him shall receive a gun and a matchcoat."[10] According to Brickell, white slaveholders commonly employed Indians to retrieve their lost property:

> They are also very expeditious in finding out the *Negroes* that frequently run away from their masters into the Woods, where they commit many outrages against the *Christians* . . . . The *Indian* Kings are sent for on these Occasions, who soon find out their Haunts, and commonly kill many of them whenever they are sent in pursuit after them, for they never cease pursuing 'till they destroy or hunt them out of the Woods.[11]

In 1763 whites agreed to pay Indians one musket and three

blankets, the equivalent of thirty-five deerskins, for each black slave captured and returned.[12]

The fear that runaways might establish maroon communities in the relative safety of the Cherokees' mountains motivated slaveholders to offer such lavish rewards for the recovery of their slaves. In 1725 a prominent South Carolina planter expressed concern that some slaves had become well acquainted with the language, the customs, and the hill country of the Cherokees. The possibility that slaves and Indians might join forces against the whites made the colonists shudder. In 1712 Alexander Spotswood of Virginia wrote the Board of Trade that he feared "the insurrection of our own Negroes and the Invasions of the Indians." The dread of such an alliance continued throughout the colonial period and gave rise to "law and order" political parties. John Stuart's North Carolina rivals, for example, successfully capitalized on this anxiety because, as Stuart pointed out in 1775, "nothing can be more alarming to the Carolinas than the idea of an attack from Indians and Negroes."[13] The fear of raids by maroons also partly shaped colonial Indian policy:

> In our Quarrels with the *Indians,* however proper and necessary it may be to give them Correction, it can never be our interest to extirpate them, or to force them from their Lands: their Grounds would be soon taken up by runaway *Negroes* from our Settlements, whose Numbers would daily increase and quickly become more formidable Enemies than *Indians* can ever be, as they speak our Language and would never be at a Loss for Intelligence.[14]

This fear was not wholly unfounded, as the following deposition given in 1751 by Richard Smith, the white trader at Keowee, demonstrates:

> Three runaway Negroes of Mr. Gray's told the Indians, as they said that the white people were coming up to destroy them all, and that they had got some Creek Indians to assist them so to do. Which obtained belief and the more for that the old Warriour of Kewee said some Negroes had applied to him, and told him that there was in all Plantations many Negroes more than white people, and that for the Sake of Liberty they would join him.[15]

The colonists went to great lengths to prevent conspiracies of Indians and slaves. They soon discovered that the most effective way to accomplish their goal was to create suspicion, hatred, and hostility between the two peoples. The colonists not only employed Indians to find escaped slaves but also used blacks in military campaigns against Indians. In 1715 during the Yamassee war a company of black militiamen participated in the invasion of the Cherokee Nation and remained after other troops departed to assist the Cherokees in an attack against the Creeks. After the Yamassee war the colonists ceased using black soldiers although the South Carolina Assembly during the Cherokee war of 1760 defeated by only one vote a bill to arm five hundred blacks. Nevertheless, slaves continued to contribute to the war effort in other ways, and over two hundred blacks served as wagoners and scouts for Colonel James Grant's expedition against the Cherokees in 1761.[16]

In another move to prevent the development of congenial relationships between Africans and Indians, the southern colonies enjoined whites from taking their slaves into Cherokee territory. Trade regulations imposed by both Georgia and South Carolina under various administrations almost always made it illegal for the traders to employ blacks in their dealings with the Indians.[17] The traders frequently ignored the provision, however, and took their slaves into Indian territory to act as teamsters and to paddle their canoes. As early as 1725 Colonel Chicken noted infractions. "I must take Notice to your Honour that [John] Sharp and [William] Hatton have brought up their Slaves altho' by law they are forfeit one hundred pounds for so doing and I should think myself Negligent in my Duty if I did not Acquaint your Honor."[18] That the offenders made no effort to conceal slaves indicated that they did not expect to be penalized by the Indian commissioner. In fact Hatton sent one of his slaves on an errand to Colonel Chicken: "This day was brought to me by one of Capt. Hattons Slaves the Young french Fellow."[19] As more traders with even more scorn for the rules entered Indian territory during the mid-eighteenth century, the number of black slaves increased. In 1757 Cornelius Doherty, a trader near Hiwassee, owned at least four slaves, and Samuel Benn of Tennessee Town used a slave to help him transport his goods over the mountains by packhorse. Benn's slave Abram won his freedom for his heroic feats during the Cherokee war. He carried dispatches between besieged Fort Loudoun and Fort Prince George and ultimately died trying to get through with a message.[20]

Stringent efforts to keep Africans and native Americans separate and hostile sometimes failed. When red and black men successfully resisted or overcame the misconception fostered by whites, they probably recognized certain cultural affinities between themselves. Both emphasized living harmoniously with nature and maintaining ritual purity; both attached great importance to kinship in their social organization; and both were accustomed to an economy based on subsistence agriculture.

African and Cherokee relationships to their environments reflected similar attitudes toward the physical world. The spiritual merged with the environmental. Common everyday activities, such as getting up in the morning, hunting, embarking on a journey, and particularly curing illness, assumed for both a religious significance, and even topographical features were invested with religious meaning. Africans associated mountains and hills as well as caves and holes with spirits and divinities while Cherokees viewed streams and rivers as roads to the underworld and "keep pools in the river and about lonely passes in the high mountains" as the haunts of the *Uktena,* a great serpent with supernatural powers.[21]

Animal symbolism was prominent in the myths of both Cherokees and Africans. Some Africans believed that snakes were immortal; others prohibited the killing of sacred snakes. Africans often portrayed the lizard as a messenger between god and mortals, and the spider as a symbol of wisdom. Similarly, in Cherokee myths the Great Buzzard created the mountains with his wings and the Water Spider devised a way to get fire.[22] Men, animals, and plants formed distinct categories, and each group was part of and essential to the cosmos as a whole. Man could respectfully draw his sustenance from nature, but he should not mistreat it. Nature had a valid existence apart from its profitability to man. Cherokees and Africans eschewed the gross exploitation of nature by which Europeans eventually wreaked havoc on their environment. Both red and black belief systems discouraged the misuse of nature and their economies did not demand it.

Olaudah Equiano, a slave who eventually obtained his freedom, described the economic system of the Kingdom of Benin in which he lived before he was captured and brought to the New World. The subsistence-level agriculture practiced by this society limited the division of labor: "Agriculture is our chief employment; and everyone, even the children and women are engaged in it."[23] According to Equiano, Africans used "no beasts of husbandry; their only instruments are hoes, axes, shovels, and beaks, or pointed iron, to dig with." While most African societies had advanced further technologically than those of native Americans, particularly in their use of metal tools, the production of iron remained limited and Africans depended on the cultivation of rice, yams, millet, sorghum, and bananas for their livelihood.[24] Although Africans probably produced enough surplus to support iron artisans, they did not develop a capitalistic economy. Equiano reported that "our manners are simple, our luxuries are few." The people were satisfied if they had enough to support life and saw no need to strain: "As we live in a country where nature is prodigal of her favors, our wants are few and easily supplied."[25]

Neither the Africans described by Equiano nor the Cherokees placed a premium on material wealth, and a person who acquired more than the accepted norm risked suspicion and censure. Both native Americans and Africans believed in the finitude of resources and realized that one person's gain was another's loss. The welfare of the community superseded the aspirations, desires, and even rights of a particular individual.[26] The African and Indian sense of community contrasted sharply with the trend in Western culture toward glorification of personal wealth, free enterprise individualism, and the destruction of a corporate ethic.

Kinship rather than economics ruled the lives of most Africans. Kinship groups governed marital customs and relationships between individuals, settled most disputes, and enabled individuals to exercise their personal rights. Kinship was also a major factor in shaping the nature of indigenous West African slavery since a slave generally lacked kinship ties and he therefore lacked the personal rights and claim to humanity which stemmed from kinship.[27]

African slavery did not, however, conform to a rigid, relatively uniform pattern as did the enslavement of blacks by Western Europeans. The Ashanti, for example, distinguished four unfree statuses: *odonko* or "foreign-born slave," *awowa* or "pawn," *akoa pa* or "pawn become slave," and *akyere* or criminal awaiting death. The *odonko*'s master gave him land to work and permitted him to retain the product of his labor. Economically he was on a par with his master, but the *odonka*'s exclusion from the kinship system denied him the activities, rights, and obligations of the Ashanti and thereby isolated him socially. The *awowa* on the other hand maintained his position in the kinship system while serving another in payment of a debt incurred by his clan or lineage. The *akoa pa* was also enslaved for debt, but his kinsmen did not redeem him, and so his situation became permanent and his kinship ties were severed.[28]

Accounts of West African slavery confirm that a man could be enslaved through a variety of circumstances. William Snelgrave, a British slave trader along the Guinea Coast in the eighteenth century, reported that African bondage ensued from either capture in war, commission of a serious crime, or enslavement for debt. Equiano recalled seeing coffles of slaves traveling through his village and described them as "only prisoners of war, or such among us as had been convicted of kidnapping or adultery, or some other crimes, which we esteemed heineous." The only slaves used by Equiano's society were captives taken in battle, and masters treated slaves much better in Benin than in the New World. "Those prisoners which were not sold or redeemed, we kept as slaves: but how different was their condition from that of the slaves in the West Indies! With us they do not more work than other members of the community, even their master; their food, clothing, and lodging were nearly the same as theirs."[29]

An African anticipated only temporary enslavement, for rarely did slavery become a perpetual state. Most societies expected slaves to marry, and the responsibility for procuring a spouse for a slave often fell to the master. The offspring of these unions gained their freedom or at least could not be sold. Africans generally permitted or even encouraged slaves to marry free persons including members of their master's lineage. Ashanti society provided that an *odonko* become free after marriage to a citizen, thus preventing the development of a slave class in the Ashanti State.[30]

The social mobility that Africans and Cherokees allowed their slaves derived from the economic insignificance of slaves as laborers. After contact with Europeans slaves did become central to the economies of many African states, such as Ashanti and Dahomey, but as articles of commerce rather than as workers. Warfare, the previous purpose of which had been revenge and not conquest, supplied the slaves to European traders.[31] Equiano gave the following acccount of hostilities between African states:

> From what I can recollect of these battles they appear to have been irruptions of one little state or district on the other, to obtain prisoners or booty. Perhaps they were incited to this, by those traders who brought the European goods I mentioned, amongst us. Such a mode of obtaining slaves in Africa is common; and I believe more are procured this way, and by kidnapping, than any other. When a trader wants slaves, he applies to a chief for them, and tempts him with his wares. It is not extraordinary if on this occasion he yields to the temptation with as little firmness, and accepts the prices of his fellow creature's liberty, with as little reluctance as the enlightened merchant. —Accordingly he falls on his neighbors, and a desperate battle ensues. If he prevails and takes prisoners, he gratifies his avarice by selling them.[32]

The establishment of commercial relations with European powers altered the traditional African institution of slavery in a somewhat different way than it did indigenous Cherokee slavery. The development of a market for black slaves among Europeans eventually led West Africans to distinguish between domestic slaves and commercial slaves. Snelgrave reported the following thwarted attempt to purchase slaves from the king of Dahomey's factor. "I understood afterwards the King had no slaves by him for sale, tho' he had great numbers of captive Negroes, which tilled his Grounds, and did other Work. For, it seems, after they are once inrolled in that Service, his Majesty never sells them, unless they are guilty of very great Crimes." Europeans encouraged warfare in Africa so that the demand for slaves in their American colonies might be satisfied. The European presence in Africa did not drastically alter domestic slavery, however, until long after abolition had ended the demand for commercial slaves.[33] On the other hand the rapid economic changes experienced by the Cherokees in the eighteenth century transformed the status of unfree people, and domestic slaves became commercial slaves. Eventually, political and military policy dictated the end of warfare for marketable captives, and the indigenous Cherokee system of domestic bondage had been so irretrievably altered by the Indian slave trade that a vacuum existed which plantation slavery ultimately filled.

From the beginning of their permanent settlement of North America, Englishmen desired Indian land more than Indian slaves. They gradually realized that their existence on the same continent with the Indians called for pacification of the various tribes until they could devise some less hazardous plan to divest the "savages" of their land. In pursuance of the ultimate objective, entirely dispossessing the native inhabitants of North America, Englishmen attempted to persuade the Indian that his interests coincided with those of the whites and that native Americans were "savage" versions of Europeans who needed only to be "civilized" in order to become equivalent to Europeans.

The presence in North America, as well as Africa, of men who appeared to be vastly different from Europeans posed a real problem for seventeenth- and eighteenth-century scientists. Genesis provided for a single creation of man and theories therefore had to be developed to explain how the differences came about. The most visible difference between Europeans and Indians was skin color but in their determination to establish that native Americans were exactly like them except for their "uncivilized" customs, Europeans refused to admit that Indians possessed genetically darker skin. James Adair gave the following explanation for this very obvious difference in hue:

> The parching winds, and hot sun-beams, beating upon their naked bodies, in their various gradations of life, necessarily tarnish their skins with the tawny red colour. Add to this, their constant anointing themselves with bear's oil, or grease, mixt with a certain red root, which, by a peculiar property, is able alone, in a few years time, to produce the Indian colour in those who are white born. . . . The colour being once thoroughly established, nature would, as it were, forget herself, not to beget her own likeness.[34]

Convinced that the European and native Americans were practically identical, whites simultaneously insisted that Africans were the exact opposite of Europeans and Indians. By emphasizing the actual, exaggerated, and imagined differences between Africans and Indians, whites successfully masked the cultural similarities of the two as well as their mutual exploitation by whites. Thomas Jefferson in *Notes on the State of Virginia* described both the Indian and African and found the African's color to be a "powerful obstacle to the emancipation of these people" while regretting that "an inhuman practice once prevailed in this country of making slaves of the Indians." Jefferson expressed a suspicion that blacks were "inferior to the whites in the endowments both of body and mind." Indians, on the other hand, differed from Europeans north of the Alps before the Roman conquest in number alone, and Jefferson implied that with time, literacy, and an increase in population, the American Indian might produce an individual comparable to Newton.[35] Jefferson's views became embodied in laws such as the South Carolina Supreme Court decision that an Indian could not be classified as a "free person of color" for the following reason:

> The whole State policy in making slaves of Indians, was temporary. . . . It was to deter their inroads by intimidations of slaverv, so hateful to Indian instricts. . . . Thev never made valuable slaves, but withered awav in a state so alien to the red man's nature. . . . But all history assures us that the negro race thrive in health, multiply greatly, become civilized and religious, feel no degredation, and are happy when in subjection to the white race.[36]

The argument for the resemblance of Europeans and Indians and the profound difference between these two peoples and Africans convinced many Cherokees, particularly those who sought the white man's "civilization," and they came to perceive the subjugation of blacks to be in their own self-interest. Cephas Washburn, missionary to the Cherokees relocated in Arkansas, reported that Ta-Ke-e-tuh gave him the following explanation for differences in men's color:

> The first human pair were red; and the varieties in the color of the human race he accounted for by the influence of climate, except in the case of blacks. Black was a stigma fixed upon a man for crime; and all his descendants ever since had been born black. Their old men, he said, were not agreed, as to the crime thus marked by the signal of God's displeasure. Some said it was for murder, some cowardice, and some said it was lying.

Such an account of the origin of racial differences spawned racial hostility which the Cherokees openly expressed as early as 1793. In that year Little Turkey sent a letter to Governor William Blount of Tennessee in which he described the Spaniards in the most derogatory terms he could as "a lying, deceitful, treacherous people, and . . . not real white people, and what few I have seen of them looked like mulattoes, and I would never have anything to say to them."[37]

Cherokees acted upon their newly fashioned assumptions about blacks, and when they founded their republic in 1827, the Cherokees excluded blacks from participation in the government. The founding fathers granted all adult males access to the ballot box except "negroes, and descendants of white and Indian men by negro women who may have been set free." The Constitution restricted office-holding to those untainted by African ancestry: "No person who is of negro or mulatto parentage, either by the father or mother side, shall be eligible to hold any office or trust under this Government." The Cherokees also sought to discourage free blacks from moving into the Nation and enacted a statute warning "that all free negroes coming into the Cherokee Nation under any pretence whatsoever, shall be viewed and treated, in every respect as intruders, and shall not be allowed to reside in the Cherokee Nation without a permit."[38]

By the third decade of the nineteenth century, therefore, the Cherokees had come to view themselves as radically different from Africans. Originally the "slaves" in Cherokee society had been war captives who were considered to be less than human because they were bereft of kinship ties, but as kinship receded in importance and as Indians began to identify with whites, Cherokees began to consider Africans to be more suitable for slavery than other Indians or Europeans. At the same time kinship became less crucial in a person's claim to humanity and freedom than his skin color.

4

The Development of Plantation Slavery

The Cherokees identified Africans with servitude long before a need for additional laborers led a Cherokee elite to adopt plantation slavery. This demand for labor came about as a result of the official United States Indian policy which continued the post-1755 British policy of pacification. The new government forced termination of the warfare by which slaves had traditionally been acquired and from which the developing upper economic class in Cherokee society had derived its income. The United States government also inaugurated a program to "civilize" the "savages," and it was to this program that the Cherokee elite turned in order to maintain their status.

In compliance with the government's "civilization" program, the Cherokees quickly adopted the white man's farming implements and techniques, and those who had substantial capital to invest in agricultural enterprises soon came to need additional workers. Following the example of their white mentors, the Cherokee upper class began using African bondsmen. However, the shift to plantation slavery was gradual because, while the government's "civilization" program produced an economic demand for laborers, the exclusive utilization of a carefully defined group of bondsmen for a particular task was alien to Cherokee culture. Plantation slavery developed only after the alteration of traditional sexual roles, the kinship system, the division of labor, and the political system.

Although the white traders, soldiers, and Indian agents who managed or supervised commerce with the Cherokees frequently married Indian women and fathered children, the matrilineal kinship system which had largely determined the nature of aboriginal bondage at first remained unaffected by the economic changes generated by the Indian slave trade. The Indian wife of a white man usually assumed the surname of her husband as did their children but, since the children belonged to the clan of their mother, the absence of a kinship affiliation with their father's people meant little to the children and absolutely nothing to the kinship system as a whole. The father's surname and possessions descended patrilineally while clan affiliation and the property belonging to lineages continued to descend matrilineally.[1] When the United States government embarked on its policy of "civilization," however, many Cherokees came to view matrilineal kinship as an aspect of their "savage" existence which had to be abandoned. Consequently Cherokees began practicing the European pattern of inheritance, and in 1808 the council pledged "to give protection to children as heirs to their father's property and to the widow's share."[2]

As members of matrilineages, women had not only traditionally had the power to decide whether a captive would be adopted or tortured but also held the title to houses and fields. The eighteenth-century naturalist William Bartram remarked that "marriage gives no right to the husband over the property of his wife; and when they part she keeps the children and the property belonging to them." But intermarriage with whites resulted in a problem with property titles. In English common law a woman relinquished all rights to her property when she married and white men accustomed to this practice assumed that they had similar power over the property of their Cherokee wives. The council finally dealt with the problem in 1819 by prohibiting white men from disposing of their Indian wives' property.[3]

Even after the passage of the law, some white men tried to exercise absolute control over the property of their Cherokee wives. General Isaac Wellborn of Alabama, for example, instituted a suit against James Vaught, a white man, and his Cherokee wife Catherine for the recovery of two slaves whom Wellborn had purchased from the husband in 1836 and whom Catherine Vaught had seized and taken to Indian territory during removal. Principal Chief John Ross replied to Wellborn's suit by explaining that Mrs. Vaught had inherited the slaves from her father.

Although she was married to James Vaught at the time of the sale, the transaction had occurred without her knowledge or consent, and Ross informed the General that "by the laws of the Cherokee Nation, the property of husband and wife remain separate and apart and neither of these can sell or dispose of the property of the other." On these grounds, Ross refused to aid General Wellborn in the recovery of the slaves.[4]

Although Cherokee women retained the right to their own property, they lost real economic power when they ceased to have an essential role in production and were replaced by either Cherokee men or African slaves. Although men traditionally helped women in the clearing of fields and the planting of crops, the Cherokees primarily associated agriculture and fertility with the female sex. In "Kana'ti and Selu: The Origin of Game and Corn," one of the myths collected by James Mooney, Kana'ti kept game in a hole covered with a rock and killed only that which his family needed for food. His son and Wild Boy, who had come from the river and had been tamed by Kana'ti and his wife Selu, discovered the source of the deer, turkeys, and bears that the hunter brought home. The mischievous boys removed the rock and allowed the animals to escape so that it became necessary for men to search for game to kill. Shortly thereafter the boys saw Selu providing corn and beans for the family by leaning over a basket and rubbing her stomach and armpits and decided to kill her as a witch. Before she died Selu instructed the boys to clear a circle of ground and drag her body over the circle seven times, but they neglected to complete the task and as a result corn only grows in a few places and Indians must strenuously labor over their crops.[5] Because Kana'ti, the first man, was responsible for the presence of game in the world and because corn originated with Selu, the first woman, it became the duty of males to hunt and provide game and females to cultivate the soil. In the Cherokee marriage ceremony, the man usually brought game to his prospective bride's house and she presented him with corn.[6] Thus men were primarily meat-producers and women were primarily vegetable-producers, and Cherokees affirmed sexual roles by the performance of their respective tasks.

While the division of labor was not exclusively sexual, the intimate association of farming and female sexuality prevented the formation of a class of enslaved agricultural workers in aboriginal Cherokee society, but this situation could only last as long as game abounded, warfare continued, and men pursued their traditional occupations. By the final decade of the eighteenth century, however, the federal government's pacification policy had effectively ended Cherokee warfare, and the Cherokees had seriously depleted their supply of game. The hunters' attempt to satisfy adequately their need for manufactured goods through the sale of deerskins contributed to the scarcity of game. Furthermore, a few Cherokees in 1775 illegally sold to the Transylvania Company their greatest expanse of hunting grounds, the territory between the Kentucky and Tennessee rivers. In return the Indians received £2,000 sterling and £10,000 in trading goods.[7] This cession and others, both legal and illegal, coupled with excessive hunting had a profound effect on the Cherokee economy and on the division of labor. Cherokee men could no longer hunt as they once had, and whites often criticized them for their laziness. Benjamin Hawkins, the first superintendent of Southern Indian tribes for the United States, noted that the women did most of the work while the men only helped occasionally in the cultivation of corn.[8] Gradually men began to take over more and more of the agricultural tasks traditionally reserved for women, and their sexual roles became blurred. Only when the identification of women with agriculture had ended was the introduction and utilization of slave labor for cultivation by even a minority of Cherokees possible. The modification of traditional sexual roles and the transformation of aboriginal definitions of male and female sexuality coincided with the sudden need for additional laborers as a result of the United States' "civilization" policy.

George Washington outlined his proposal for the "civilization" of the Cherokees in direct response to the serious economic depression confronting the tribe as a result of compulsory peace and the depletion of their hunting territory. In this distressing situation the Cherokees gratefully received the president's suggestion for relieving the economic crisis:

> Some of you already experience the advantage of keeping cattle and hogs; let all keep them and increase their numbers, and you will have a plenty of meat. To these add sheep, and they will give you clothing as well as food. Your lands are good and of great extent. By proper management you can raise live stock not only for your own wants, but to sell to the White people. By using the plow you can vastly increase your crops of corn. You can also grow wheat (which makes the best of bread) as well as other useful grain. To these you will easily add flax and cotton which you may dispose of to the White people, or have it made up by your own women into clothing for yourselves. Your wives and daughters can soon learn to spin and weave.

Washington instructed the Indian agent to procure looms, spinning wheels, plows, and other implements and to hire people to instruct the Cherokees in their proper use.[9]

Washington selected Benjamin Hawkins, the scion of a wealthy North Carolina family, as the man to supervise the civilization of the "savages." In his position as superintendent of Indian tribes south of the Ohio River, Hawkins tried to set an example for his wards by establishing a plantation complete with black slaves on the Flint River.[10] On his initial visit to the Cherokees, Hawkins discovered that the Cherokees avidly sought the tools of civilization. The Terrapin, a Cherokee whose farm was fenced and well stocked with cattle and hogs, asked Hawkins when the Cherokees might expect the plows and other implements promised by the government. A group of women at Etowah told Hawkins that "they would plant cotton and be prepared for spinning as soon as they could make it, and they hoped they might get some wheels and cards as soon as they should be ready for them."[11]

Under the direction of Hawkins and his successor, Return J. Meigs, the Cherokees advanced rapidly along the road to "civilization." In 1826 Elias Boudinot, one of the most prominent leaders of the Cherokee Nation, documented his people's amazing progress in *An Address to the Whites:*

> In 1810 there were 19,500 cattle; 6,100 horses; 19,600 swine; 1,037 sheep; 467 looms; 1,600 spinning wheels; 30 wagons; 500 ploughs; 3 saw mills; 13 grist mills & c. At this time there are

> 22,000 cattle; 7,600 horses; 46,000 swine; 2,500 sheep; 762 looms; 2,488 spinning wheels; 172 wagons; 2,943 ploughs; 10 saw-mills; 31 gristmills; 62 blacksmith-shops; 8 cotton machines; 18 schools; 18 ferriors; and a number of public roads. In one district there were, last winter, upwards of 1000 volumes of good books; and 11 different periodical papers both religious and political, which were taken and read.[12]

As the Cherokees accumulated the material evidence of "civilization," they realized that traditional tribal methods of safeguarding property no longer sufficed, and they began instituting changes that curtailed individual freedom and consolidated and centralized political power.[13] White greed brought about the first restrictions on personal property. Although Cherokees originally considered an individual's house and fields to belong to him or to his lineage and to be disposable at will, the attempts by whites to gain control of Cherokee land forced the Nation to apply the rules of communal ownership to this property as well as to the hunting grounds. In their initial step toward the acceptance of the concept of inalienable property, the Cherokees substituted the possession of an estate in occupancy for the possession of a fee simple. By this later arrangement a Cherokee still owned and could sell any improvements he made on the property. Ultimately, however, it became necessary to prohibit the sale of improvements in order to discourage Cherokees from migrating to the West.[14]

The enforcement of such stringent laws required a far more powerful central government than the Cherokees possessed.[15] Under their traditional government each town had a war chief and a peace chief, but neither could force anyone to obey his will because the power of the chiefs stemmed solely from the respect which their wisdom and valor commanded. Since the Cherokees recognized the war chief as leader only during military crises, he had little power in peacetime. However, warriors steadily gained more power throughout the eighteenth century as they became financially successful through the sale of deerskins and particularly war captives. Moreover, the Europeans increasingly insisted on dealing with the warriors to enlist allies for their own imperialistic rivalries. Warriors also became important to the peaceful operation of government because they assumed the task of controlling the actions of recalcitrant individuals whose unauthorized raids on white frontier settlements brought vicious retaliation against the nation as a whole.[16]

The rise of an economic inequality and an acquisitive spirit further led to the creation of a far more uniform and centralized political and judicial system. Adair observed the way in which Cherokees responded to this need. "In their former state of simplicity the plain law of nature was enough; but, as they are degenerating very fast from their ancient simplicity, they, without doubt, must have new laws to terrify them from committing new crimes, according to the usage of other nations, who multiply their laws in proportion to the exigences of the time."[17] Written Cherokee laws dated from 1808 when the council passed and recorded a law establishing a national police force, commonly called the lighthorse guard, for the purpose of suppressing "horse stealing and robbery of other property." Two years later the council abolished clean revenge, and in 1822 the Nation established a Supreme Court. The process of political centralization and the formalization of legal and judicial institutions culminated in 1827 with the organization of a republic under a written constitution patterned after that of the U.S. federal government. Approximately 40 percent of the laws passed by the General Council under the new Constitution involved matters such as debts, interest rates, tolls, contracts, and wills. The large number of laws dealing with property rights is not surprising since the founders of the new government were clearly members of the economic elite. The twelve framers of the Constitution whose names appear on the Census of 1835 farmed an average acreage four times that of other heads of households. Their mean corn production was over 1,500 bushels while that of other Cherokees was only slightly more than 207 bushels, and they averaged six times as much wheat as other heads of households.[18]

A corollary to the growing concern of the economic elite over the regulation of individual actions and over the protection of realty and improvements was their desire to safeguard investments in human property. The republican government of the Cherokee Nation rested largely in the hands of slaveholders, and of the twelve signers of the Constitution of 1827 who are listed on the 1835 census, eleven owned bondsmen. The preponderance of slaveholders is even more surprising when one considers that they comprised less than 8 percent of the heads of households.[19] Furthermore, these twelve men owned 22 percent of all the slaves in the Cherokee Nation. The Cherokee founding fathers clearly realized that plantation slavery required police power and effective government.

Laws controlling the activities of slaves actually preceded the Constitution of 1827. An act passed by the council in 1820 prohibited the purchasing of goods from slaves and provided that anything bought from a slave that proved to be stolen property had to be restored in fact or value. The law proscribed masters from allowing their slaves to buy or sell liquor and imposed a fine of fifteen dollars on violators. Later laws forbade the marriage of whites and Indians to slaves or the freeing of slaves for the purpose of marriage and made it unlawful for slaves to own property.[20] The Cherokees enforced their slave code in two ways. First of all, the laws passed offered an incentive to the prosecutor to seek out offenders and bring them to justice by providing that one half of the fines collected accrued to the prosecuting official. Second, corporal punishment was administered by "patrolers of the settlement or neighborhood in which the offence was committed, and every settlement or neighborhood shall be privileged to organize a patrolling company."[21]

The paucity of laws governing the behavior of masters and slaves in the preremoval Cherokee slave code stands in stark contrast to the multitude of provisions of the white antebellum South.[22] Noticeably lacking in the Cherokee code are laws dealing with insubordination and rebellion, and the majority of punishments are reserved for the masters and not the slaves. The law penalized the person who bought goods from slaves, the masters who allowed their slaves to buy or sell liquor, and the whites or Indians who married slaves. Even the hysteria which usually accompanied any suggestion of sexual relationships between white women and blacks is missing, and white or Indian women who indulged in interracial sex suffered fourteen fewer stripes than men.[23] The discrepancies between the slave code of the Cherokee Nation and the codes of the white society which many Cherokees were trying to emulate can only be explained in terms of the enduring power of Cherokee cultural traditions. The government of the Nation only reluctantly interfered in a matter which Cherokees customarily dealt with on an individual basis or through traditional means. As a result, the master continued to be responsible for the actions of his slaves just as he was for his own behavior. Thus the slave code aptly demonstrates the position occupied by the Cherokee slaveholder in the two decades before removal. The Cherokee planter, driven by the desire to make a profit, amass a fortune, and protect his financial investment, attempted to imitate the plantation society of the white South. Yet he could not entirely escape his Indian heritage.

Although Cherokee culture tended to ameliorate some of the harsher aspects of plantation slavery, the slave was a species of property and Cherokee law protected property rights. The court often ordered slaves sold in order to satisfy debts and judgments to settle estates. *The Cherokee Phoenix,* established in 1828 and published in English and Cherokee, carried announcements of approaching sales. According to one notice the marshal would sell on a certain date corn, fodder, cattle, and a slave named Gabriel to satisfy a judgment against James Petit for $500. In another advertisement the *Phoenix* listed Joe, his wife and child, corn, fodder, horses, cattle, hogs, oxen, wagon, loom, rifle and furniture as the items to be sold in the execution of a will.[24]

In spite of the unpleasant realities of plantation slavery, the image evoked by a discussion of wealthy planters is popularly one of moonlight and magnolias, white columns, and hundreds, even thousands of slaves. The moon probably shone as bright and the magnolias smelled as sweet in the Cherokee Nation as anywhere else in the South and a few mansions with white columns dotted the landscape, but no one in the Nation owned vast numbers of slaves. Joseph Vann had 110 slaves in 1835, but only two other planters held title to more than 50 slaves and of the 207 slaveholders, 168, or 83 percent, owned fewer than 10 slaves.[25] Even some of the large slaveholders lacked the trappings of wealth associated with white planters. George M. Waters who owned 100 slaves lived in a hewed log house which was appraised at $250 after removal. The valuation of Waters's improvements was one of the largest in the Nation but totalled only $7,346.50 and included such items as seven "negro cabins," a smoke house, cribs, fencing, cow pens, a mill-house, and a ferry.[26]

In 1835 John Ross, David Vann and John Ridge owned nineteen, thirteen, and twenty-one slaves, respectively, and possessed estates that were fairly typical of the large slaveholders. The three men lived in two-story, weather-boarded houses with brick chimneys and glass windows and had lumber houses, loom houses, improved fields, orchards, smith shops, mills, and ferries. An analysis of the Census of 1835 indicates a strong positive correlation between slaveholding and the number of acres which Cherokees cultivated, the houses and farm buildings they owned, and the bushels of corn which they raised. Since these factors as well as the ownership of mills and ferries determined one's economic status, Cherokee slaveholders such as Ross, Vann, and Ridge primarily composed the upper class. There were exceptions, however, such as Samuel Mays, the master of only 5 slaves who lived in a house worth $700 and owned several farms, with houses as well as a fishery and a ferry, the total value of which was $11,935.[27]

Although the valuations of the estates of small slaveholders included the same kinds of improvements as those of the large slaveholders, their houses were simpler, farms and buildings less numerous, and nonagricultural assets fewer. Edward Adair's improvements totalled $2,292, including a house worth $700, a barn, separate kitchen, smoke house, a house for his seven slaves, orchards, and a grape arbor. Poorer and perhaps more typical of small slaveholders were Green Fox Baldridge and Watie. Watie's loss amounted to $477. He owned a double cabin with two chimneys and a small house for his two slaves as well as a smoke house, stable, corn crib, two fields, and fruit trees. Baldridge's slave must have lived in the loft of his master's one room cabin because the Baldridge claim did not list a "negro house." The $250 valuation of his estate included a kitchen, crib, 2 stables, 2 fields, a spring house, and fruit trees.[28]

Slaveholders such as these controlled the government of the

Cherokee Nation partly because they had created it but also because their wealth and situation gained them the respect of fellow tribesmen and enabled them to deal more effectively with whites. According to the Census of 1835 the slaveholders cultivated more acres and produced more corn than nonslaveholding Cherokees, and they owned most of the nascent industries in the Nation. Slaveholders farmed an average of seventy-five acres, each of which yielded approximately 1,040 bushels of corn while nonslaveholders averaged eleven acres and 141 bushels of corn. Slave labor apparently enabled the slaveholders to produce more corn per acre as well—13.86 bushels per acre under cultivation compared to the 12.81 bushels per acre that the nonslaveholders managed to produce. The slaveholder accumulated more than he could use himself and the profit made by the sale of the surplus gave him capital to invest in various enterprises. The 75 percent of the mills and 42 percent of the ferries owned by slaveholders represented an investment of this sort.[29]

The slaveholders' advantage over nonslaveholders in relationships with whites stemmed from intermarriage as well as from wealth. Only 17 percent of the people living in the Cherokee Nation in 1835 had any white ancestors, but 78 percent of the members of families owning slaves had some proportion of white blood. Contact with a white parent or grandparent gave these people a head start toward "civilization," and it influenced them to identify linguistically with white society. Among the people living in slaveholding families (including infants and small children), 39 percent could read English, while only 13 percent were proficient at reading Cherokee. In the case of nonslaveholding Cherokees, less than 4 percent were capable of reading English, and 18 percent could read Cherokee. Literacy in English clearly gave the slaveholders a tremendous advantage at a time when troubles with whites over the issue of removal were mounting.[30]

This advantage became apparent very early in the nineteenth century when Thomas Jefferson planted the seeds of the removal crisis of the 1820s and 1830s. In 1802 Jefferson agreed that the United States government would extinguish the titles of all Indian lands within the limits of the state of Georgia if that state would relinquish its claim to the western lands included in the original charter. Advised by the Cherokee agent Return J. Meigs and Secretary of War Henry Dearborn, Jefferson decided to incorporate removal into the "civilization" program which had spawned plantation slavery. He proposed that the Cherokees move west of the Mississippi River where game still abounded and where they might continue to live in their natural state and acquire civilization at a more cautious pace.[31] A few Cherokees accepted Jefferson's offer, but most of "the children of nature" whom Jefferson had hoped to protect from civilization and its attendant evils chose to remain in the East. Another major migration occurred from 1817 to 1819. In both migrations, some conservative Cherokees did elect to go west in search of game and their traditional way of life, but many who chose to remove, particularly in the 1817-19 migration, were the "civilized" and relatively wealthy progressives.[32]

The majority of the conservatives in the valley towns continued to cling as tenaciously to their land as they did to their old ways. A New Englander who visited the Cherokees in 1830 wrote the following letter to the editor of the *Connecticut Observer:* "I was repeatedly informed, both by full Cherokees and by others, that most of those that had enrolled to go to the Arkansas were either white men having Indian families, or half breeds, but that very few full Cherokees had enrolled. This class are evidently the most opposed to a removal." Jefferson's plan for the salvation of these conservatives was anathema to them, for they continued to view the world as an island suspended by strings from the vault of the sky and themselves as the "principal people" who occupied the center of the island. In spite of the fact that some Cherokees had permanently migrated to the West in the late eighteenth century and others had traveled there to hunt, the territory west of the Mississippi remained to most conservatives a largely unknown land at the edge of the island. West was the direction in which the spirits of the dead traveled, and it was the cardinal point associated with darkness and death.[33] Jefferson had hoped that such conservatives would find a haven in the west where the government could protect them from the corrupting aspects of "civilization," but he failed to realize how inextricably the Cherokee belief system was tied to the land and how inconceivable it would be for most of these people willingly to exchange their location at the center of the world for western lands.

Removal was unacceptable to the central government of the Cherokee Nation from its inception, and in 1808 the Principal Chief, Black Fox, temporarily lost his position because of his sympathy for Jefferson's removal proposal. In 1819 the council passed an act providing that "the authority and claim of our common property shall cease with the person or persons who shall think proper to remove themselves without the limits of the Cherokee Nation." Finally in 1829 in an attempt to prevent the unauthorized signature of a removal treaty, the council codified what had been an unwritten law for two decades and declared that anyone who became a party to such a treaty "shall suffer death."[34]

The removal issue reached the crisis point with the election of Andrew Jackson in 1828. In his first annual address to Congress, the military hero, who owed his victory over the Creeks at the Battle of Horseshoe Bend in 1814 to his Cherokee allies, made clear his intention to fulfill the Georgia Compact of 1802 by extinguishing Indian titles and removing the "five civilized tribes" west of the Mississippi. Jackson maintained that the Indians had no claim to land which they were not actually cultivating and that no organized Indian nation could exist within the borders of a sovereign state.[35] The Cherokees, governed by a bicameral legislature under a written constitution, educated in the schools of missionary societies, and informed by a bilingual newspaper, resolved to resist any attempt on the part of the United States government and the state of Georgia to force them west of the Mississippi.

The events which followed Jackson's election, however, rendered all resistance useless. With the discovery of gold on Cherokee land, Georgia intensified its demand for Cherokee removal. The state extended its laws over the Cherokee Nation, and the legislature passed an Indian Code that prohibited Cherokees from testifying against white persons, mining gold, speaking against removal, and meeting in council. The legislature also provided for a survey and the division of Cherokee land preparatory to a lottery for the distribution of homestead lots of 160 acres and gold lots of 40 acres. In 1830 Congress passed the Indian Removal Act which gave Andrew Jackson the authority to negotiate with the Cherokees and other southern Indians for their relocation west of the Mississippi.[36]

A glimmer of hope flickered briefly in 1832 when the U.S. Supreme Court ordered the state of Georgia to release Samuel Austin Worcester, one of the missionaries who had been convicted and sentenced to prison under a Georgia statute which required all white men living in the Cherokee Nation to take an oath of allegiance to the state. In the majority opinion, Chief Justice John Marshall declared that "the Cherokee Nation, then is a distinct community, occupying its own territory, with boundaries accurately described, in which the laws of Georgia can have no force, and which the citizens of Georgia have no right to enter but with the assent of the Cherokees themselves or in conformity with treaties and with the acts of Congress."[37] Rejoicing in the Cherokee Nation was tempered, however, by the warning of John Ridge, one of the Cherokee leaders who had been educated in New England, that "the chicken snake Genl. Jackson has time to crawl and hide in the luxuriant grass of his infamous hypocrisy."[38] Ridge's assessment of the situation proved accurate, for the president refused to enforce the decision of the Supreme Court, and allowed attacks by Georgians on Cherokees and their property to become more brazen and vicious. In February of 1833 Ridge wrote Principal Chief John Ross that "the usual scenes of which our afflicted people experience are dreadfully increased since your departure, and they are robbed and whipped by the whites almost every day."[39]

Chief Ross received a steady stream of poignant accounts of numerous atrocities committed by whites against his virtually defenseless people. For example, in April 1834, Ayuque wrote Ross that "the whites are now threatening me and my family out of doors and to take my field our only dependance for support," and Dianna filed the following complaint: "I hereby certify that about 2 months ago a company of white men came to my house drunk. They made a great noise and I was afraid they would hurt my children and I ran out to another house. In the morning after sunrise I came back found the house broke down to the joist and one wheel broken . . . Rich, Edmondson has taken possession of my field and is now plowing it."[40]

The Cherokees had no means by which to protect themselves from the invasion by Georgians. The courts of the Cherokee Nation had ceased operation and Cherokees could not testify against whites in Georgia courts for the recovery of their property or in satisfaction of assaults against their persons. The Nation's police force no longer functioned, and the Georgia Guard certainly afforded no protection to Indians. In fact, this body actively engaged in the dispossession of the Cherokees. John Howard Payne, whom the Guard took prisoner along with his host John Ross, gave the following account of a conversation of Guard members which he overheard while he and Ross were in captivity:

> Long before morning several got up and sat around the fire, smoking and talking. "Ah," said one, "there must have been some beautiful slicking done last night!" And then stories were recounted of exploits upon people around. One small house had been tipped over, to dislodge the tenants; into another they had broken through the roof.
>
> "First one timber fell—and the family tumbled on their knees."
>
> "Ha! ha! ha!"
>
> "And one began to beg."
>
> Here was another roar.
>
> "And the little ones squalled 'mammy-mammy'!"
>
> Now they all mimicked crying children.
>
> "And then the old woman fell to praying."
>
> Here was a deafening shout of laughter, which was so long continued that they became exhausted and we had some repose.[41]

Even when the Nation's lawyers managed to obtain injunctions prohibiting whites from seizing the property of individual Cherokees, the Cherokees found themselves thwarted by the refusal of Georgians to honor them. Lawyer David Irwin wrote Ross, "You have been informed no doubt of the difficulty we have encountered in getting those Bills served, owing entirely to the disobediance of the clerks and sheriffs of the different counties in this Territory."[42] Individual attempts by Cherokees to protect themselves or their property generally failed, and the federal government declined to intervene. Evan Jones, the Baptist missionary to the conservative valley towns, reported that "a man named Bell, at Sixes, took away or rather took possession of James Proctor's Fish-trap, though not his lot. He attempted to take Proctor's gun from him, but failing to do so, he struck him on the head with a stone and knocked him down senseless, and then effected his purpose. . . . Proctor applied to the troops at Canton, without success."[43]

As a valuable form of property, slaves were subject to seizure by the Georgians, and their Cherokee masters had no legal means by which to seek their return. The only hope Cherokees had for the recovery of or compensation for stolen bondsmen was through congressional action or the promise that claims filed after removal would be honored. In 1830, for example, the House and Senate passed a joint resolution directing the secretary of war to ascertain the value of three slaves taken from Anthony Foreman, a Cherokee, by a white man and instructing the secretary of the treasury to pay the amount determined. Ten years later Thomas Woodward filed a claim for the value of "one negro woman Aggey or Akee who was forcibly seized and feloniously taken away from his plantation on the Etowa River in the Cherokee Nation East of the Mississippi some time about the year of ____ by white men citizens of the U. States."[44]

In the face of mounting attacks on Cherokee citizens, Principal Chief John Ross persisted in his refusal to recognize Georgia's claim to Cherokee land or to come to terms with the invaders. The Georgian who had drawn Ross's lot evicted the chief from his comfortable home in Rossville, south of present-day Chattanooga, and forced him to move into a primitive log cabin across the state line. Even in Tennessee Ross was not safe from the harrassment of the Georgia Guard, which arrested him and Payne and imprisoned them for several days. Ross continued, however, to encourage the Cherokees to maintain their unity and to endure the incursions of Georgians; he realized that any evidence of wavering or of factionalism would give added impetus to Georgia's plan. Many Cherokees, including Ross, believed that the Georgians who had already taken up the lots they had drawn were generally disappointed with what they had received and that if the Cherokees remained steadfast and united, the State of Georgia would settle for a cash payment to relieve the United States of its obligations under the Compact of 1802.[45] Ross and other leaders of like mind found many supporters particularly among the nonslaveholding Cherokees who were the most conservative and least acculturated and for whom removal had originally been proposed.

Gradually a small faction of highly acculturated, wealthy slaveholders began to doubt that the Cherokees' resistance would succeed. This group, which became known as the Treaty party, stood in opposition to Ross's National party. They coalesced around the leadership of Major Ridge, a hero of the Battle of Horseshoe Bend and a consistent proponent of Cherokee adoption of white culture, his son John Ridge who aspired to be principal chief, Elias Boudinot, the editor of the *Cherokee Phoenix,* and Stand Watie, Boudinot's brother.[46] George Paschal, the white son-in-law of Major Ridge, gave the following explanation for the Treaty party's decision to reach an agreement with the United States government and the State of Georgia:

> Nevertheless after Georgia had surveyed the Cherokee lands—granted them out to her citizens—after thousands had overrun the country—upturning every foot of soil which contained gold—dispossessed the most wealthy Cherokees, particularly those who had taken reservations under former treaties—prostrated the largest forests, organized ten new counties—erected as many flourishing villages—consigned their Missionaries to the Penitentiary, and in fact completely annihilated their social and political existence; the conditions of the people became intolerable—and the most intelligent minds in the Cherokee country as well as their best friends out of it, began to look round for the means of relief.[47]

Although it is quite possible that humane and honorable motives alone guided these men, Governor Wilson Lumpkin of

Georgia surreptitiously promised special consideration and some degree of protection to the faltering Cherokees who stood to lose the most in terms of material wealth. The lots on which members of the Treaty party had improvements were either withdrawn from the lottery or declared exempt from immediate confiscation. In December 1834, Lumpkin instructed the federal enrolling officer to "assure Boudinot, Ridge, and their friends of state protection under any circumstance. I shall feel it my imperative duty to pay due regard to the situation and afford them every security which our laws will justify or authorize."[48] On December 29, 1835, Lumpkin's strategy paid off. Major Ridge, John Ridge, Elias Boudinot, Stand Watie, and other members of the Treaty party met at New Echota, the capital of the Nation, and in the presence of approximately five hundred Cherokees (including children) signed a treaty by which the Cherokee Nation relinquished all claim to land east of the Mississippi in exchange for five million dollars and agreed to migrate to the western lands already occupied by Cherokees who had previously removed.[49] The wealthy members of the Treaty party chose to depart almost immediately. They arrived in the West with their slaves and whatever possessions they could carry in the spring of 1836. Thus the signers of the removal treaty were spared the forced removal of 1838 by which those people most firmly attached to the land were rounded up at bayonet point and herded into overcrowded stockades to await a westward march in the dead of winter.

The Treaty of New Echota may have had as profound an impact on the lives of slaves as it did on the lives of Cherokees. Ten years after the signing of the treaty, Elizur Butler, a white missionary to the Cherokees, wrote a colleague that in 1835 a group of "influential men" were making arrangements for emancipating the slaves and receiving them as Cherokee citizens. The treaty and the disruption which followed, according to Butler, prevented the abolition of slavery in the Cherokee Nation.[50]

John Ross continued to resist removal. He collected the signatures of 15,665 Cherokees on a petition protesting the Treaty of New Echota. Furthermore many whites rallied to the Cherokee cause. The legislature of the state of Massachusetts passed a resolution which was introduced in the U.S. House of Representatives protesting the treaty. The citizens of Burlington, New Jersey, sent a memorial to the House expressing sympathy for the Cherokees and protesting the "unjust" treaty. Some citizens of the state of Pennsylvania also came to the defense of the Cherokees and sent a memorial to Congress. Pennsylvanians in particular offered the Cherokees support in their battle against removal. John Ross noted this in a letter to supporters in 1838. "It is another evidence of sympathy of the descendants of William Penn with the wronged red man, of which Pennsylvania has so often, and especially of late, afforded us testimonials that we should be ungrateful indeed if we could ever forget."[51]

The support of the Quakers and the New England missionaries would not be forgotten by the conservatives who had been betrayed by Indians who had adopted white southern ways. Another great moral issue lay dormant in both the Cherokee Nation and the United States in 1838, but when the issue of slavery divided the United States and set North against South, the same lines of cleavage which developed along with plantation slavery and had been magnified by removal would once again surface in the Cherokee Nation. These conservatives associated slavery with the white southerners who had forced them from their homes and with the slaveholding Cherokees who signed the fraudulent treaty by which the despicable deed was accomplished while those who spoke out against the nefarious institution of slavery were the very ones who had come to their defense in 1838. Many conservatives came to accept the position expressed in the following excerpt from a letter written by a Quaker woman with whose family John Ross had stayed during the removal crisis: "I remember well that evening and our talk about slavery, for then I first learned that the Cherokees held slaves. And I said that the love of right, and of justice, and humanity which made us feel any wrong done to the Indian, made us unwilling it should be done to the less powerful, and less capable African."[52]

The development of plantation slavery helped create two distinct classes within Cherokee society not only in an economic sense but also in terms of values and world views. While most leaders of both the National party and the Treaty party owned slaves, the interests they represented and the views they espoused differed radically. Members of the Treaty party had abandoned "savagery" including traditional Cherokee kinship, economics, laws, and beliefs. These men sought the life-style and shared the values of white southern planters and felt no compunction over the ceding of Cherokee land. The majority of Cherokees, however, preferred to maintain their traditional values and way of life and therefore refused to support the Treaty party. Although he was a wealthy slaveholder, John Ross as well as other leaders of the National party drew support from this group because they verbalized and defended those traditional values which bound the Cherokees to their land, made them satisfied with a mere subsistence, and caused them to view slavery as an aspect of the white southern "civilization" that had forced them from their homeland.

5

Post-Removal Chaos

The division within the Cherokee Nation which slavery helped produce and removal magnified did not end with the migration of the Cherokees to the western Indian country. In fact, the experience of removal intensified the animosity between progressives and conservatives and left the Cherokees unable to deal with the divisiveness socially, politically, or psychologically. One manifestation of the division within Cherokee society and of the Cherokees' inability to reconcile their differences was political factionalism; another was chaos and violence. The turmoil which characterized the decade after removal disrupted the carefully structured republican political institutions of the Cherokee Nation, retarded the growing capitalist economy, and virtually destroyed any link which the upper class had with traditional Cherokee social organization and culture.

The cultural and economic gulf between rich progressives and poor conservatives, slaveholders and nonslaveholders, widened with removal as wealthy, highly acculturated Cherokee planters transported their slaves to Indian Territory along with other chattel property. In order to escape the seizure of more of their possessions by invading Georgians, many slaveholders departed for their new homes in the West before the forced removal of 1838–39 during which 4,000 of the 12,000 Cherokees who participated died.[1] Most members of the Treaty party fled the Nation in 1836; and many Ross partisans also left, including Joseph Vann, who conveyed his family and slaves on the Ohio, Mississippi, and Arkansas rivers to Webbers Falls in 1836 aboard his own steamboat.[2] Unlike Vann some slaveholding members of the National party and their bondsmen awaited forced removal along with the conservative nonslaveholding Cherokees. Even those slaveholders who chose to share the arduous journey to the West with the conservatives were far more comfortable, had better provisions, and suffered fewer casualties than their nonslaveholding companions. For example, George Hicks's detachment of 156 households totaled 1,031 people and included 13 slaves who belonged to Thomas Woodward (4), Te-Kah-se-na-ky (1), Philip Inlow (5), and Hicks himself (3). In this particular detachment, which traveled overland, the slaveholders owned an unusually high proportion of the draft animals and conveyances —5 of the 12 wagons, 1 of 2 carryalls, 16 of the 36 wagon horses, and 2 of the 14 oxen.[3] John Ross himself used 18 horses and oxen to transport his household of 31 kinfolk and slaves to the West. Ross also commissioned his Nashville agent, Thomas Clark, to purchase an additional carriage, 2 horses, and a baggage hack; and at Clark's recommendation, he hired 2 free blacks as drivers for his family.[4]

The slaves who accompanied the detachments of Cherokees in the removal of 1838–39 occasionally performed useful services for the group as a whole. They went ahead of the wagons with axes and cleared obstructions from the trail. Slaves also acted as watchmen at night and, armed with guns, protected encampments from the wild animals that prowled nearby. However, slaves primarily benefited their masters. They hunted for game to help supplement the inadequate provisions and worked for their owners as teamsters, cooks, and nurses. The labor of slaves and the services that they performed spared slaveholders some of the suffering experienced by other Cherokees in the course of removal.[5]

Not only did slaves tend to make their masters' migration more comfortable, but slaveholders possessed a distinct advantage over the nonslaveholders in re-establishing themselves in the West. After arrival slaves helped their masters clear and fence fields, cut logs, build houses and barns, construct docks, and plant crops. Since the Cherokees had transferred their practice of holding land in common to the West, slave labor was a tremendous boon to planters. A Cherokee was free to clear and cultivate all the land he desired, and he held title to the improvements on that tract of land. Therefore, a man with additional laborers in the form of slaves could clear more acreage and make more improvements than the nonslaveholder. His assets increased, not in relation to the capital which he invested in land, but in proportion to the number of men whose labor he could command. Consequently, the economic class structure, which had developed prior to removal and was grounded in slavery, continued and perhaps became more rigid and distinct as a result of this advantage which slaveholders had over nonslaveholders. Josiah Gregg, a trader who frequently traveled across Indian country on his way to Sante Fe, observed:

> The traveler, passing through the Cherokee Nation, is struck with the contrast between an occasional stately dwelling, with an extensive farm attached, and the miserable hovels of the indigent, sometimes not ten feet square, with a little patch of corn, scarce large enough for a family garden. . . . Most of the labor among the wealthier classes of Cherokees, Choctaws, Chickasaws, Creeks, and Seminoles, is done by negro slaves; for they have all adopted substantially the Southern system of slavery.[6]

Slaves clearly made a difference in economic productivity among the Cherokees and consequently a good market for slaves existed in the Indian country immediately following removal. In an effort to satisfy the demand, Lewis Ross, the brother of Principal Chief John Ross, chartered a boat in 1838 and transported five hundred slaves from Georgia to the Cherokee Nation. An armed guard met the boat and escorted Ross's property to his plantation for sale to other Cherokees. Some slaveholders went to Arkansas, Tennessee, or New Orleans to purchase slaves. Still others bought chattels from individuals who took advantage of the chaos which followed removal by stealing slaves or kidnapping free blacks. The tremendous demand for slave labor certainly stimulated this illegal trade which was carried on by men who ranged from merely unscrupulous traders to real desperados.[7]

Removal magnified political as well as economic divisions in the Cherokee Nation. The Treaty party joined forces with the Western Cherokees, or Old Settlers, in opposition to Ross and the National party. The Old Settlers were Cherokees who had emigrated to Arkansas before 1828 when they ceded the Arkansas territory and moved further west. The Treaty of New Echota provided for the removal of the Eastern Cherokees to the land governed by the Old Settlers, who had established their own distinctive form of government in which three equal chiefs exercised severely restricted power. Although a minority, the Old Settlers felt that the newly arrived emigrants should accept their previously established government, laws, and chiefs. Hoping to render Ross powerless, the Treaty party supported the position of the Old Settlers.[8]

At a general council held at Takattokah in June 1839, Ross proposed that a commission composed of the chiefs of the Cherokee Nation and of the Old Settlers along with elected representatives draft a new set of laws under which all Cherokees would be governed. This proposal omitted representatives of the Treaty party and so that faction influenced the Old Settlers to reject Ross's plan and to reaffirm their intention to maintain the original Western Cherokee government and law code and to extend it over the Eastern Cherokees. The Old Settlers did agree to a second council but any promise of union that this agreement signified was dashed the day following the adjournment of the Takattokah council when Major Ridge, John Ridge, and Elias Boudinot were executed by a group of Cherokees in accordance with the law of 1829 which had made the cession of Cherokee land a capital offense. Although Eastern and Western Cherokees did meet in convention before the close of 1839 and adopt a constitution patterned after the Eastern Cherokee constitution of 1827, many Old Settlers and members of the Treaty party considered the document fraudulent and refused to accept the validity of any government organized according to its provisions.[9]

The absence of a unified, centralized, and effective government meant that the Cherokees could neither cope with the chaos nor prevent the violence that followed the deaths of the leaders of the Treaty party. Furthermore, federal troops stationed at Fort Gibson under the command of General Matthew Arbuckle had no legal authority to interfere with the internal affairs of the tribes relocated in the western Indian country. Although troops illegally interrogated Cherokees about the killings and relentlessly sought the assassins' identities, they declined to aid Ross in suppressing the violence and ending the bloodshed.

Much of the early violence resulted from political factionalism. Members of the Treaty party including James Starr, G. W. Adair, John A. Bell, and Stand Watie reportedly formed a conspiracy in 1839 "for the purpose of killing and robbing the most prominent men of the opposite party." In fact James Starr and many of the members of his family did ultimately organize an outlaw band and terrorize both Cherokees and white citizens in the neighboring state of Arkansas. The Starrs aroused so much fear that the son of John Ridge wrote Watie that the people of Fayetteville "had rather meet the devil himself." Political factionalism soon ceased to be the primary motivation for the lawlessness and violence, and the Starrs came to be viewed as common criminals. The gang's exploits provoked the editor of *The Cherokee Advocate* to declare that "The deed performed by the notorious Tom Starr in murdering and robbing the poor old negro, "Squire" Jacobs, who lived on Lee's Creek seems to have confirmed the good citizens of the state to the honorable determination to arrest, or drive off this cowardly villain and his infamous companions in crime."[10] Individuals as well as gangs did a great deal of violence. The personal letters of this period almost always chronicle recent crimes. For example, John Ross's son James wrote his father that "There has been more murdering in the nation since you left. The great man Archilla Smith has killed John McIntosh . . . David Miller has also killed one John Phillips some place near the mouth of the Illinois." Stand Watie's wife Sarah wrote her brother that Elick Cockrel had been arrested for stealing horses, Charles Reese, Joseph Lynch, and James Clem Thompson had been arrested for arson, a boy had been whipped for stealing, and Wheeler Faught had been hanged for murder. John Candy reported the theft of slaves and horses, a stabbing, and a scalping to Watie and commented: "Murders in the country have been so frequent until the people care as little about hearing these things as they would hear of the death of a common dog."[11]

The chaotic legal and judicial situation made it unlikely that official justice could be dispensed, and many criminals openly flouted the law. For example, following an altercation between Bluford Alberty and a black man by the name of Harry in which Harry was injured, the *Advocate* reported that Alberty had fled. Alberty defiantly denied that he feared apprehension and trial, and in the next issue of the *Advocate* a correction appeared: "Mr. Alberty says he is at home, and intends remaining there." In the absence of a formal judicial system many Cherokees possibly even reverted to the aboriginal practice of blood revenge. James Ross informed his father that the murderer of John Phillips "was taken by Ellis Phillips and some few men. I have understood that they killed him without having any trial whatever." In despair Candy wrote Watie. "You will doubtless remember that Stand, the murder of James Starr, was killed and scalped. . . . I think there is now to be no end to bloodshed, since the Starr boys and the Riders have commenced revenging the death of their relatives. A dozen or so are implicated, and I am afraid that some of them will be more desperate than the first."[12]

The rampant violence in the Cherokee Nation stemmed not only from political factionalism and the absence of an effective government but also from the psychological impact of removal. The United States had destroyed the constitutional government, the schools, the missions, and the newspaper of the Cherokee Nation as well as the homes, crops, and personal property of individual Cherokees. Armed troops had forced the Cherokees from their land "at the center of the world," escorted them on a death march west of the Mississippi, and deposited them in the strange land "at the edge of the earth." The Cherokees no longer felt that they controlled their own destiny, and a sense of rootlessness and the feeling that life had little meaning pervaded the Nation. Sarah Watie expressed such sentiments in a letter to her brother. "I am so tired of living this way. I don't believe I could live one year longer if I knew that we could not get settled. It has wore my spirits out just the thought of not having a good home. I am so perfectly sick of the world." Many Cherokees turned to alcohol in an attempt to cope with their feelings and their situation. In 1845 William P. Ross, the editor of the *Advocate,* identified the causes of lawlessness as removal and whiskey. With each burst of violence, the Cherokee self-esteem sank lower. In an editorial Ross commented that "It is made our duty to again record the execution of one citizen and the murder of another. The frequence with which we have been called upon to make similar records during the short career of the *Advocate* is the subject of much mortification to our national pride." For such a humiliated and depressed people, human life and property could have little value.[13]

The lawlessness which afflicted the Cherokee Nation placed all forms of property in jeopardy and particularly slaves who were a valuable and easily disposable commodity on the frontier. The most susceptible to theft were children and the *Advocate* frequently carried reports of their seizure. In one such theft several men went to "the residence of Mrs. Elizabeth Pack, pushed themselves into the negro houses, and kidnapped a couple of negro children." The masters who lost slaves often placed advertisements in the *Advocate* such as the one in which Johnson Whitemire offered $100 for the return of "2 boys, one a Mulatto, about 12 or 13 years old, lower lip inclined to hang down, name, Robin—the other darker complexion than the mulatto, about 8 or 10 years old, lips thick, the sight of the right eye lost, name, Daniel." Whitemire recovered his slaves when a man from Arkansas who was traveling along the Red River heard that two boys fitting the publicized description had just been sold. He identified the youths and notified Whitemire who determined that they had been "run from this country by Mat Guerrin and Creek Starr, by whom a bill of sale was given—the former placing thereto his own signature—the latter, that of Mr. Whitemire himself."[14]

Free blacks in the Cherokee Nation also became subject to seizure and sale. In one episode of 1848, a white man and his black companion kidnapped a woman named Aiky and her daughter Nannie both of whom had been freed by their mistress at her death. In 1847 Aiky's two other daughters, one of whom was married to a Cherokee, had been kidnapped while their mother and sister fled to the woods. At that time Aiky and Nannie took refuge at the home of Archibald Campbell, a Cherokee, but the kidnap victims were never recovered. A year later during the absence of their protector Campbell, the felons approached the two women, knocked Aiky to the ground, bound her hands, and compelled her and Nannie to get into their canoe. Whenever the canoe passed a settlement the kidnappers forced the women to lie down. Finally they arrived at an Arkansas river port and took passage aboard a steamboat which carried the party to Memphis where the women were to be sold. Fortunately a group of Memphis citizens suspected foul play and applied to the mayor who managed to secure the release of the captives and instituted suit against the kidnappers.[15]

The frequent kidnapping of free blacks incensed many Cherokees. The *Advocate,* for example, reported a "very gross and daring outrage" in which two little mulatto girls were kidnapped and taken out of Indian Territory. According to the newspaper's account, "the wretches entered the house, enquired of the mother where her children were, tied them while in bed in her presence and took them off." Fortunately for the victims a party of Cherokees and whites recovered the children near Warsaw, Missouri, where one of the Starrs and the infamous Mat Guerrin, a member of the Starr gang, had left them for sale. The rescuers promptly "restored them to their freedom."[16]

In other cases, slaves and free blacks were not so easily recovered, especially when the thieves left the Nation immediately with their captives and headed to Arkansas or Texas for quick and easy sales. This was probably the fate of slaves who were not recovered within a year or so of their disappearance. Furthermore, kidnapping required some degree of violence and it was not uncommon for the victim to be injured or killed. When James Starr took the two boys from Whitemire, he hit a third boy over the head and injured him so badly that he released him after half a mile. Reports of legal cases involving fatal kidnappings occasionally appeared in the *Advocate.* John McIntosh, for example, was tried for "murder in the attempt of theft, a negro man belonging to David Vann."[17]

The kidnappers of free blacks and slaves were often apprehended in either the Cherokee Nation or the neighboring states. The *Advocate* was pleased to report arrests of felons such as that of Calvin and William Shores in Arkansas "for dealing in certain free negroes from this Nation" and commented that the Cherokees would "be glad to see justice done." In a similar episode within the Nation, the *Advocate* gave the following account:

> A case of some interest was to be tried last Monday in Canadian District. It was that of a Cherokee man named Kah-lan-to-li-ka, who had been arrested on a charge of having sold as slaves, certain free negroes, who have been taken off South and again sold. . . . We have heard of other cases similar to the alleged above, and are gratified that measures have been taken to place the questions involved in their true light before the public. At best, the situation of the colored race is an unenviable one, and he who rises up in defense of any right they may have, especially the right of freedom, against the cupidity of those who would deprive them of it by unjust means, deserves the thanks of all friends of humanity and justice among us.

Kah-lan-to-li-ka was acquitted, but the case was to be retried and "its actual merits," according to the *Advocate,* "be thus reached." Justice, however, was not the only concern of the *Advocate* in the capture and trial of the kidnappers of blacks as the editor demonstrated by posing the following questions to his readers: "Will someone be kind enough to inform us, where a numerous company of NEGRO DEALERS obtain their right to overrun every section of our country, at pleasure, in pursuit of their unholy traffic? and whether the interests of those who hold slaves among us to not demand an enquiry into that right?"[18]

While slaves were frequently victims of the lawlessness following removal, the disruption equipped them psychologically to resist bondage. For the first time slaves saw their masters in a powerless, subordinate position. Slaveholders in Ross's National party found themselves impotent against the State of Georgia and the United States and forced to submit to removal while slaveholding members of the Treaty party lost popular support and became generally ostracized for signing the Treaty of New Echota. Thus removal dispelled any notion that the slaves might have had about the omnipotence of their masters. This realization coupled with the sense of restlessness and disregard for law and order which slaves shared with their masters prompted slaves to run away and rebel and the absence of effective police power meant that disruption by slaves could be dealt with no more easily than the lawlessness of Cherokees and whites.

The turbulent political situation made the Cherokee Nation an ideal haven for runaways from surrounding states and the editor of the *Advocate* lamented:

> . . . our country is traversed by numbers [of slaves], who have escaped from their rightful owners; either of the Nation or the State, or the Creek country, we have every reason to believe. Some of these have become associated with the band of Seminole slaves under the guardianship of Gen. Jessup—and the mere fact of being thus protected, has infused into them a spirit which leads them with the most bare faced impunity to trespass upon peaceable Cherokees.

Advertisements which offered handsome rewards for the return of runaways frequently appeared in the *Advocate* as planters who lived as far away as Louisiana suspected that the Cherokee Nation might be the destination of their fugitive bondsmen. Arkansas and Missouri were more common sources of runaways. Many whites from these neighboring states who placed advertisements in the *Advocate* speculated that the fugitive slaves probably had "gone to some of the neighboring Indian Nations."[19]

The presence of runaways as well as the psychological impact of removal and the subsequent disorder in the Nation influenced many slaves owned by Cherokees to abscond. Before removal Cherokee slaves seem never to have run away since the *Cherokee Phoenix* carried advertisements placed by whites for runaways and by Cherokees for stray horses and cows, wives who had deserted their husbands, and slaves who had been stolen, but in over six years of publication not one notice of an escaped slave belonging to a Cherokee appeared. The *Advocate,* however, which commenced publication in 1843, frequently published advertisements for runaways. A typical advertisement gave date and place at which the slave was last seen and a description of his clothing and physical appearance including any distinguishing characteristics such as a speech impediment, scars, or a limp. In such advertisements, the master offered a reward, usually $20, for the recovery of his chattel and instructed whoever apprehended the runaway to return him or to lodge him in the local jail. The anarchy which prevailed in the Nation made the recovery of runaway slaves extremely difficult and advertisements usually ran some time. If the advertisement failed to produce results after several months, a planter often increased the amount offered for the runaway's capture and return, but even an inflated reward sometimes went unclaimed.[20]

Fugitive slaves sometimes obtained aid from nonslaveholding Cherokees. Martha Phillips told an interviewer for the WPA Writer's Project (part of a federally funded relief measure for artists during the Great Depression of the 1930s) that upon hearing of the intended sale of Martha and her brothers, her mother escaped with the children. The frantic woman attempted to swim the Grand River with the two small children on her back but turned back when fourteen-year-old Martha failed to master the strong current. The family hid in the mountains and probably would have starved if it had not been for the kindness of an Indian woman who gave them some parched corn. After a month of hiding Martha's mother killed a wild hog, but the small fire that they built to cook the meat attracted the attention of a passerby. Fortunately the Indian man who discovered the family had sympathy for them and conducted them to Martha's cousin's house where they hid in an attic until they could make a final escape to freedom.[21]

Most flights by slaves seem to have been made quietly and without violence as in the case of the escape of "Nigger Dave" who "borrowed Mr. Storey's horse Charly to go to Park Hill and kep going toward Californ."[22] Other slaves accomplished their escapes more violently as Hanna Grover remembered:

> I have referred to mother's invalid sister, Aunt Cyntha, who lived with them. Years before the war she and Uncle Henry lived on the Illinois River. They owned a darkey called "Nigger Smoot" whom they had had many years and trusted. One night, Uncle Henry, expecting to go turkey hunting the next morning had Smoot help him mold bullets to use. That day, Uncle had sold a good horse and had the money in the house. That night after

> they had gone to sleep, Smoot took an ax, killed Uncle Henry and pounded Aunt Cyntha until he thought she was dead. Then taking the money, a good horse, and an old rifle he left the place.

The injured woman's brother found her and her dead husband a day and a half later and immediately began pursuit of Smoot, trailing him to Fredonia, Kansas, where he captured the fugitive. The two returned to Indian Territory and, according to Grover, "the negro was hung in the yard where he had committed the crime ten days before."[23]

Not all slaves who were retaken relinquished their freedom willingly. In one such incident, a slave belonging to Dr. R. D. Ross refused to submit to "correction" by his master for riding horses at "improper times" and ran away. A group of Cherokees discovered the fugitive in the woods several days later and attempted to capture him, but "he resisted them with weapons which compelled them to shoot him." Another slave who was being confined in the jail at Tahlequah, the capital of the Nation, until his master could claim him joined an accused murderer and, armed with bowie knives, they rushed the jailer and escaped.[24]

It is not surprising that runaways resisted capture because the punishment for running away was often sale. One former slave interviewed in the WPA Writer's Project vividly remembered the sale of two siblings: "Young Master never whip his slaves, but if they don't mind good he sell them off sometimes. He sold one of my brothers and one sister because they kept running off."[25]

Some of the fugitive slaves who successfully escaped and avoided capture headed for California or one of the free states. Henry Bibb, for example, first escaped to Ohio and then moved to Michigan where he became famous as an abolitionist lecturer and as the author of a narrative about his life in bondage. In addition to northern free states, the discovery of gold in California resulted in an epidemic of "gold fever" in the Cherokee Nation and many Cherokee slaves, lured by the promise of wealth as well as freedom, made California their destination.[26] Other slaves chose to remain in Indian Territory and took refuge with the Seminoles, whose valiant resistance to removal from Florida had been strengthened by runaway slaves and who therefore tended to welcome fugitives to their Nation.[27]

The majority of slaves who escaped from Cherokees probably remained in the Nation, however, because of personal ties, lack of information about places of refuge, or ignorance of the English language. Advertisements for runaways included remarks such as "speaks the English language imperfectly, but the Cherokee well." Family as well as linguistic ties kept fugitives in the Nation as husbands frequently returned to wives and children to parents. The master of a boy named Harvey suspected his chattel to be "lurking either in the vicinity of Fort Gibson, the Bayou, Green Leaf or at his fathers on Caney." Advertisements also noted: "He has a wife living at Mrs. Taylor's in Tahlequah"; "About a year since he had a wife at Mr. N.B. Denenburg's"; or "It is supposed he is now either about Jas. Vann's Senr. or at the mouth of Illinois River as he has a wife at each place."[28]

Slaves frequently made their escapes on their master's horses and usually took a supply of food and clothing. When this supply dwindled, they often needed to steal in order to subsist. Thus the presence of fugitive slaves added to the lawlessness in the Cherokee Nation. Cherokees often discovered that runaway slaves had raided their chicken coops, smoke houses, corn cribs, or gardens. Many slaves took weapons such as rifles, pistols, and bowie knives with them when they escaped, and they used these to procure provisions. Waiting until the men in the household were in the fields or in town, these slaves usually frightened Cherokee women and children into fleeing by brandishing their weapons and then entered their houses to take what they needed.[29]

On at least one occasion slaves united in their resistance to bondage. In 1842 thirty-five slaves belonging to Joseph Vann and other slaveholders in the Canadian District of the Nation revolted. The bondsmen stole firearms from a store and proceeded on the night of November 15 to abscond into the Creek Nation after taking horses, mules, and clothing from their masters. When the sheriff of the district failed to capture the slaves, the National Council appointed John Drew to command one hundred men at national expense, to pursue the fugitives, and to deliver them to Fort Gibson for safe-keeping. Drew and his company successfully apprehended the slaves and returned them to their owners. Vann removed most of the rebels who had belonged to him from the Nation and put them to work on his steamboat which plied the Mississippi, Arkansas, and Ohio rivers.[30] Betty Robertson, who belonged to Joseph Vann, was interviewed in the WPA Writer's Project and recalled the exile of the rebels:

> My pappy was a kind of a boss of the negroes that run the boat, and they all belong to old Master Joe. Some had been in a big run-away and had been brung back, and wasn't so good, so he kept them on the boat all the time mostly. . . . My pappy run away one time, four or five years before I was born, mammy tell me, and at that time a whole lot of Cherokee slaves run off at once. They got over in Creek Country and stood off the Cherokee officers that went to git them, but pretty soon they give up and come home. Mammy says they was lots of excitement on Old Master's place and all the negroes mighty scared, but he didn't sell my pappy off. He jest kept him and he was a good negro after that. He had to work on the boat, though, and never got to come home but once in a long while.[31]

Lewis Ross uncovered and defused another plot in 1846 when he discovered that some of his slaves had been collecting guns and ammunition. Ross's questioning of the slaves failed to reveal what they intended to do with their arsenal, but exposure of their conspiracy and confiscation of the means by which they had hoped to accomplish their end effectively thwarted what might have been another significant uprising.[32]

The revolt of 1842 and both real and imagined plots resulted in a paranoia throughout the Nation, and the *Advocate* began publishing accounts of slave uprisings and conspiracies elsewhere. A story reprinted from the *New York Sun* revealed a conspiracy in Virginia which had been betrayed by a free black in New York who had heard about the plot from relatives in Norfolk. The editor of the *Advocate* commented on a Caribbean rebellion: "The accounts of the Insurrection of the blacks in Martinique and their barbarities are horrible." Reports of major crimes committed by blacks also found their way into the pages of the *Advocate,* such as the article concerning a negro man found guilty of raping a white woman in Virginia and a report of the murder of a Missouri man within three hundred yards of his house by two slaves wielding axes.[33]

Accounts of violent crimes, the many escapes and depredations, and the hysteria that accompanied the slave revolts resulted in the passage of an elaborate black code. Although the Constitution of 1827 had relegated blacks to a subject position, laws regulating the behavior of blacks before removal had been cursory (see chap. 4). The Constitution adopted in 1839 reaffirmed the inferior status of residents of the Nation who possessed African ancestry: "No person who is of negro or mulatto parentage . . . shall be eligible to hold any office of profit, honor, or trust under this Government." In response to the lawlessness and violence and as a consequence of the destruction of many traditional Cherokee values that had tended to mitigate harsher aspects of plantation slavery, the National Council and Committee also passed a series of repressive laws which governed the activities of slaves and free blacks within the boundaries of the Nation.[34]

The first law passed by the council after removal was entitled "An Act to Prevent Amalgamation with Colored Persons." Although a similar law had existed before removal, the earlier version had merely prohibited whites or Indians from marrying slaves or freeing slaves for the purpose of matrimony while the new law provided that "intermarriage shall not be lawful between a free male or female citizen with any slave or person of color." The latter law prescribed fifty stripes for convicted females of both races and a hundred lashes for black males whereas the earlier laws had punished black and Cherokee males equally but more severely than females.[35]

Nevertheless illegal sexual liaisons and marriages between Cherokees and blacks continued to occur as they had before removal. In 1824 Shoe Boots had petitioned the council to recognize the legitimacy and citizenship of his three children by a black slave. The council granted the request on the condition that "Capt. Shoe Boots cease begetting any more children by his said Slave *woman.*" Shoe Boots was not the only violator of the miscegenation law, and the census of 1835 confirms that a small group of Cherokee citizens readily admitted having African ancestry.[36]

"Amalgamation" did not cease with the more stringent law which was passed after removal. Missionaries reported that intermarriage continued and laws were not enforced. Aiky, the free black woman who was kidnapped along with her daughter, stated that another daughter Betsy who had been kidnapped earlier was married to a Cherokee named De-gar-tea-dees-ke and had a child by him. Intermarriage also took place between Cherokee women and blacks. Agnes Walker told the WPA interviewer, "My maternal grandmother was a full blood Cherokee and my grandfather was a negro." Sarah Wilson identified her father as Ned Johnson, the son of her Cherokee master, and noted that at the age of eight her grandmother had explained that her parentage was "why old Mistress picked on me so." Although marriages and liaisons occurred, sometimes openly, the fact remained that such relationships were against the law, and the *Advocate*'s accounts of infractions such as the following served as a reminder of their illegality: "A case of practical amalgamation was tried at this place last Friday, which resulted in the conviction of the parties, and their punishment with stripes. Gay gallants should be cautious how they take to their bosoms ebon companions."[37]

Before removal Cherokee law required free blacks to obtain a permit to reside in the Nation and after removal the council significantly extended the liabilities imposed on free blacks. An 1840 law declared it illegal for "any free negro or mulatto, not of Cherokee blood, to hold or own any improvement within the limits of this Nation." In 1842 the council passed an act that required all free blacks who had not been emancipated by Cherokees to leave the Nation. The same act also provided that a master who chose to free his slaves continued to be held responsible for the conduct of his former bondsmen. In the event that the former master died, the law demanded that the freedmen post a bond for their good behavior or leave the Nation. The final section of the bill indicated why Cherokees may have sud-

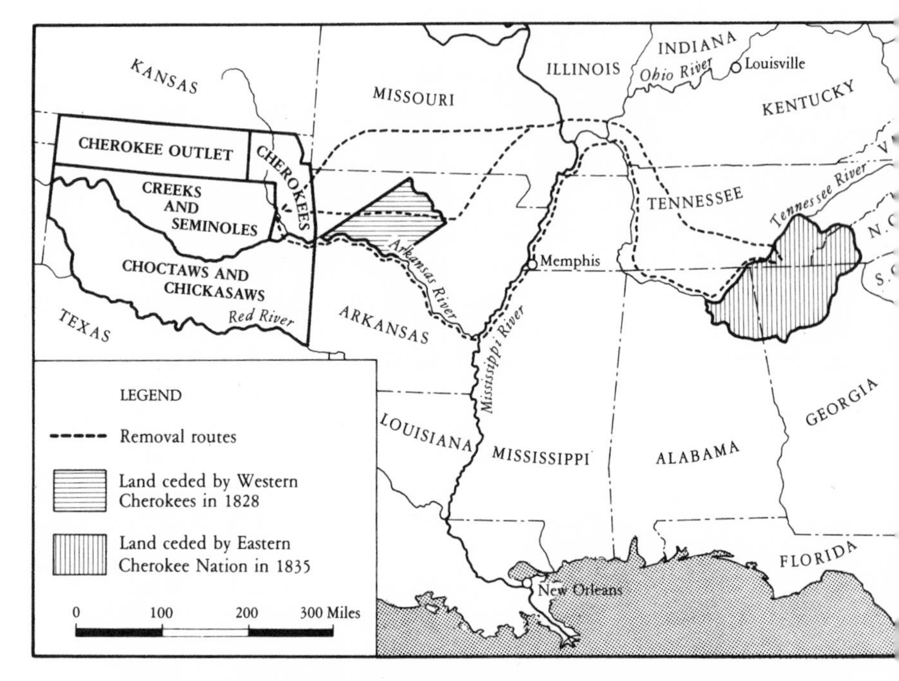

Map 4. Land Cession and Removal (From John W. Morris and Edwin C. McReynolds, *Historical Atlas of Oklahoma,* Norman, Okla., 1932; Grant Foreman, *Indian Removal: The Emigration of the Five Civilized Tribes,* Norman, Okla., 1932)

denly become so concerned about the free blacks in their midst. "Should any free negro or negroes be found guilty of aiding, abetting or decoying any slave or slaves, to leave his or their owner or employer, such free negro or negroes, shall receive for each and every such offence, one hundred lashes on the bare back, and be immediately removed from this Nation.[38]

The council in 1840 also made it illegal for slaves to own any property and empowered the sheriff in each district to confiscate horses, cattle, hogs, and firearms belonging to slaves that had not been disposed of in accordance with the law. The sheriff was instructed to offer the contraband for sale at public auction, "the proceeds of such sale to be paid to the said violator, after deducting eight per cent for the Sheriff's fee." The purpose of this law was reportedly to relieve slaves of the temptation to steal corn. Some slaves, however, continued to own livestock without opposition. The council further restricted the property rights of slaves when it passed a law which made it "unlawful for any person to trade with a negro slave, in any way whatever, without first having obtained permission from the owner of such negro slave."[39]

In 1841 the repressive tendency developed as the council authorized the appointment of patrol companies in the various districts of the Nation and instructed the patrolers to "take up and bring to punishment any negro or negroes, that may be strolling about, not on their owners' premises, without a pass." In an attempt to avert a slave revolt and to control the lawlessness which was rampant in the Nation, the act also empowered the patrol companies to punish any black whom they discovered to be carrying "weapons of any kind, such as guns, pistols, Bowie-knives, butcher-knives or dirks."[40]

The patrol companies seem to have become gradually lax in the performance of their duties, and many districts discontinued patrols after a semblance of harmony and order returned to the Nation in 1846. Memories of the chaotic early 1840s, however, prompted the *Advocate* to print the following editorial in 1853:

> We would take this time to say to all slave-holders in our country, to draw the reigns of government over the slaves with a

> steady and firm hand. The permitting of our slaves at any and all times without our consent to run about over the country generates a spirit of insubordination. They forget their stations and become impertinent and insulting.
>
> They are permitted to meet and congregate in large crowds in various neighhoods [*sic*] where drinking, gambling, and places of mischief are concocted and executed to their own detriment and the safety and good order of society.

The *Advocate* urged that the patrol companies be reinstituted under the provisions of the law of 1841 "to guard the interest and property of the country."[41]

A law enacted by the council in 1841 prohibiting the teaching of free blacks or slaves to read and write represented a major departure from the rudimentary preremoval slave code which had lacked such a provision.[42] Cherokee planters in the East rarely objected to their slaves receiving instruction and claimed that it made them better bondsmen. Therefore, missionaries of the American Board of Commissioners for Foreign Missions openly conducted "Sabbath schools" for both red and black parishioners throughout the Nation. Sometimes the missionaries held separate schools for the two races after the fashion reported by one missionary. "A Sabbath school is held in the morning for Cherokees, and in the afternoon for the black people." Other Sabbath school teachers, however, wrote to their headquarters in Boston about integrated instruction: "I have generally taught a Sabbath school for the blacks, and occasionally several adult Cherokees." Jeremiah Evarts, one of the missionaries, described the amazing success of the schools:

> A Sabbath school for the instruction of blacks, has been kept up since last summer. The improvement which a number of them have made, is truly wonderful. A man of thirty years, who only knew the alphabet when the school commenced, can now read a chapter, or a psalm, very decently. A boy of fifteen, who did not know a single letter, can now read very well in the Testament. Several others have begun to read the Bible.

Cherokees occasionally benefited directly from the instruction received by blacks in the Sabbath schools. One Cherokee youth even learned to spell from black servants who attended the Sabbath school conducted at Brainerd.[43]

A few Cherokees permitted the children of their slaves to attend the regular mission schools along with their own children, but only some missions accepted slave children as students. In 1820 American Board missionaries resolved to leave the admission of black children to the discretion of teachers in local schools. The teachers at Dwight Mission in the West decided to refuse black students in 1822 after an incident between a black boy and a Cherokee girl nearly caused parents to withdraw their daughters. Missions in the East usually accepted black children. A problem arose, however, when the State of Georgia began trying to enforce its laws in the Cherokee Nation because the Georgia slave code prohibited the instruction of blacks. In 1832 the Georgia Guard invaded the classroom of Sophia Sawyer, a missionary of the American Board, and informed her that she was in violation of the law because two black children were in her class. The guard threatened to have her arraigned at the next term of court if the instruction of the children did not cease.[44]

In surrendering to southern white supremacy and their own growing racism, the Cherokees passed the 1841 act that made the instruction of blacks illegal and provided for the collection of a fine by the Nation from offenders. An amendment to the act was passed in 1848 which empowered the sheriff to expel from the Nation any white person guilty of this crime. Still, the strict laws against teaching blacks to read and write did not prevent some blacks from acquiring basic literacy skills. The five members of the Moore family who resided in the Nation until they emigrated to Liberia all knew how to read and the youngest child could write as well. Some missionaries encouraged Cherokees to break the law which prohibited teaching slaves to read, and they apparently met with some success. Chaney McNair, a Cherokee slave, recalled that a neighboring slaveholder, Benjamin Franklin Landrum, believed in educating his bondsmen and "taught them all to read and write, from the time they were children." Richard Taylor even sent his slave children to the mission school. In 1845 one missionary reported that half the slaves in his congregation could read.[45]

Although Cherokee planters strengthened their laws concerning slaves and free blacks, many of their sentiments regarding slavery seem to have remained basically unchanged as their disregard for various provisions indicates. The planters' attitudes about the institution of slavery are clearly revealed in the two newspapers published by the Nation, the preremoval *Cherokee Phoenix* and the postremoval *Cherokee Advocate.* These newspapers do not necessarily reflect the views of the readers, of course, but the ideas which the two presented no doubt partly reflected and shaped the thinking of the readers. Furthermore, the newspapers probably found more subscribers among the wealthier, more highly acculturated Cherokee slaveholders than among the poorer, nonslaveholding conservatives.

The *Phoenix* frequently addressed itself to the question of the international slave trade and came out in solid opposition to its continuation. The newspaper exposed the techniques employed by traders to evade existing laws and vehemently condemned them. One article entitled "A Scene in Africa" and reprinted from the American Colonization Society's *African Repository* vividly portrayed the cruelty of the capture of slaves in Africa and their transportation to the New World. "Here every day for centuries, has the human body been bound in chains, the ties of kind fellowship, of nature's strongest affections, ruthlessly sundered, and hope which smiles in death, made to perish by living agony. . . . My God! who can describe the miseries of those crowded to death in the dungeons of a slave ship?" Articles also appeared which lamented the condition of slaves after their arrival in this hemisphere and described bondage as "a situation as debasing to the human mind, and infinitely worse as regards physical sufferings, than the ordinary condition of the brute creation."[46]

Following removal to Indian Territory, the *Advocate* continued the condemnation of the slave trade. A speech by Lord Aberdeen to the British House of Lords on the suppression of the traffic in slaves appeared as did an "Important Proclamation" by which the governor of Cuba warned that all ships arriving at that island with slaves on board would be confiscated. Another angry article accused United States ships of concealing their involvement in the illegal trade by changing colors midway in their journey to Brazil, and a similar essay claimed that the practice by British West Indian planters of using contract labor from Sierra Leone masked a "revival of the slave trade by Great Britain."[47]

Advancing beyond mere disapproval of the slave trade, the editor of the *Phoenix* appeared to favor gradual and compensated abolition and voluntary manumission everywhere. The *Phoenix* concerned itself with the matter of slavery in the District of Columbia not by taking a direct stand but by reprinting resolutions introduced and memorials presented to Congress for the gradual abolition of slavery in the capital of the United States. On an individual level, notices such as the one which disclosed that William Brown, a Tennessee judge, had freed his fifteen slaves in his will seemed to offer a subtle suggestion to Cherokee slaveholders.[48]

The abolition movement was well under way by the time the *Advocate* commenced publication, and the newspaper frequently printed fairly neutral articles about the movement indicating a tolerance of abolitionist ideas if not their wholesale acceptance. Perhaps the presence of proabolitionist missionaries whom the Cherokees admired tempered criticism of abolitionism. The editor, for example, reported that "after years of perseverance John Quincy Adams has at length accomplished repeal of the Rule of the House of Representatives which precluded the reception of Abolition petitions." Another article dispassionately announced the abolition of slavery on the Island of Saint Bartholemew. The *Advocate* did, however, castigate those abolitionists whom the editor termed "slave stealing miscreants." One article blamed abolitionists who hid escaped slaves for "violence and bloodshed" although it seems that the violence was on the part of the slave catchers and the blood belonged to the slaves and the abolitionists. Another unsympathetic account of an abolitionist involved in "aiding and abetting the abduction of slaves" pointed out that in Maryland "the offence is punishable by imprisonment in the Penitentiary."[49]

Although the *Advocate* on occasion condemned the activities of the abolitionists, the newspaper did not undertake a systematic or even haphazard attempt to defend the institution of slavery. In 1830 the *Phoenix* had labeled as a "queer doctrine" a speech by South Carolina Governor Stephen D. Miller in which he said, "Slavery is not a national evil; on the contrary, it is a national benefit," and the *Advocate* echoed the sentiments of its predecessor. The strongest statement ever made by the editor of the *Advocate* in defense of slavery predicted how people in the future would view slaveholders. "*Slavery in 1875*—When we look back one hundred and thirty years, we shall find that our Eastern and Northern ancestors were slaveholders as well as those in the South, and no one will dispute that there were a race of sober, discreet, pious men, as religious, as well and humanly disposed as any of succeeding generations." In general the Cherokees neither heartily condemned nor strongly defended the institution of slavery but preferred reticence. William Shorey Coody, a wealthy planter, wrote John Ross from Philadelphia after he witnessed the burning of Pennsylvania Hall by antiabolitionists that the event had convinced him that where the issue of slavery was involved "our *Silence* was the better and indeed only proper course."[50]

Since most Cherokees apparently did not subscribe to the theory that slavery was a positive good, they sometimes admitted that blacks possessed the ability to progress politically, socially, and intellectually under the proper conditions. The *Advocate* reported that blacks and mulattoes held positions as chief justice, attorney general, judge, governor, magistrates, legislators, jurors, newspaper editors, and clergymen in the Caribbean islands. The paper also noted items such as the story which reported that "Macon B. Allen, a colored man, has been admitted to practice at the Boston bar" and referred to an eighteen-year-old slave as "a remarkable black boy" because he could solve multiplication and division problems "which would require a long process of figuring on the slate, with perfect ease in his mind."[51]

Some Cherokees hoped that the colonization movement would provide a solution to the problem of the continuing slave trade and would make it possible for blacks to establish their own political, social, and economic institutions apart from white and Cherokee societies and lands. David Brown wrote the editor of a Richmond, Virginia, newspaper in 1825:

> There are some African slaves among us. They have been, from time to time, brought in and sold by white men. They are, however, generally well treated, and they much prefer living in a nation, to a residence in the United States. There is hardly an intermixture of Cherokee and African blood. The presumption is, that the Cherokees will, at no distant day, cooperate with the humane efforts of those who are liberating and sending this proscribed race to the land of their fathers.[52]

Endorsements of colonization appeared frequently in the *Phoenix.* One article expressed the hope that "the exile, sufferings, and degredation of the Africans, may be succeeded by their return, felicity and honor." The paper noted approvingly that the Kentucky Assembly had passed a resolution favoring colonization and that Virginians had organized a state colonization society. The *Phoenix* closely followed the activities of the American Colonization Society. The obituary of "Mr. Ashmum, the friend of Africa & late agent of the American Colonization Society" was reprinted from the *New Haven Journal,* and the *Phoenix* happily announced the appointment of Ashmum's successor. The paper also noted the society's success in recruiting colonists for Liberia and reported on the arrival of repatriated Africans.[53]

Cherokee planters before removal allowed their slaves to establish the African Benevolent Society in affiliation with the American Colonization Society. William Chamberlain, a missionary of the American Board of Commissioners at Willstown, supervised the founding and operation of the slave association and sent the following report to the national office in 1830: "This society is composed entirely of Slaves having Cherokee masters. They meet on the evening of the first Monday in each month to pray for the blessing of God on the colony at Liberia and on the ACS." The members of the Wills Valley Benevolent Society anticipated "making out enough to carry one emigrant to Liberia" but never realized their goal although the slaves did make remittances to the national treasurer in 1830 and 1831 of twelve and eight dollars, respectively. The contribution in 1831 would have been more substantial according to Chamberlain had it not been for the fact that "some busy persons succeeded in prejudicing many of the members against the object and in persuading them to spend their money another way."[54]

The Cherokee slaves do not seem to have reestablished their auxiliary of the American Colonization Society after removal, but interest by Cherokee planters in colonization continued as a means of ending the slave trade. One article in the *Advocate* which reported an attempt by the colony of Liberia to buy land between Monrovia and Cape Palmas pointed out that the purchase would halt the slave trade along eight hundred miles of the African coast. Other related items concerned the continuing prosperity of the colony and the desire of blacks to return to their native continent.[55] The *Advocate* failed to mention any desire on the part of Cherokee planters to manumit and repatriate their bondsmen.

The only interest in active colonization after removal seems to have been among the free blacks in the Nation. In December 1852, a family of free blacks from the Cherokee Nation embarked for Liberia aboard the brig *Zebra* but all of the emigrants died of cholera except eighteen-year-old John who arrived in Monrovia in March. Following the tragedy, the *Advocate* printed the following notice: "Died at sea, in the month of January last, Abraham Moore and his wife, Nancy, their daughter Violet and their son Charles, free black people, on the way from the Cherokee Nation to the Republic of Liberia. Abraham and Nancy had been for many years exemplary professors of religion, and at the time of their departure, were members of the Mission Church at Park Hill."[56]

The Cherokee planters' waning interest in emancipating and colonizing their slaves can best be explained in the context of removal, the chaos which followed and the alteration of traditional Cherokee values. Postremoval chaos involved not only whites and Cherokees but also blacks, and the planters who formed an economic, political, and social elite reacted to escapes and rebellions by passing a series of strict laws governing the activities of slaves and free blacks. Although slavery among the Cherokees continued to be different from the institution practiced by white southerners, the differences became less perceptible. The Cherokees persisted in their condemnation of the slave trade and reacted only mildly to the abolition movement. Slaveholders did not defend the enslavement of Africans but recognized slavery merely as a means of providing the large labor force that had become a necessity for producing the surplus which distinguished the "progressive" Cherokee from his conservative brother. As wealth became one of the major values of this upper class any attempt to undermine the means by which they had achieved status was discouraged. Thus colonization as well as other solutions to the "problem" of slavery was abandoned or redefined so that the peculiar institution and the fortunes that it had produced could be protected.

6

Masters and Slaves

While the controversy over removal exacerbated the economic and cultural divisions within Cherokee society and the postremoval chaos resulted in a hardening of attitudes toward blacks and a strengthening of the slave code, Cherokee planters continued to live in much the same way as they had before removal. Agriculture provided the economic foundation for most Cherokee slaveholders but other enterprises supplemented their incomes both before and after removal. Whenever possible, planters expanded their commercial, industrial and agricultural holdings and such expansion necessitated the purchase and effective utilization of more slaves. Consequently, the slaves themselves found their lives shaped by the fluctuating demand for labor and by the activities in which their masters were engaged, but they managed nevertheless to maintain a viable family life and a social existence apart from the impositions placed on them by their masters.

Most of the fortunes possessed by Cherokee planters originated in the colonial Indian trade. As the descendants of white traders who lived among the Cherokees in the eighteenth century and warriors who had invested capital obtained through trade in slaves, many planters were second and third generation slaveholders who had inherited their position in the upper economic class of Cherokee society. Although these heirs shifted their attention to agriculture in the 1790s and the first decade of the nineteenth century, trade continued to be an element in the incomes of many slaveholders. Lewis Ross, the brother of Chief John Ross and the descendant of traders, for example, owned two or three large stores in the Nation before removal, and New

England missionaries who visited him in 1829 reported that he also had "an elegant white house near the bank of the river, as neatly furnished as almost any in Litchfield County [and] negroes enough to wait on us." In stores such as the ones operated by Lewis Ross, Cherokees sold surplus agricultural produce and purchased manufactured goods. The planters usually managed to harvest more cotton and corn than they could use and sold the excess to merchants who shipped the produce by boat down the Tennessee and Mississippi rivers to New Orleans for sale.[1]

Before removal the majority of Cherokee slaveholders lived in northwestern Georgia, northeastern Alabama, and southeastern Tennessee where the soil was fertile and the broad plains offered excellent pasturage for large herds of cattle, horses, sheep, goats, and swine, most of which belonged to the wealthier Cherokees. James Vann, the largest slaveholder and perhaps the richest man in the Cherokee Nation in the first decade of the nineteenth century, reportedly owned "a hundred head of horses, 400 head of cattle and plenty of hogs." Because the Cherokee custom was to allow livestock to forage in the forests, the herds commanded little time on the part of slaves until late fall, when the Cherokees rounded up some for butchering or sale.[2]

Cherokee planters used slave labor in the cultivation of tobacco, wheat, oats, indigo, and potatoes as well as corn and cotton. In 1829 James Vann's son-in-law had "about six or seven hundred acres of the best land you ever saw, and negroes enough to manage it and clear as much more as he pleases; raised this year about five thousand bushels of corn." Occasionally the planters employed an overseer to supervise the operation of their plantations. James Vann had a white overseer as early as 1800, and even as late as 1831 when problems with whites were mounting George M. Waters requested a permit from the council to hire a white man "of good character" as an overseer.[3]

The slaves of Cherokees also acted as servants in their masters' private homes and in public houses and taverns which some planters such as James Vann and his son Joseph owned. In addition the Vanns were the proprietors of a ferry located just below the point where the Chestatee empties into the Chattahoochee. A traveler gave the following description of the Vann ferry:

"[The ferry boat] was a broad, shallow, flat-bottomed thing, with double floor, built of very thick planks, having space enough for a large wagon and team, and making one think of an ordinary plank-bridge turned bottom upwards. A rope of twisted hide was stretched across the river and fastened to a tree on each side. The flat was pulled across by means of the rope."[4] Vann no doubt entrusted the arduous task of towing the crude vessel across the current to some of his slaves.

Although Cherokee planters required hard work from their bondsmen, they probably treated their slaves much better on the average than did their white counterparts. Following a brief stay with a Cherokee planter in Arkansas in 1819, a member of an expedition to the Rockies recorded in his journal: "The Cherokees are said to treat their slaves with much lenity." Samuel Worcester, the American Board missionary, reported from Park Hill shortly after removal that Cherokee masters treated their slaves better than whites in the surrounding states. According to Worcester, Cherokee masters did not interfere with marriage among their slaves and most allowed their bondsmen to own horses, cattle, and pigs despite the law forbidding such. The missionary maintained that he had never heard of the murder of a slave by a master and that great severity in corporal punishment would bring odium to the perpetrator. A decade later Daniel Butrick, another missionary, wrote that the Cherokees did not enforce the laws prohibiting intermarriage and teaching slaves to read. Butrick also expressed the opinion that slaves in the Cherokee Nation did not work half as hard as workers in the North. Thus relative leniency on the part of masters seems to have been characteristic of Cherokee slavery both before and after removal.[5]

The obvious exception to this generalization was James Vann. This wealthy planter was good and generous when sober as demonstrated by his kindness to Moravian missionaries who in 1800 decided to locate their school and church at Springplace near his home. Despite his disdain for religion, Vann offered the Moravians assistance, sent a slave to help with the heavy labor, and allowed his slaves to attend services at the mission. Vann's frequent and immoderate consumption of alcohol, however, evoked great cruelty, and his slaves reacted to the abuse he gave them in kind. On one occasion a group of slaves attacked their master and robbed him. The irate planter responded by burning one of the participants alive, and upon hearing that another slave was plotting against his life, shot him on the spot.[6] Vann's drunken brutality and his slaves' insubordination were apparently exceptions in the period before removal. The absence of advertisements for runaways in the *Phoenix* probably indicates that slaves did not become so dissatisfied that they ran away. One slave who belonged to a Cherokee and was sold to a white man from whom she escaped told the sheriff who captured her that she belonged to a fictional Cherokee in the hope that someone in the Nation would redeem her. Although many slaves did run away after removal, one of them, Henry Bibb, insisted: "If I must be a slave, I had by far, rather be a slave to an Indian, than to a white man."[7]

While removal probably did not produce drastic changes in the treatment of bondsmen or in the personal relationships between masters and slaves, relocation in the West did alter Cherokee agriculture to some extent. Indian country was located slightly above the cotton belt, and the climate made the production of cotton unprofitable on a large scale. After removal planters grew cotton primarily for domestic consumption and built no cotton gins until 1844, when George W. Gunter erected a gin on the Arkansas River. Many Cherokees raised sheep and made their clothing of wool or wool mixed with cotton rather than fabric woven from cotton alone. The western Indian country was well suited for grains, however, and the Cherokees planted and exported large quantities of wheat, corn, and millet.[8]

The larger planters or those planters who primarily concerned themselves with other ventures employed overseers to operate their plantations. When Joseph Vann was editor of the *Advocate,* he placed the following notice in the newspaper: "Wanted—A white man to take charge of a farm and negroes. A young man of good moral character, and who has had some experience in the management of negroes, can get employment by enquiring at this office." Planters frequently imposed restraints on overseers in meting out punishment. One of John

Ross's overseers complained, "I am not bound for the conduct of your negroes in no way because I could not be sustained if I was to try to correct them." Instead of employing overseers some planters used slaves to supervise the operation of their farms. Morris Sheppard, a former slave interviewed in the WPA Writer's Project, recalled that his master, Joe Sheppard, had some kind of business in Fort Smith and left his uncle in charge while he was gone. "When he got home he called my uncle in and ask about what we done all day and tell him what we better do de next day. My uncle Joe was de slave boss and he tell us what de Master say do."[9]

Whether the operation was supervised by an overseer or a slave boss, a fairly sophisticated division of labor existed on the larger plantations. Ella Coody Robinson, whose father, William Shorey Coody, owned one of the largest estates in the Cherokee Nation, recalled that her mother supervised a head cook, an assistant cook, a housemaid, a serving girl, a nurse for her children, and a man who helped with the cleaning. The Coody household also included a laundress and a coachman. The plantation community consisted not only of these house servants and the field hands but also a shoemaker, a carpenter, and a blacksmith. According to Mrs. Robinson, social classes existed among the bondsmen, and the house servants and the skilled workers considered themselves to be above the field hands.[10]

Slaveholders found tasks to occupy their slaves year round. In spring the wheat, corn, millet, and cotton had to be planted along with vegetable gardens. Spring was also the season for shearing sheep whose wool would provide the next winter's clothing and for making soap out of cracklings left over from the winter hog-killing and lye which had been extracted from ashes. In summer the slaves cultivated the crops and kept them free of weeds, gathered the fresh produce, and picked ripe fruit, which they placed on the roof of the smokehouse to dry. In fall the wheat had to be harvested and ground and the surplus produce taken to market. Slaves also cut millet and pulled corn. Some masters instructed their slaves to remove the blades from the corn stalks and bind them in bundles for fodder for the livestock. The slaves picked cotton if their master had grown any and took it to his house, where they placed it by the fire to dry. Unless a planter took his cotton to a gin, the slaves had to pick out the seeds by hand and they often spent their evenings at this task. Also at night and after the crops had been laid by, the slaves helped spin the cotton fiber into thread and weave the thread into cloth. Planters who owned pecan or walnut groves employed their slaves in the gathering of nuts and occasionally had enough surplus to send some nuts to market. In winter slaves chopped wood and butchered livestock for their masters. Morris Sheppard reminisced: "When it git good and cold and de crop all gathered in anyways, they is nothing to do 'cepting hog killing and a lot of wood chopping and you don't get cold doing dem two things." Some planters killed as many as twenty hogs at one time, salted them down in troughs hewed out of trees, and when the meat had cured sufficiently, hung the sides of pork in the smokehouse over a smoldering fire of hickory chips. As Sheppard remembered butchering, the household enjoyed some of the meat fresh: "De hog killing mean we gits lots of spare ribs and chitlings, and somebody always git sick eating too much of dat fresh pork. I always pick a whole passel of muskatines for old master and he make up sour wine, and dat helps out when we git the bowel complaint from eating dat fresh pork."[11]

The financial situation of Cherokee slaveholders varied and therefore they lived in vastly different styles. Morris Sheppard described the house belonging to his master who owned two families of slaves: "The big house was a double log house wid a big hall and a stone chimney but no porches, wid two rooms at each end, one top side of de other." Some planters weatherboarded their houses; others did not. Sarah Wilson's master lived in "a double log house made of square hewed logs, and with a double fireplace out of rock where they warmed theirselves on one side and cooked on the other." This house also boasted a front porch where the family sat and even slept in the summer. A few Cherokee planters owned cooking stoves but most had only fireplaces with pot hooks over which the slave cook labored. The wealthier planters, however, lived in far more elaborate houses. Colonel Ethan Allen Hitchcock, an army officer who inspected the Indian country for the U.S. government, gave the following description of the home of Lewis Ross near Park Hill:

> Lewis Ross the merchant is wealthy and lives in considerable style. His house is of the cottage character, clapboarded and painted, his floor carpeted, his furniture elegant, cane bottomed chairs, of high finish, two superior mahogany Boston rocking chairs, mahogany ladies work table with drawers, a very superior Chickering piano on which his unmarried daughter, a young lady of about 17 or 18, just from school at Rawway in New Jersey, plays some waltzes, and sings some songs.[12]

Lewis Ross, like many of the wealthier planters, had nonagricultural assets which enabled him to live in such a style. Following removal, Ross reopened his mercantile business and ultimately operated two stores in Salina and one at Fort Gibson. Ross told Hitchcock that "he sold a great proportion of domestics, some ready-made clothing, especially pantaloons and overcoats, and a great many shoes." Ross transported his dry goods from Van Buren aboard wagons pulled by teams of oxen, and one of his slaves later recalled that the business was so prosperous that "several wagons were kept busy on the road as long as he ran the store."[13]

The export of grain and the import of manufactured goods from the east lured some planters into the shipping business. Joseph Vann found this enterprise not only economically rewarding but also personally satisfying and spent most of his time aboard his boats while overseers looked after his agricultural interests. Boats transported passengers and mail to Indian Territory as well as farming implements and supplies, such as sugar, coffee, tea, rice, and spices. Generally planters purchased these staples once a year where they sold their crops and the provisions had to last until they placed the next annual order. The boats usually docked at Webbers Falls on the Arkansas River when they unloaded cargoes from as far away as Cincinnati or New Orleans, but some of the wealthier planters constructed docks near their homes to facilitate the receipt of supplies.[14]

At first Vann's fleet consisted of a steamboat ferry on the Illinois River and flatboats which his slaves floated down the river and then poled back upstream. Encouraged by the profits which ownership of a steamboat promised, Vann built a steam powered, side-wheel vessel and named her the *Lucy Walker* after his favorite and fastest race horse. Vann used his bondsmen including those who had participated in the abortive insurrection of 1842 to operate the *Lucy Walker.* In the fall of 1844 the boat exploded on the Ohio River a few miles below Albany, Indiana, and about 50 of the 130 passengers on board, including Vann, his son-in-law Preston Mackay, and twelve slaves, were killed. R.P. Vann, the grandson of Joseph Vann, repeated the following account which one of the surviving Vann slaves had told him:

> He said that my grandfather was on the top deck, entertaining the passengers at a ball and dinner and there was a good deal of drinking. They were having a race with another boat on the river and though they were a little ahead of the other boat my grandfather came down to the boiler deck drunk and he told the negro to throw another side of meat on the fire in order to get more steam so that they could gain on the other boat. The negro told him that the boat was carrying every pound of steam it could stand and Joe Vann pulled his pistol on the negro and told him that if he did not obey him he would shoot him. The negro threw the side of meat on the fire as he was ordered and then turned and ran to the stern of the boat and jumped into the river, and he had not much more than got into the water when the boilers blew up.

Considering Vann's penchant for racing and drinking, this is probably a fairly accurate account of the disaster. A passenger who survived commented to the *Advocate* that "he discovered some time previous to the explosion, that there was at least a very gross mismanagement of the engine."[15]

Steamboating usually proved to be a hazardous investment not only in terms of possible loss of life but also because accidents occurred quite commonly and even those which did not result in fatalities could delay a boat long enough to make it unprofitable. The House Committee on Naval Affairs reported that in the period 1830–40 eight boiler explosions such as the one aboard the *Lucy Walker* claimed 780 lives, and fire destroyed 25 vessels resulting in 255 deaths. Steamboats frequently hit snags in the muddy western rivers or ran aground on sand bars.[16]

Such accidents plagued John Ross, who invested in the steamboat *Victoria.* Ross began his venture with high expectations which one of his partners countenanced in writing the chief, "If we can have good luck we can make money with her this summer." Ross should have accepted the events of the voyage which the *Victoria* had just completed as portentous. His partner encountered difficulty descending the Ohio River to Louisville because of low water and one of the water shafts broke above the mouth of the Arkansas River. In the winter of 1840 the boat struck a log, and the collision forced her on a sand bar. The shipping business entered a slump about the same time, and the proprietors had to borrow money to pay off the crew. By early summer the *Victoria* was running again, but a June gale inflicted new damages. At this point Ross and the other investors decided to sell the steamboat but discovered that the *Victoria* had claims against her amounting to more than the sale price she could command.[17]

Cherokee slaveholders found a safer investment and a more certain source of profit in salines. Josiah Gregg noted that "the most valuable perhaps, and the most abundant mineral production of the Prairies is *Salt* . . . and in the Cherokee nation salt springs are numerous." The first people to operate the salines in Indian Territory were not Cherokees but white men. The Cherokees who had removed in 1808 and 1819 located first in what is now Arkansas and then moved across the river into Indian Territory in 1828, at which time the whites had to relinquish their salt works to the Old Settlers. In 1833 the Old Settlers passed an act making the salines national property to be leased to the highest bidder for a term of five years. When the Eastern Cherokees arrived in 1839 some of the Old Settlers were well established in the business and producing considerable quantities of salt. The government instituted by John Ross and the Eastern Cherokees enacted a law in 1841 which reaffirmed the law of 1833 but provided that all salines would revert immediately to the nation and be opened to bids and that their operators would be paid by the Nation for improvements. The payments received by the Old Settlers for their improvements were small consolation for the loss of their profitable industries, the leases for which the legislature awarded to others.[18]

Lewis Ross leased one of the salines and employed slaves in its operation. Ross reportedly paid fifteen hundred dollars for a slave to be overseer of the saltworks which occupied the time of most of his 150 slaves in the winter when it was too cold to farm. Ross's saline contained several wells that poured salt water. The slaves filled huge pots with the water and placed them on furnaces while others cut the vast quantities of wood needed to keep the furnaces burning. When the water evaporated, pure coarse salt remained in the pots and the slaves then placed the salt in bags so that Ross could sell it.[19] Other salines did not have free-flowing salt water. Salt on the surface of the ground after a rain signaled the presence of subterranean deposits of the valuable mineral and lessees usually employed slaves to drain wells. Once they struck the salt-laden water, the slaves hollowed out trees to use as conduits. After salt was obtained, it was bagged and sold locally, transported overland by ox-pulled wagons, or shipped down the Arkansas River aboard keelboats.[20]

Slaveholders used their slaves in other nonagricultural enterprises. In addition to leasing the saltworks at Lynch's Prairie near Grand River, for example, Joseph Lynch also owned a tannery which his slave Boson operated when his master was busy with his farm, sawmill, or gristmill. Avery Vann, another large slaveholder, provided bricks fired by slaves in his kiln for local residents as well as for his own buildings. Joe, an African-born slave in the Tahlequah district, wove white oak bushel baskets so tightly that they reportedly held water and his master sold the baskets to residents of the district who used them to carry corn for livestock. Other masters used their slaves' particular skills and knowledge to provide needed services to the neighborhood. Tom Foster's grandfather owned a woman remembered only as Aunt Martha who acted as midwife to most of the families in the community including her masters' and delivered Tom himself. Also renowned for her knowledge of herbal medicines, Aunt Martha used "different herbs for different ailments"—a tea made from butterly root for pneumonia, horsemint tea for typhoid, and polecat bush tea for "summer complaint."[21]

In addition to the highly acculturated slaveholders who had diversified economic interests, a few conservative Cherokees owned slaves but they seem to have valued their slaves less for labor than for companionship and particularly for the ability to speak English. New Thompson reported that "the only negroes who had to work hard were the ones who belonged to the half-breeds. As the Indian didn't do work he didn't expect his slaves to do much work." Cudjo who belonged to Yonguska, chief of the extremely conservative Qualla Cherokees who remained in North Carolina after removal, informed Charles Lanman of their unique master-slave relationship: "He never allowed himself to be called '*master*,' for he said Cudjo was his brother, and not his slave."[22]

In the households of Cherokee traditionalists the only English-speaking person was frequently a bondsman. American Board missionaries reported in 1818 that all blacks in bondage to Cherokees spoke English. The missionaries, who had tremendous difficulty mastering the Cherokee language, occasionally relied on bilingual slaves to translate their sermons. Furthermore, masters often turned to their slaves for aid in communicating with English-speaking visitors. In 1818 Ebenezer Newton spent a night in the home of a Captain Foster, "an Indian of some consequence in the Nation; he could not speak a word of English, that I know of, but he had some negroes who could speak very well." The members of the expedition to the Rocky Mountains in 1819 visited the Old Settlers at Rocky Bayou, Arkansas, where Tom Groves graciously received them as guests and sumptuously entertained them. Major Stephen H. Long, a member of the expedition, recorded in his journal, "Groves, our landlord, though unable to speak or understand our language, held some communication with us by means of signs, being occasionally assisted by a black girl, one of his slaves who interpreted the Cherokee language." Another expedition that journeyed to Indian country in 1832 counted among its number the English artist Charles Joseph Latrobe and the American writer Washington Irving. Latrobe noted that a slave girl belonging to Frenchman Jack (who was of French and Cherokee descent) was the only member of the household who spoke anything other than Cherokee and she acted as interpreter. Long after the final removal some slaves in Indian Territory seem to have been continuing to perform this service for their masters. R.R. Meigs recalled that near Park Hill lived an old Cherokee woman known as Granny Wolfe who relied on her slave to translate. Meigs told the WPA interviewers: "The spectacle seems strange to some of the visitors, no doubt, the coal black girl speaking both English and Cherokee and keeping the old woman informed as to what was being said."[23]

The services performed by most slaves were not so essential and, when slaveholders discovered that they did not need the labor of some of their bondsmen temporarily, they usually hired them out. Renting a slave's labor for a period of time also offered an alternative to sale when a planter's financial situation became strained. John Rollin Ridge, the son of John Ridge, wrote his cousin Stand Watie: "I need money or what can be converted into money right away. I might sell the negroes or I might high them out." Slaveholders who needed a steady income and could not supervise their bondsmen hired them out. For example, following her husband's death the wife of Major Ridge arranged to hire out the slaves inherited by her retarded son Watty so that he would be provided for financially.[24]

The practice of hiring out slaves proved a boon to those who needed additional laborers but were unable to purchase them for various reasons. The cost of hiring a slave from his master was considerably less than his purchase price and therefore more economically feasible on a short-term basis. A twenty-year-old slave, for example, valued at $800 to $1,000, commanded a per annum fee of $100 to $125. In many cases the hiring of a slave was far more practical than the purchase of one. Since Major Ridge's slaves were divided among his children at his death, only a few remained to assist his widow. In 1857 Mrs. Ridge was an elderly woman and had only one servant remaining so she instructed J.W. Washbourne to write Stand Watie: "Old Uncle Phil is about done. He has all the work to do at Ms. Ridge's; to cut and lift wood, and he can hardly drag himself along. Ms.

Ridge wishes to know if you could not send William to help him."[25]

Even American Board missionaries who opposed slavery hired slaves to help them. Most missionaries had scruples about the practice but an acute labor shortage compelled them to use slave labor. The hiring of slaves was a troublesome issue. Daniel Butrick caused dissension in the mission family in 1826 by protesting the hiring of slaves at Brainerd, and the Dwight Mission in the West even passed a resolution not to employ slaves. The resolution was repealed, however, because as Charles Cutler Torrey wrote, "We were obliged to hire slaves from their owners if we wished extra help." Perhaps in an attempt to salve their consciences, the missionaries, according to Rev. Torrey, "always gave them some money for themselves in addition to what we paid their masters."[26]

When planters needed additional workers and decided that it would be more profitable to acquire their own slaves, they had several possible sources for their purchase. Professional slave traders brought their merchandise from states in the Old South to Indian country or more frequently to Arkansas where Cherokees purchased them. In addition Cherokee planters bought slaves from residents of other Indian nations. Many slaveholding pioneers passed through the Cherokee Nation on their way west and sometimes relinquished their chattels. Stand Watie, for example, bought a woman and two children from Jacob and Sebrina Croft, Mormons en route to Salt Lake. Cherokees who traveled abroad also frequently bought slaves and returned them to the Nation. On a trip to New Orleans William Shorey Coody's wife persuaded her husband to buy a woman and her six children who were on their way to New Orleans to be sold. The woman feared that they would be separated and Coody obliged her by purchasing the whole family for $1,500. Coody was not the only Cherokee planter to receive a request from a distraught slave to be bought. Morris Sheppard recalled how his mistress was thwarted in an attempt to purchase a runaway slave:

> One night a runaway negro came across from Texas and he had de blood hounds after him. His britches was all muddy and tore

> where de hound had cut him up in de legs when he clumb a tree in de bottoms. He come to our house and Mistress said for us negroes to give him something to eat and we did. Then up came de man from Texas with de hounds. . . . Mistress try to get de man to tell her who de negro belong to so she can buy him, but de man say he can't sell him and he take him back to Texas with a chain around his two ankles.[27]

When planters needed to dispose of slaves they sold them either within the Nation or to a professional slave trader who transported them out of the Nation for sale. When Andrew Nave advertised "a likely young Negro man twenty-two years of age" in the *Advocate,* he insisted that this "first rate hand" was being sold "for no fault in him at all, only I have no use for him at present." Such assurance apparently paid off, for the advertisement did not appear in the next issue of the *Advocate.* Another advertiser in the *Advocate* was P.H. White and Company of Van Buren, Arkansas, the proprietors of which wanted to buy "fifty likely young negroes suitable for field-hands and house-servants, for which cash will be paid." Slave traders from more distant locales also expressed interest in buying surplus bondsmen in the Cherokee Nation. John Staples, the owner of a "Negro mart" in Memphis, Tennessee, wrote John Drew to inquire about current market prices in the Nation as he desired "to by from 100 to 200 Likely young negroes in which i will pay the highest cash pryces."[28]

At times professional traders offended the sensibilities of Cherokees who preferred to ignore the more unpleasant aspects of slavery. A trader who purchased a group of slaves from Joe Sheppard just after the beginning of the Civil War put his inventory in a pen until he could begin his journey. Morris Sheppard, one of the fortunate slaves who had not been sold, recalled that the trader "never come until the next day, so dey had to sleep in dat pen in a pile like hogs. . . . It made my Master mad, but dey didn't belong to him no more and he couldn't say nothing." In the meantime another slave trader appeared and the first purchaser decided to conduct an auction right on Sheppard's plantation. According to Morris Sheppard, the sale was conducted as follows: "The man put dem on a block and sol 'em to a man dat had come in on a steamboat, and he took dem off on it when de freshet come down and de boat could go back to Fort Smith. It was tied up at de dock at Webber's Falls about a week and we went down and talked to my aunt and brothers and sister. . . . Old Mistress cried jest like an of de rest of us when de boat pull out with dem on it."[29]

Occasionally masters permitted slaves whose services were no longer needed to find their own masters. Sarah Paschal wrote her cousin Stand Watie about disposing of her slave property: "If Tom's & Peggy's wishes can be indulged without compromising my interest, let them be indulged, but if such Masters as they may choose do not give me as much as I think right, I cannot indulge them in the choice of a Master."[30]

Other Cherokee slaveholders arranged for their bondsmen to purchase freedom. Of the five members of the free black family who emigrated from the Cherokee Nation to Liberia, Abraham and Nancy Moore and their oldest child, Violet, had bought their own freedom and the parents had managed to accumulate enough to redeem the second child while the third child had been born free. William Shorey Coody agreed to allow an elderly slave known as Rabbit to purchase himself and permitted the old man and his wife to sell cider and gingerbread to travelers who forded the river on Coody's property and to charge a fee for directing strangers across the river which was full of eddies and suction holes.[31]

Cherokee planters seem to have made little effort to keep families together as Morris Sheppard's account of the sale of his family by a relatively kind master demonstrates. Sheppard's mother had been sold even earlier and had died soon after delivery to her new master. Some bills of sale listed a mother and her offspring but rarely was the father included in such family sales.[32] Occasionally mothers and children were sold to reunite them, but even then financial considerations were paramount. Sarah Paschal wrote Stand Watie: "I would sell Elie to Mr. Tucker for $250. You can take that for him if you cannot get more. I want all I can get for him. I do not want to dispose of him, but as Mr. Tucker has the Mother, perhaps I had better let him have the child." The sale of both parents and the retention of children occurred fairly often. Gilbert Vann told a WPA interviewer: "My father, whom I never saw, was named Toby Vann. He was sold by his master to a plantation owner in Texas. My mother, too, was sold and taken to Texas. My father died soon after his arrival there and before my birth." Rarely did a family remain completely intact. When listing the names of the members of her family for an interviewer, Betty Robertson added, "I had one brother and one sister sold when I was little and I don't remember the names." Chaney McNair was sold at the age of ten to Colonel William Penn Adair for a legal fee incurred by his master Dick Ratcliff. Sarah Wilson recalled that her sister "was sold off to a Starr because she wouldn't have a baby." Sarah's mother found some small consolation in the sale however. Her mistress had insisted that she name all her female children "Annie" after her, and so Sarah's mother called them "Annie" in front of her mistress but "Sarah" and "Lottie" behind her back because "she hate old Mistress and that name too." When her owner sold the older daughter, "Mammy tell her to call herself Annie when she was leaving but call herself Lottie when she git over to the Starrs. And she done it."[33]

Missionaries sometimes tried to influence slaveholders to honor family ties. When Richard Taylor decided to sell a man and his wife without their children, J.C. Ellsworth, an American Board missionary, admonished Taylor about the evils of slavery. When Taylor offered to sell the man to the mission, Ellsworth accepted the offer, emancipated the slave, and took his note for the purchase price. The mission then employed the freedman as a shoemaker and miller.[34]

When a planter bought a slave, the bondsman abandoned the surname of his old master and assumed that of his new one. Chaney McNair explained: "Up to the time my father was sold [to John Drew], he went under the name of Bob Ratcliff, after he was sold he changed his name to Bob Drew, but my mother was still a Ratcliff." A few masters permitted their bondsmen to continue to use the name of a former master. Chaney Richardson's parents belonged to a man by the name of Tucker and when he sold them to Charley Rogers, the new master did not object to their use of the name Tucker "because last name didn't mean nothing to a slave anyways." Richardson pointed out the "folks jest called my pappy 'Charley Rogers' boy Joe'."[35]

In spite of sales, most slaves maintained family ties. Cherokee planters usually allowed men who had been sold away from their families to visit their wives and children, but the frequency of the visits varied. Chaney McNair's father came home once a week after he was sold to a neighbor. On the other hand, Sam Vann's father was united with his family only once a month. In this case the settlement of his master's estate had resulted in Sam, his mother, and ten brothers and sisters becoming the property of a daughter who lived ten miles away from the son who retained Sam's father. Fortunately for this family, the brothers and sisters remained together because frequently when siblings were separated, they never saw each other again. McNair told the interviewer, "My two oldest brothers were sold and I never heard of them anymore."[36]

Slave families who had been separated probably had an opportunity to meet at social, recreational, and religious gatherings. Many Cherokee slaves attended church with their masters. Most slaves belonged to Methodist and Baptist churches. Those who were members of American Board congregations fully participated along with Cherokees in decision-making, and male slaves voted on receiving new members. Most slaves, however, tended to remember their own "singings" better than the more formal church services. The slaves in a particular neighborhood obtained passes from their masters if the masters did not disapprove and gathered at some central location or in one of the cabins to sing, pray, or perhaps be baptized. Many slaves whose masters opposed these meetings slipped away, and those without passes had to be very careful to avoid the patrol companies. In late summer or early fall when the farming was over but the weather was still good, many slaves no doubt accompanied their masters to annual camp meeting. One camp meeting site about two miles north of Stillwell, Oklahoma, was located next to a bubbling spring in a deep secluded valley surrounded by wooded hills. The whole family went to the camp meeting and took camping equipment and food. The participants held worship services twice daily at 11:00 A.M. and at 8:00 P.M., and these services often lasted as long as two hours each. The rest of the time people visited with their neighbors, relatives, and distant acquaintances.[37]

A more secular and perhaps more popular entertainment in the Cherokee Nation was horse racing. The most widely attended races were those held at a track near the Arkansas state line because it attracted whites as well as Cherokees and also because liquor could easily be obtained. Some Cherokee planters, such as the Vanns, owned stables of blooded race horses, and many of the jockeys were black slaves. Slaves also seem to have attended the races sometimes as unwilling spectators because their masters took them there in search of a buyer and often met success. Henry Bibb's Cherokee master, for example, purchased him at a horse race. Promoters advertised the day of the race a week or so in advance and some avid fans arrived early and began placing their bets which ranged from very small to very large the day before the actual race.[38]

Cherokees and probably their bondsmen also gathered and bet on ball games but the slaves did not participate. The Cherokees played two types of ball games, the less competitive of which was between men and women. Players erected a tall pole and attached either a bush over which the ball had to be hurled or a movable object which had to be struck. Only men played the second type of ball game, in which contestants of opposing teams tried to hurl the ball with racquets over their own goal post and to prevent the enemy from scoring at the other goal, which was located at the opposite end of the field.[39]

Cherokee slaves attended Green Corn festivals with their masters but did not take an active part in the stomp dances. This ceremony took place in July when corn had reached the roasting stage. The celebrants cooked the corn in ashes while they roasted their meat over the flame. After feasting all the Cherokees attached shells to their ankles and wrists and joined in the stomp dance. According to one observer, the feasting and dancing continued for days.[40]

Although some opportunities for seeing relatives existed, Cherokee slaves often encountered obstacles in their attempts to sustain familial bonds. Some planters, such as John Lowery, did not allow their slaves to leave the plantation. Jane Battiest recalled, "We did not mix and mingle with other people very much. . . . He kept us at home and did not give us the privilege of visiting anyone except the other slaves he had on the farm." Morris Sheppard's master required him to get a pass before visiting his brothers who lived five miles away in Webbers Falls. Not only was a pass a prerequisite to his visit but if the patrol companies happened to discover a slave who was away from home without a pass, "dey wore him out good and made him go home" according to Sheppard.[41]

Even if their fathers were absent, most slave children seemed to have fared well. Ella Coody Robinson contended that her father refused to allow female slaves to work for one month following the birth of a child. However long postpartum recuperation was, when mothers returned to their chores they usually took their children with them. Chaney Richardson, whose mother was the "house woman," recalled: "Mammy worked at the Big House and took me along every day." The children of field hands either accompanied their parents to the fields or remained near their living quarters in the care of one of the elderly people. Chaney McNair's master, Dick Ratcliff, was a very old man and he took care of the children while his sons supervised the slaves in the fields. The children entertained him by singing "Polly Put the Kettle On" and other songs and by dancing, and the old man staged wrestling contests and foot races.

As soon as they were old enough children began working. As her first chore Chaney Richardson held the hank for her mistress when she was spinning thread, and Morris Sheppard as a child tended twenty calves while the adults grazed and milked the cows. Sarah Wilson's mistress hired her out as a seamstress before she was eight and by the time she reached ten she was making almost all the clothes for her master's family. Sarah Wilson, however, had an unusually hard childhood. She was the granddaughter of her mistress and the old woman, who was a "hellion" in the first place, was particularly cruel to Sarah. The abused child recalled, "She took most of her wrath out hitting us children all the time. She was afraid of grown Negroes. Afraid of what they might do while old Master was away, but she beat us children all the time." At the age of eighty-seven Sarah had scars on her legs from stripes that her master had inflicted with a riding quirt because she told a lie.[42]

In general Cherokee planters seem to have treated elderly slaves well perhaps as a result of the respect elderly slaves received from their peers. Even Sarah Wilson's exceptionally cruel master and mistress did not cross her grandmother, and when the child feared punishment she fled to her grandmother for protection. Furthermore, the old woman seems to have harbored little fear of her owners. Sarah recalled, "One day I was carrying water from the spring and I run up on Grandmammy and Uncle Nick skinning a cow. 'What you-all doing,' I say, and they say to keep my mouth shut or they kill me. They was stealing from the Master to piece out down at the quarters with." Sarah's grandmother's only chore was to mind her master's grandchild: "Grandmammy set on Master's porch and minded the baby mostly." Some masters allowed elderly slaves to retire completely. According to Moses Lonian, Lewis Ross had two slaves in their eighties, Uncle Farrar and Aunt Sarah, who no longer worked for him. They may, however, have had to contribute to their own support because Lonian reported that "the old man set traps and caught wolves, coons, opposums, and skunks and sold the hides."[43]

Most slaves who belonged to Cherokee masters received sufficient food and clothing and adequate housing. The slaves usually ate in their own cabins and their diet consisted of corn bread, cured meat, fresh vegetables, and occasionally chicken, goat, and sheep. A few slaves had their own gardens and chicken houses but most received vegetables, chicken, and eggs from their master. Most slaves supplemented these provisions with deer, turkeys, fish, fruits, berries, nuts, wild potatoes, and greens. Some masters, such as Joe Sheppard, provided their slaves with brown sugar, cane molasses, and sometimes coffee. One of the few planters who rationed provisions and restricted slaves to their rations was Ben Johnson, the master of Sarah Wilson. She recalled: "The slaves would get rations every Monday morning to do them all week. The overseer would weigh and measure according to how many in the family, and if you run out you just starve till you get some more. We all know the overseer steal some of it for his own self but we can't do anything, so we get it from the old master some other way." Johnson's slaves, of course, appropriated what he considered to be his for their own use. Sarah's grandmother and uncle stole his cows and Sarah herself took green peas, beans, and radishes from her mistress's vegetable garden. Even then, Sarah remembered that the slaves ate sweet potatoes most of the time and only occasionally received a ration of goat or sheep along with the potatoes and corn meal.[44]

Housing also varied from one plantation to another. All slaves (and many of their masters) lived in log cabins. Some cabins had floors, stone or brick chimneys, and only a door for light and ventilation. The cabin Sarah Wilson grew up in had no furniture except shelves attached to the walls which served as beds for the children. Other slaves such as Morris Sheppard slept on wooden beds with rope springs and trundle beds which could be pulled out at night for the children and pushed away during the day. Sheppard's cabin was also furnished with a table and chairs held together with wooden dowels instead of nails because "nails cost big money."[45]

Cherokee planters usually provided adequate clothing for their slaves. Children wore long shirts made of cotton or wool-mix that had been dyed with copperas, while adults had shirts and trousers or dresses made of the same fabrics. Slaves sometimes had sheepskin jacks, wool socks and stockings, and wool gloves for winter. Most slaves went bare foot in summer unless they wore their shoes to church. Shoes as well as clothing were generally manufactured on the plantation, although the Vanns provided their house servants factory-made high top shoes with brass caps on the toes. The homemade shoes were of cow hide tanned with bark and had soles nailed on with wooden pegs.[46]

When they became seriously ill, most slaves received professional medical care. Minor ailments were left to home remedies, but as Morris Sheppard phrased it: "If somebody bad sick he [the master] git de doctor right away, and he don't let no negroes mess around wid no poultices and teas and sech things like cupping-horns neither." Planters may have had an ulterior motive for their concern about the health of slaves, as Joseph Scales pointed out: "Should a slave get sick he was given the best medical attention possible, for to get him well, meant more labor on the plantation."[47]

Just as the food, housing, and clothing of slaves differed from one plantation to another so did working hours. Morris Sheppard's master had two families of slaves who cultivated a fifty acre field. Sheppard recalled: "They was so many of us for dat little field we never did have to work hard. Up at five o'clock and back in sometimes about de middle of de evening, long before sundown." Chaney McNair compared the situation of Cherokee slaves to that of slaves belonging to whites: "There were no restrictions set as to how much work we should do in a day. I was told that down in Texas the slave owners set a rule that each slave was to do so much work each day and any who failed to come up to their rule received so many lashes when night came." According to Sarah Wilson, however, all masters were not as lenient as those of McNair and Sheppard because Ben Johnson had made his slaves work "from daylight to dark."[48]

The harshness of the punishment meted out by Cherokee planters varied as well. Most reminiscences of former slaves indicate kind treatment by their masters. Chaney Richardson told the interviewer: "I was always treated good when I was a slave. . . . None of the Cherokees ever whipped us, and my mistress give me some might fine rules to live by." Morris Sheppard's mistress took him to the "Big House" after the sale of his mother and he remembered that "she was kind to me like I was part of her own family." On the other hand, some masters, such as Ben Johnson, mistreated their slaves terribly. Sarah Wilson remembered the following event and cited it as an example of Johnson's cruelty:

> One time he whipped a whole bunch of the men on account of a fight in the quarters, and then he took them all to Fort Smith to see a hanging. He tied them all in the wagon, and when they had seen the hanging he asked them if they was scared of them dead men hanging up there. They all said yes, of course, but my old uncle Nick was a bad Negro and he said, "No, I ain't a-feared of them nor nothing else in this world," and old Master jumped on

> him while he was tied and beat him with a rope, and then when they got home he tied old Nick to a tree and took his shirt off and poured the cat-o-nine-tails to him until he fainted away and fell over like he was dead. I never forgot seeing all that blood all over my uncle, and if I could hate that old Indian any more I guess I would, but I hated him all I could already I reckon.[49]

Since the Cherokee legal code placed no restrictions on the extremes to which a slaveholder could go in correcting his bondsmen, all masters had the power to abuse their slaves just as Ben Johnson did. Slaves were at the mercy of their owners and the treatment they received depended on their master's disposition and the extent to which he was willing to go in order to increase his profits. Most slaves saw a direct correlation between the treatment they received and the results their masters hoped to obtain. Even kind masters had profit uppermost in their minds as Joseph Scales recalled; "The Vanns were good to their slaves, believing that they had to be well fed, clothed well and properly housed to get the best labor obtainable from them." Sarah Wilson had accurately assessed the situation when she said of Johnson, "The way he work the Negroes so hard, old Master must have been trying to get rich."[50]

7

Civil War in the Cherokee Nation

Cherokee planters watched the growing conflict in the United States over slavery with apprehension. The editor of the *Advocate,* who expressed concern over the California statehood controversy in 1850 less for the threat to the balance between free and slave states in the United States Senate than for the grave danger to the Union, rejoiced when the news arrived that "a compromise will be effected between the North and South, upon the slavery question, and that the Union will finally be saved, and California admitted as a free State." For many Cherokees the possible destruction of the government on which they had based their own legal system portended domestic disaster. Although the Cherokees had projected a façade of unity since the 1846 agreement between the Ross party and the Treaty party led by Stand Watie, factionalism was rife in the Cherokee Nation. The editor of the *Advocate* could have easily applied his wishful thinking to the Cherokee Nation when he wrote of the United States: "There is too much patriotism in the Union, to permit such a noble edifice as this glorious Union, having for its corners one love of liberty—its materials, patriotism—and cemented by the blood of '76 to be ruthlessly torn asunder."[1]

The Cherokees might have been able to view the developments in the United States in the decade before the Civil War impartially and dispassionately had not the moral question of slavery involved the white missionaries in the Nation whose history had been inextricably intertwined with their own. Building on the failures of eighteenth-century mission activities, missionaries had begun their ministry in earnest among the Cherokees in 1800 when the Moravians received permission to organize a school, and Presbyterians, Methodists, and Baptists soon followed the Moravians. They had guided the Cherokees along the tedious path to civilization, had gone to prison to protest removal, and had followed the Indians to the West to help them get reestablished.

The missionaries who had the most profound effect on the Cherokees and scored the most notable success were the representatives of the American Board of Commissioners for Foreign Missions. The Boston-based American Board expressed concern from the beginning of their labors among the Cherokees that their potential converts owned slaves. At first the Prudential Committee, which coordinated the Board's mission activities, permitted missionaries to hire slaves as laborers in the mission stations with the slave's permission. Some missionaries even purchased slaves from their masters with the intention of emancipating them. Several years later the committee amended the rule to prohibit any hiring of slaves. Many missionaries among the southern Indians, such as Samuel Austin Worcester of the Cherokees, protested that the only alternative to the occasional hiring of slaves was the abandonment of the stations and surreptitiously continued the practice.[2]

Another matter of contention between the missionaries and the committee centered on the admission of slaveholders to membership in the church. For the first three decades of the board's ministry among the Cherokees the committee agreed with the missionaries that conversion of the slaveholders and their acceptance into the church should come first and that emancipation of the slaves would soon follow as slaveholders recognized that slavery was inconsistent with the concept of Christian brotherhood. In response to growing pressure on the board by New England abolitionists, however, the committee revised its view in 1848 and insisted that the missionaries deny church membership to slaveholders and preach against slavery even it if meant the alienation of many members of the congregations and their possible expulsion from the Nation.[3]

Samuel Worcester, Elizur Butler, and other American Board missionaries among the Cherokees replied in a letter to the committee which the *Advocate* published in full so that there would be no doubt about where the missionaries stood on the questions of slavery and abolition. The missionaries began by pointing out their dilemma. "We are aware that we stand between two fires; in danger of displeasing, by what we may write, on the one hand the people for whose good we labor, and on whose esteem and confidence our success must depend, and, on the other, the Christian community by whom we are sustained in our work. We do not say, in danger of displeasing one *or* the other, but both at the same time, for opposite reasons." The missionaries candidly explained their position on the various aspects of the slavery question. They affirmed that no slave had ever been purchased by an American Board missionary "except with a view to emancipation" and that no missionaries held bondsmen. The missionaries did admit that they had hired slaves with the bondsmen's consent and, furthermore, they believed that "when his condition is improved by it, and his privileges increased, and he is brought into the way of religious instruction, and so, perhaps of salvation, to hire him is no violation of the law of love, but rather an act of kindness." Still, the authors of the letter recognized that a relatively humane practice tended "to uphold and encourage the system of slavery" and agreed to halt the hiring of slave labor.

The missionaries pointed out that their churches were congregational and therefore governed themselves despite the fact that the financial support for their ministries came from the board. In this context they broached the subject of admission of slaveholders into the church. The correspondents asserted that the Bible did not explicitly condemn slavery, that the nefarious institution was only "implicitly condemned by the general law of love." The apostles received slaveholders into the church and following their example, the American Board missionaries admitted "all to our communion who give evidence that they love the Lord Jesus Christ" regardless of their status as slaveholders. The missionaries defended the admission of those who bought and sold slaves because as they pointed out "occasional exchanges of masters are so inseparable from the existence of slavery," that most slaveholders had at some time participated in the traffic and that sales rarely worsened the condition of the slave and sometimes improved it. The missionaries intimated that they would bar professional slave traders who sold slaves in "manifest disregard to the welfare of the slave" if such a situation ever presented itself.

As for preaching against the evils of slavery, the missionaries in the field informed their northern brethren that the laws of the Nation sustained the institution and that the Cherokees resented interference by missionaries in "what is generally regarded as simply a political institution." They proceeded to remind the committee that at times it was unwise to attempt to accomplish something that was "impracticable, though in itself desirable" and that their own position on slavery represented not what they would like to do but merely what they were capable of doing under the circumstances.[4]

The editor of the *Advocate* applauded the missionaries' letter and in the next issue wrote with a slight touch of sarcasm: "The position of the Missions, as defined by themselves is one that ought to satisfy people in the North, whose minds are not overcast by the darkness of slavery, but beaming with the light of benevolence and the desire to do the greatest amount of good in a Christian point of view, without dragging religion into the mud and dirt of civil affairs and political dissensions and conflicts."[5] Other denominations were not able to keep their missionaries out of the "mud and dirt," however, and ultimately even the American Board was drawn into the furor.

Religious debates over slavery went beyond the confines of the American Board and precipitated far more serious consequences among other denominations, such as the Methodists and Baptists who had missionaries among the Cherokees. In 1844 the Methodist General Conference enacted a strong antislavery policy and the following year southerners withdrew to form the Methodist Episcopal Church South. In the same year a group of disaffected Baptists founded the Southern Baptist Convention to protest the antislavery stance of the national organization. Since slavery was the issue that caused the split, it is not surprising that Methodist and Baptist missionaries were less than quiet on the subject. William S. Robertson wrote his parents:

> There has been nothing done with our translation since I last wrote. The Methodist translator being out in the Seminole country at the head of a party of armed men hunting negroes; they killed one man and caught some very old women and children. . . . The ears of the north would tingle if they could hear the enormities that are being practiced by missionaries supported by the Baptist and Methodist Churches South.[6]

The Southern Methodist Church originally supplied the ministers to the Cherokee Nation, and in 1849 they were joined by a missionary from the northern Methodist Church. According to the account in the *Advocate,* this new arrival, a Mr. Gurley, held a meeting at his home "to lecture his disciples secretly upon matters which he deemed prudent not to broach in a public congregation." The Cherokees must have suspected that the matter under discussion was abolition because a crowd gathered outside the house, broke up the meeting, and compelled Mr. Gurley to flee. The irate mob then proceeded to wreck the church by breaking the windows, tearing down the stoves, and thoroughly vandalizing the interior.[7]

The most highly respected Baptist missionaries in the Nation, Evan Jones and his son John, were supported by the northern church and freely admitted being active abolitionists. Evan Jones began his ministry in 1821 among the conservative Cherokees in the Valley Towns of North Carolina. He accompanied those of his flock who were forced to migrate and reestablished his ministry among the traditionalists in Indian Territory, where his son joined him. These conservatives not only tolerated the abolitionist sympathies of Jones and his son but became open advocates. In 1853, Jones reported to the American Baptist Missionary Union that all slaveholding members of the Baptist churches in the Cherokee Nation had voluntarily withdrawn, but Worcester maintained that Jones had excommunicated those who refused to withdraw. In 1859 the Joneses helped the conservatives organize a group known as the Keetowahs, whose stated purpose was to preserve tribal traditions but who came to function as an abolitionist organization and as Union partisans during the Civil War. In 1860 George Butler, the U.S. agent to the Cherokees who was a southerner, expelled John Jones from the Nation because of his uncompromising devotion to the cause of abolition.[8]

The Moravians, who had owned and hired slaves prior to removal, also began to assume an antislavery stance. This change in sentiments meant that the Moravians began to find more followers among the conservatives than among the highly acculturated slaveholders. The fate of the two missions which Moravians established in the West illustrates the effect of the missionaries' growing opposition to slavery. Canaan, which ministered primarily to progressive slaveholders faltered and was abandoned while New Springplace prospered because it served nonslaveholding traditionalists.[9]

Abolitionism soon spread to the American Board when the Prudential Committee sent younger men from New England to aid Worcester, Butler, and other aging missionaries. Having come from the heart of the abolitionist movement, these arrivals were less concerned about the sensibilities of their congregation than they were about the evil of slavery, and slaveholding Cherokees came to suspect the American Board missionaries of abolitionism. The ministers unwittingly encouraged this view by offering a warm welcome to abolitionists who did visit Indian Territory. One particular opponent of slavery who found refuge at one of the American Board's missions had been living in Fort Smith until he declined to join a group of proslavery volunteers bound for Kansas because of his moral opposition to slavery. The volunteers responded to his refusal and admission by cutting up his clothes and saddlebags, blacking his face with lampblack and turpentine, shaving his head, and pouring turpentine and whiskey down his throat with a funnel before throwing him in the river and forcing him to swim to the other side. (One missionary commented that this was "a strange cure for abolitionism.")[10]

Suspicion that the American Board missionaries were really active abolitionists led slaveholders to accuse them of helping slaves to escape. When a slave named David borrowed Charles Cutler Torrey's horse to go to Park Hill and did not return, Worcester and Torrey "were charged with instigating him to run away, and with furnishing him with money and a horse for the purpose." The slaveholders took the matter up before the National Council and tried to pass an act requesting Torrey's removal from the Nation and requiring all missionaries to appear before the Indian agent to "give an account of themselves." Both acts were barely defeated after Torrey signed an affidavit in which he stated that he "knew nothing whatever of David's purpose." Reverend Torrey's son later recalled that in another episode "Mr. Torrey was once sought by drunken Indians who planned to tar and feather him because they said he had objected to the cruel beating of a slave." Torrey was away from home at the time on a preaching tour and never even heard of the punishment of the slave. Nevertheless, suspicion of the missionaries grew. A political faction formed around the issue of getting rid of abolitionist missionaries, particularly Jones and Worcester, and in the decade before the Civil War several candidates for council were elected on an antimissionary platform.[11]

The missionaries' more open opposition to the institution of slavery failed to satisfy the Prudential Committee. The Cherokees did not appear to be traveling very rapidly down the road to emancipation despite forty years of American Board ministry and an almost universal acceptance of Christianity. Therefore when the most stalwart of all the American Board missionaries, Samuel Austin Worcester, died in 1859 the committee decided to end its missionary activities among the Cherokees. The committee refused to admit that slavery was the issue over which the missions closed and insisted instead that the Cherokees no longer needed the American Board's ministry because they had become "a Christian people." As soon as war broke out the Baptists also decided to close their Cherokee mission and recalled Evan Jones, who joined his son in Kansas where they spent the war ministering to pro-Union Cherokee refugees while the Keetowah society, which they had organized, defended the Union within the Cherokee Nation.[12]

When the Civil War finally began, both North and South looked anxiously to the southern Indians to see what these residents of the territory between Kansas and Texas would do. As a grain- and livestock-producing area, Indian Territory could provide ample food for the western troops of the side with which the Indians decided to align themselves. Furthermore, Indian Territory offered an access route by which an invasion of either Kansas or Texas could be launched.

At the time of southern secession, the Cherokees were having their own problems with the United States government over squatters on their neutral land bordering Kansas which the government had offered to buy on insultingly unfair terms. The Cherokees desperately needed to sell the neutral lands which they did not use in order to finance their press, schools, and government. The Confederacy determined to exploit this situation and immediately commissioned Albert Pike, an Arkansas resident well-acquainted with the southern Indians, to treat with the Cherokees and the other "civilized" tribes. Confederate Indian Commissioner David Hubbard empowered Pike to buy the neutral land on the same terms which had been asked from and refused by the federal government and to guarantee continuation of the annuities that had been stipulated in treaties between the Cherokees and the United States.[13]

Even before Pike could contact John Ross, Governor Henry M. Rector of Arkansas wrote the principal chief a letter in which he pointed out the affinities and mutual interests of the Cherokee Nation and the Confederacy and urged him to join the seceding states. In his letter Rector expressed the basic argument that Confederate officials and southern sympathizers would use in the attempt to secure a Confederate alliance: "Your people in their institutions, productions, latitude and natural sympathies are allied to the common Brotherhood of the Slaveholding States. —Our people and yours are natural allies in war, and friends in peace. —Your country is salubrious and fertile and possesses the highest capacity for future progress and development by the application of " 'Slave labor.' "[14]

In his reply to the chief executive of the neighboring state Ross clearly indicated that his position and that of the Cherokee Nation in the conflict would be one of neutrality. Ross, whose major concern was the preservation of the independence and territorial integrity of the Cherokee Nation and the lives and property of its citizens, believed that only a policy of neutrality could accomplish these aims. In a letter written in May to Confederate Lieutenant Colonel J.R. Kannady at Fort Smith, Ross again expressed his desire to remain neutral and requested that the Cherokee Nation not be used as a battleground. In June Ross outlined his position to the Confederate commander at Fort Smith, Brigadier General Benjamin McCulloch:

> In regard to the pending conflict between the United States and Confederate States, I have already signified my purpose to take no part in it whatever. . . . Our country and institutions are our own. However small the one and humble the others, they are as sacred and valuable to us as are those of your own populous and wealthy State to yourself and people. We have done nothing to bring about the conflict in which you are engaged with your own people, and I am unwilling that my people shall become its victims.[15]

Ross realized that the Cherokees had a dual heritage, which made a decision to support either North or South an extremely difficult one. In an address to the National Council he pointed out the dilemma facing the Cherokees: "Our locality and situation ally us to the South, while to the North we are indebted for a defense of our rights in the past and that enlarged benevolence to which we owe our progress in civilization." Gratitude for support during the removal crisis and for the work of the missionaries overshadowed the desire on the part of some slaveholders, such as John Ross, Joseph Vann, and John Drew, to go to battle in defense of the institution of slavery from which they had derived much of their wealth. They also believed that the right of Cherokees to their property which had been spelled out in treaties with the United States included slave property and therefore the institution within the Nation could not be altered by an act of the United States.[16]

The treaties themselves provided a more concrete reason why John Ross believed that neutrality was the only viable alternative open to the Cherokees. A policy of neutrality meant that treaties with the United States which recognized the political and property rights of Cherokee citizens would continue to be honored. Perhaps naïvely, Ross insisted that Cherokee "political relations are with the government of the United States and our rights are protected by the enforcement of the Laws under the Constitution." Ross viewed it as a matter of honor to abide by those treaties and to respect the obligations set forth in them, and he wrote Pike: "We doubt not that no other course [than neutrality] is left for us to follow; unless we ourselves set the example of bad *faith* which is dishonorable to any nation and dangerous to a weak one."[17]

Ross resented the scare tactics employed by some southerners in their over-zealous attempt to convince the Cherokees of the desirability of an alliance with the Confederacy. In his letter to Ross Governor Rector wrote, "It is well known that the Indian country west of Arkansas is looked upon by the incoming administration of Mr. Lyncoln as fruitful fields ripe for the harvest of Abolitionism, Free Soilers, and Northern Mountebanks." Ross tersely replied that he was certain that "the Laborers will be greatly disappointed." Ross insisted that he was not aware of "any such disturbing of the peace" and considered it to be an insult to his people that Rector and others believed the Cherokees could be so readily manipulated. In a letter to his nephew, Ross wrote that he "had often been pained by the uncalled for falsehoods circulated in the face of all the facts" and asserted that the Cherokees "were not Dogs to be helped on by Abolitionists against any people"[18]

In an effort to prove that the Cherokees could not be so easily influenced, Ross began trying to unify the Nation behind his policy of neutrality. In early June Ross and Joseph Vann, the assistant principal chief, wrote the wealthy and politically powerful Captain John Drew: "There is no reason why we would split up and become involved in internal strife and violence on account of the political condition of the States." Ross implemented his program for the maintenance of relations with the United States and the avoidance of involvement in the Civil War when the council met later that month. After presenting the correspondence concerning the question of neutrality, Ross issued a proclamation to the Cherokee people "imposing neutrality and observance of treaty obligations during the difficulties pending between the United States and the Confederate States."[19]

Ross and other Cherokee leaders who supported his policy of

neutrality assumed that slavery was not a divisive issue in the Nation and that their official sanction of the institution would not interfere in the continuation of relations with the United States. In his address to the National Council Ross gave his views on the subject:

> It is a cause of deep regret that the subject of slavery has become paramount to all other considerations in opposite sections of the United States and is producing so much harsh recrimination and alienation among those who are bound together by the glories of an unequalled history and the sacred ties of one blood and one interest. Slavery has existed among the Cherokees for many years, is recognized by them as legal and they have no wish or purpose to disturb it or agitate it—others have no excuse for doing so come from whatever quarter they may. It is not an open question among us but a settled one. Agitation in regard to it of any kind can be productive of good to no one.[20]

Ross failed to realize or at least did not admit that slavery, through the life style it supported and the attitudes it fostered, partly produced the division within the Nation that predated removal and became pronounced following the forced migration. In 1861 the highly acculturated slaveholders in the Nation lived and thought more like white upper-class southerners than they had at the time of removal despite the fact that traditionalists had become increasingly disillusioned with the white man's "civilization," including the institution of slavery. As a result of the growing disparity in values and of the deep-seated factionalism, unity in the face of the impending crisis proved to be more elusive than ever for the Cherokee Nation.

Well before Ross enjoined the Nation from participation in the conflict a group of Cherokees under the leadership of Stand Watie, brother of the slain Elias Boudinot, organized the Knights of the Golden Circle or, as they later became known, the Southern Rights party. Although the stated purpose of this group was to bring the Cherokees into the Confederate fold, the leaders acknowledged that they had seized upon this particular crisis to oust Ross and the National party from power and establish themselves "on an *honorable* equality with this old Dominant Party that for years has had its foot upon our necks."[21] The factionalism which had developed over removal was reviving under new banners.

Watie's party effectively utilized southern proslavery rhetoric to mask the group's real motives. Proponents of a southern alliance circulated the rumor that a "Black Republican" had been appointed United States agent among the Cherokees to replace George Butler, who had resigned to return to his native South and enter the service of the Confederacy. The party also predicted the immediate "subjugation of the Cherokees to the rule of Abolition" unless the Nation formed an alliance with the Confederacy. The adoption of this rigid proslavery, antiabolition stance came easily to men who were in the main highly acculturated slaveholders.[22]

In opposition to the Knights were the Keetowahs, or Pins, who protested the Cherokees' acceptance of slavery as well as other aspects of the white man's "civilization" and favored Ross's policy of neutrality which in effect maintained an alliance with the Union based on previous treaties. A confrontation between the two groups finally occurred in the summer of 1861 at Webbers Falls when some southern supporters attempted to raise the Confederate flag and approximately 150 "armed and painted" conservatives prevented them from accomplishing their aim. In reaction to this event, Ross characteristically reminded his supporters that only through unity could the Cherokees maintain neutrality and avoid being drawn into the conflict.[23]

Ross's attempt to conceal the factionalism in the Nation and to project the image of a united people failed miserably. Both Cherokee citizens and outsiders were aware of the division. Elizabeth Watts clearly remembered the factionalism in the Nation in 1861 and gave the following account to a WPA interviewer:

> Years passed, and the bad feeling between the two factions seemed to get worse over the question of Slavery. Ross opposed it. Stand Watie, relative of Boudinot, was for it.
>
> Missionaries came along the "Trail of Tears" and opposed it. Some Indian Agents were for it.
>
> The Indians did not want to fight. . . .
>
> Not many full-bloods owned slaves and they had a secret society called "Kee-oo-Wah." They wore two common pins crossed

on their coats for their emblem. Most all full-bloods belonged and wanted to stay with Tribal laws and customs. Most of them were the Ross faction and opposed Slavery.

Those who endorsed slavery had a society and it was made up of half-breeds and they owned most of the slaves.[24]

The southern officials who tenaciously sought an alliance from the Cherokees also perceived the factionalism. Upon first assuming his position as Confederate envoy assigned to effect a treaty with the Cherokees, Albert Pike traveled to the Cherokee Nation not only because wealth, location, and a large population made the Cherokees the most desirable Indian allies, but also because he saw "more danger of division and dissaffection than anywhere else" and therefore more likelihood that one of the factions would sign a treaty to gain a domestic political advantage. Confederates also correctly identified the lines of cleavage and the relative popularity of the opposing factions. General McCulloch wrote: "There are two parties in the Cherokee Nation—one in favor of immediate secession, the other represented by John Ross, and wishing to be neutral. This party is in the majority, and consists of all the full-bloods and a part of the half-breeds."[25]

In spite of the support for his position several developments forced Ross by the end of the summer to abandon the policy of neutrality. Federal troops had vacated the forts protecting Indian Territory and a Confederate invasion of the Nation appeared imminent. Furthermore, the general military situation indicated an early Union defeat. Confederate troops had repelled a federal invasion at Bull Run in Virginia and closer to home had trounced Union soldiers at Wilson's Creek in Missouri. Cherokees under the command of Stand Watie participated in the latter encounter and thus signified their intention to ignore Ross's directive. In addition the Watie party seemed about to sign a treaty and with the support of the Confederacy take over the government of the Nation. Faced with the prospect of a divisive internal power struggle and a minority government establishing its legitimacy by the use of Confederate troops, Ross revealed in August that he was ready to treat with Pike and commissioned John Drew to raise a regiment for defense of the Nation and ultimately for service to the Confed-

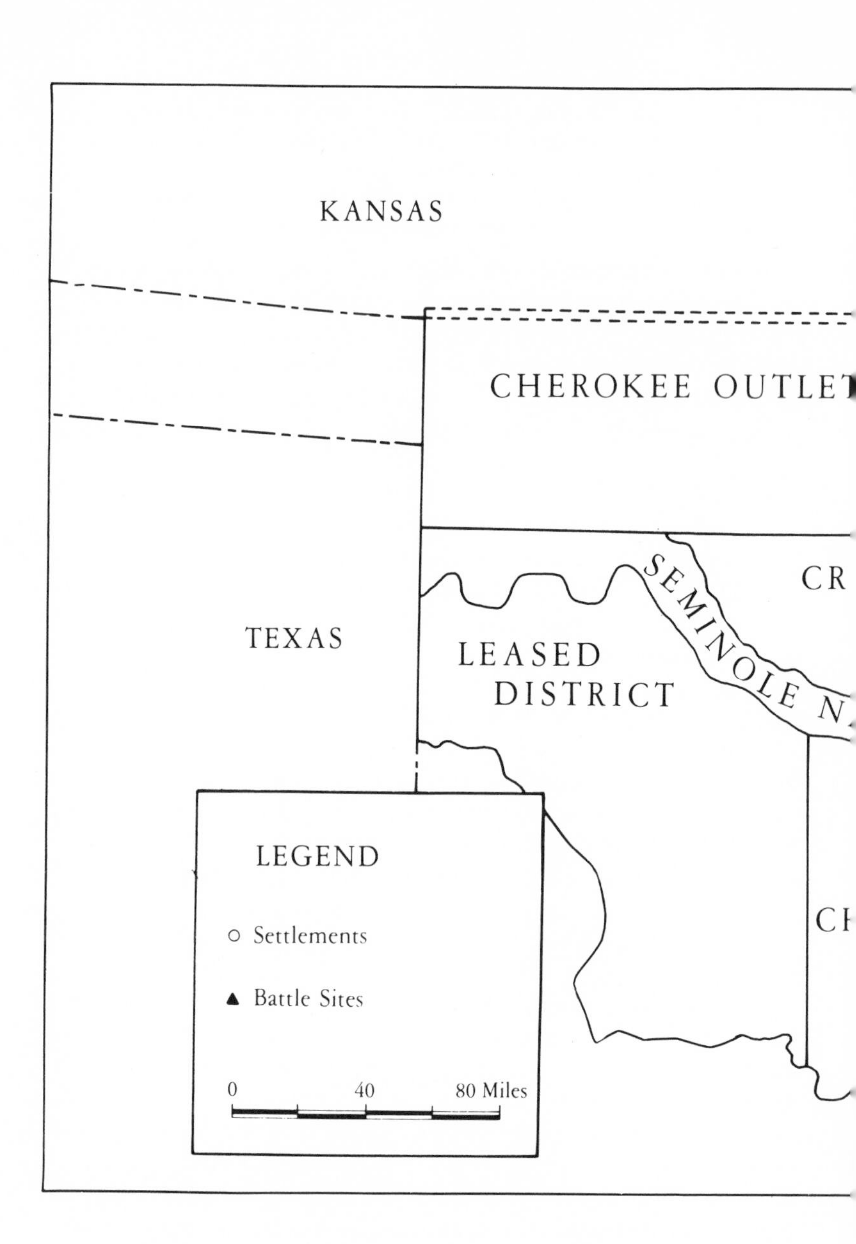
KANSAS
CHEROKEE OUTLET
TEXAS
LEASED DISTRICT
SEMINOLE
LEGEND
Settlements
Battle Sites
0
40
80 Miles

Map 5. The American Civil War in Indian Territory (From John W. Morris and Edwin C. McReynolds, *Historical Atlas of Oklahoma,* Norman, Okla., 1965)

erate cause. Following the signing of a treaty with the South in October, Ross recognized the troops that Watie had organized while the Cherokees were officially neutral but did not merge Watie's battalion with the regiment. Evan Jones who defended Ross to United States Commissioner of Indian Affairs W.P. Dole pointed out that Drew's regiment was "altogether distinct from the rebel force before mentioned. The great majority of the officers and men being decidedly loyal Union men." General McCulloch also differentiated between the two groups of Cherokee soldiers and sought to preserve the distinction:

> Col. Stand Watie belongs to the true Southern party, composed mostly of mixed bloods, and opposed to John Ross, and by whose course and influence Ross was induced to join the South. I hope our Government will continue this gallant man true friend of our country in service, and attach him and his men (some 300) to my command. It might be well to give him a battalion separate from the Cherokee regiment under Colonel Drew. Colonel Drew's regiment will be mostly composed of full-bloods, whilst those with Col. Stand Watie will be half-breeds, who are educated men, and good soldiers anywhere, in or out of the Nation.[26]

A thinly veiled disenchantment with the Confederate cause on the part of some Cherokee soldiers was clearly revealed in December 1861 when many of the men and officers of John Drew's regiment deserted and joined a group of Creeks en route to Kansas under the leadership of Opothleyohola, who had vehemently opposed the Creek alliance with the Confederacy. Colonel Douglas Cooper, who commanded the Confederate Indian troops, at first tried to dissuade the disaffected Creeks from seeking asylum behind Union lines in Kansas and, when he failed, ordered the capture of the band which was made up of women and children as well as warriors. The conservative Cherokees in Drew's regiment refused to go to battle against fellow Indians, whose sentiments concerning the war they shared, and fled their encampment the night before the battle was to take place. Many sought refuge with Opothleyohola while others returned to their homes determined to fight for the Confederacy no more. A few Cherokees remained with the Creeks who suffered defeat in battle with Cooper but who finally reached Kansas freezing and starving. Some of these men promptly enlisted in the Union army.[27]

The Cherokee deserters returned home and augmented the ranks of the Pins, who had accelerated their attacks on avid supporters of the Confederate alliance. Many of these attacks were personal while others were aimed at the property of the wealthy planters. Slaves frequently suffered most since they were an extremely valuable form of property and a major reason for the war in which the Cherokees had become embroiled. Chaney Richardson recalled the harassment of slaves in the first year of the war and recognized that it was only a new manifestation of the persisting factionalism:

> My master and all the rest of the folks was Cherokees, and they'd been killing each other off in the feud ever since long before I was borned, and jest because old Master have a big farm and three-four families of Negroes them other Cherokees keep on pestering his stuff all the time. . . .
>
> When I was about 10 years old that feud got so bad the Indians was always talking about getting their horses and cattle killed and their slaves harmed. I was too little to know how bad it was until one morning my own mammy went somewhere down the road to git some stuff to dye cloth and she didn't come back. . . .
>
> They find her in some bushes where she'd been getting bark to set the dyes, and she been dead all the time. Somebody done hit her in the head with a club and shot her through and through with a bullet too.

Morris Sheppard also had vivid memories of the activities of the Pins both before and during the war:

> Dey was a lot of dem Pin Indians all up on de Illinois River and de was wid de North and dey taken it out on de slave owners a lot before de War and during it too.
>
> De would come in de night and hamstring de horses and maybe set fire to de barn, and two of 'em names Joab Scarrel and Tom Starr killed my pappy one night just before de war broke out. . . .
>
> Them Pins was after Master all de time for a while at de first of

de War, and he was afraid to ride into Fort Smith much. Dey come to de house one time when he was gone to Fort Smith and us children told dem he was at Honey Springs, but they knowed better and when he got home he said somebody shot at him and bushwacked him all the way from Wilson's Rock to dem Wildhorse Mountains.[28]

The Pins were not the only ones responsible for property damage and personal violence in Indian Territory. As the war progressed and provisions became scarce, Watie's men began robbing those who had Union sympathies. Hannah Hicks, the daughter of Samuel Austin Worcester who had married the Cherokee Abijab Hicks, wrote in her journal of late 1862: "Today we hear that Watie's men declared their intention to come back and *rob* every woman whose husband has gone to the Federals, and every woman who has Northern principles." Only a few days later Watie's men and some other Confederate soldiers visited her and "took many valuable things, and overhauled every closet, trunk, box & drawer they could find."[29]

The chaos in the Cherokee Nation in 1862 far exceeded that in the decade following removal. Hannah Hicks, whose husband had been murdered accidentally by the Pins leaving her with five small children, recorded the following entry in her journal:

Today I went to the Printing Office. I did not know how completely it had been cleared out. The Press, Types paper & all carried off. By Watie's men, with the help of the Texians. We hear today that the "Pins" are committing outrages on Hungry mountain and in Flint, robbing, destroying property & killing. It is so dreadful that they will do so. Last week, some of Watie's men, went and robbed the Rosses place up at the mill; completely ruined them. Alas, alas, for this miserable people, destroying each other as fast as they can.[30]

The first regular federal troops to enter Indian Territory invaded the Cherokee Nation in the summer of 1862. Encouraged by the missionary Evan Jones, who insisted that Ross had unwillingly entered into the Confederate alliance, the United States decided to attempt a rescue of the principal chief. In July the Indian Expedition reached Tahlequah and the leaders contacted Ross at his home in nearby Park Hill about the possibility of his defecting to the Union. Ross refused to meet with the United States soldiers and sent copies of documents dealing with the Confederate alliance in an effort to justify his actions. Hesitating for only a few days, the federal detachment camped at Park Hill took the men guarding Ross and the chief himself captive. The expedition then retreated back into Kansas taking their prize prisoner, his family, and the records and treasury of the Nation with them. Federal authorities paroled Ross, and the chief journeyed east to Washington and then to Philadelphia, where he spent the remainder of the war.[31]

Stand Watie promptly declared the office of principal chief vacant and assumed the position himself. Other Cherokee officeholders who had shifted their allegiance to the Union were removed from office and replaced with Watie's men. This prosouthern government immediately passed an act which compelled all men from sixteen to thirty-five to enter the Confederate army, and Watie's troops began searching for, arresting, and imprisoning offenders. Many Cherokee men who were unwilling to fight for the Confederate cause went into hiding and depended on friends and relatives to conceal them from Watie's men. Because they feared detection and arrest, these fugitives offered little economic support for their families or protection against raids by Watie's troops. The conscription law, continual harassment, and alternating Union and Confederate invasions prompted other Union sympathizers to flee to Kansas, where many of the men joined the Indian Brigade of the Union Army.[32]

The majority of the Cherokees continued to support Ross and refused to recognize the government headed by Stand Watie. Thomas Pegg became acting principal chief in Ross's absence and as such called a meeting of the National Council in February 1863. Citing the absence of federal protection, the presence of Confederate troops on the border, pressure from adjoining states, the destruction of communication lines with Washington, and the factionalism within the Nation that made a minority treaty with the Confederacy likely, the council voted to revoke the Confederate treaty on the grounds that "acts performed under such duress have no binding effect in law or morals." To affirm its loyalty to the United States the council deposed all Cherokee officials who continued to support the Confederacy. Finally the council agreed to emancipate all slaves "within the limits of the Cherokee Nation" and to abolish the institution permanently. The council imposed penalties for violation of the emancipation act and admonished Cherokee soldiers to enforce its provisions. The Cherokee emancipation act had little effect on most slaves, however, because they belonged to members of the Watie party, who did not recognize the legitimacy of the government which had passed it, and many planters removed their slaves beyond the boundaries of the Cherokee Nation.[33]

In the summer of 1863 federal troops once again invaded the Cherokee Nation and devastated the entire area north and east of the Arkansas River before retiring. Many slaveholders and Confederate sympathizers fled southward and westward with their families and slaves. At first they took refuge in the Creek Nation and the northern districts of the Choctaw Nation, where they received provisions from the Confederate commissary. In 1864 Watie and his troops moved a large group of the refugees to the Red River, where they either bought or rented land in the Choctaw and Chickasaw nations or in northern Texas.

Although many manufactured items were difficult to obtain and currency was in short supply, the wealthier planters fared well because they still had their slaves to provide them with an income. Morris Sheppard recalled his sojourn in the southern Choctaw Nation:

> Old Master get three wagons and ox teams and take us all way down on Red River in de Choctaw Nation.
>
> We went by Webber's Falls and filled de wagons. We left de furniture and only took grub and tools and bedding and clothes, 'cause they wasn't very big wagons and was single-yoke.
>
> We went on a place in de Red River bottoms close to Shawneetown and not far from de place where all de wagons crossed over to go into Texas. We was at dat place two years and made two little crops.

Some planters simply hired their slaves out to Texas planters in order to avoid the expense of purchasing or renting land. Sarah Wilson recalled. "We was way down across the Red River in Texas at that time, close to Shawneetown of the Choctaw Nation but just across the river on the other side in Texas bottoms. Old Master took us there in covered wagons when the Yankee soldiers got too close by in the first part of the War. He hired the slaves out to Texas people because he didn't make any crops down there and we all lived in kind of camps." The southern refugees and their bondsmen remained in the Red River valley until the Confederate defeat compelled planters to free their chattels. Some slaveholders relinquished their bondsmen calmly while others such as the cruel Ben Johnson "went wild."[34]

The end of the war found many Cherokee citizens and slaves displaced. In addition to Union Cherokee sympathizers in northern states and southern refugees and their slaves, a large group of former Cherokee slaves had escaped and fled to Kansas. Many of these served in the First Kansas Colored Infantry and battled their former masters at Honey Springs and Cabin Creek. Confederate Cherokees, outraged at the sight of blacks in uniform, committed horrid atrocities. On one occasion when a group of southern soldiers defeated a company of blacks, they cut their throats and stripped the clothing from the bodies and then guarded the bloating bodies for two days before leaving them to be buried by Union troops. Despite their service in the Union cause, at the end of the war the surviving black soldiers were mustered out of the army and left to find their way alone back to the Cherokee Nation, where many of their families lived and their claim to citizenship rested.[35]

Former slaves probably feared returning to the Nation because the civil war between Cherokee factions did not end with the surrender of Stand Watie on June 23, 1865. The Southern Cherokee refugees also hesitated to exchange the relative safety of their haven on the Red River for the hostility of the conservatives who controlled Indian Territory. The government of John Ross and Thomas Pegg had confiscated the refugees' property, and the Pins seemed intent upon retaliation. Nancy Lynch wrote her uncle James M. Bell, who had fled the Nation, about the conservatives' acrimonious attitude toward the former slave-holders. "It lacks a good deal being peaceable times. They [the Pins] says they wont let the half breeds live among them. . . . I tell you Uncle Jim half breeds has no showing here among these pins. It is no use to think about coming back now." The Southern Cherokees were equally unwilling to forget former allegiances. Stand Watie confidently wrote his son Saladin in the summer of 1866: "You may tell the delegation that our people are steadfast, none have taken or will take the obnoxious oath [of allegiance to the United States]."[36] Thus the old factionalism, which originated over removal and was hardened by civil war, continued long after the fighting ended; and although slavery, which had partly created the division within the Nation, no longer existed, its legacy of economic and social inequality and cultural dichotomy endured.

Epilogue

The continuing factionalism in the Cherokee Nation was evident when Unionist and Confederate representatives met with United States peace commissioners at Fort Smith in September 1865. Ignoring the obvious division of loyalty, the commissioners insisted that all Cherokees had forfeited their rights under former treaties by forming an alliance with the Confederacy and refused to recognize Ross as principal chief. Despite dissatisfaction on both sides, particularly by the Ross faction, the representatives signed a preliminary agreement and prepared to meet in Washington in the spring of 1866.[1]

Much to the amazement of Ross and other Unionists, the former Confederate Cherokees who were more amenable to the proposal that railroads be built across Indian Territory received an extremely cordial reception in Washington. Ross was especially concerned because the former rebels sought an immediate division of the Nation and the establishment of the Southern Cherokee Nation. President Andrew Johnson ordered that a treaty incorporating this proposal be drawn up. In response Ross began to enlist support in the U.S. Senate and to arouse public sentiment against another minority treaty forced on the Cherokee people. Fearing that Ross would succeed, the delegates of the Southern faction wrote Watie and urged him to declare a separate government at once:

> Don't neglect to have the Southern Cherokee Government organized *immediately*. Have it done by all means, even should Gen. Watie's Proclamation not be able, in time, to collect a thousand voters. Organize it with a five hundred vote if you can't get more or less, but organize; and *afterwards* we will settle elections again.

> We have won the day and sloth and delay *must not* be suffered to endanger our work. Ross is appealing, lamely I admit, but still, appealing to the sympathies of the Radicals and the ignorant. He will *appeal also* to the sympathies of the ignorant Cherokees.[2]

However, Ross managed to get the treaty defeated and to begin work on a second agreement. Content to wait for a more opportune time to press the Southerners' demand for a division, Elias Cornelius Boudinot wrote his brother: "I have an idea the best thing to be done is to have the question of division unsettled but to secure a few simple titles to all our improvements and the restoration of all our property sold under confiscation."[3]

Ross ultimately signed a treaty with the United States on August 11, 1866 which included articles restoring confiscated property to Southern Cherokees, extending citizenship to freedmen, allowing other tribes to settle on Cherokee land, ceding the neutral land in Kansas, and granting rights of way to railroads.[4] The Southern faction agreed to accept the treaty but determined to continue lobbying for a separation. Boudinot, whose views prevailed among Southern Cherokees, wrote his uncle Stand Watie:

> We have been beaten; that is to say we have not been successful in securing an absolute separation; I am in doubt as to the proper course to pursue.
>
> Adair and the others wish to defeat the treaty the Ross's have signed, but I incline to the opinion that the better policy would be to accept what they put in their treaty as it does not commit *us* to anything, and gives us a good chance to renew the demand for a division at a more favorable opportunity.
>
> The treaty grants a general amnesty, declares confiscation laws void and gives the Ross party no jurisdiction over us in civil and criminal cases before the Court. They shoulder all the responsibility of the negro matter.[5]

The "negro matter" to which Boudinot referred was the treaty provision extending all the privileges of Cherokee citizenship, including an allotment of land, to the Nation's freedmen. Originally all former slaves of Cherokees had six months to return to the Nation and claim their acreage but many freedmen encountered great difficulty reaching the Nation within the time limit, and so the provision was amended in 1870 in order that slaves residing in the Nation in 1861 could receive an allotment and citizenship whenever they returned to Indian Territory. The Cherokee concept of communal ownership enabled the freedmen to obtain land that former slaves of white southerners never received. But the elevation of freedmen to the status of property holder in the Nation did not extirpate the racism of many Cherokees. For example, J.W. Deupree complained to James M. Bell in 1868 about cotton worms and his inability to collect overdue accounts and attributed his problems to "*Negroism* and Radicalism." Almost four decades later the *Bartlesville Enterprise* commented on the Cherokees' reluctance to include freedmen in the allotments made by the Dawes Commission. "The Cherokees have always opposed giving them [the freedmen] allotments and would have shut them out entirely had the negroes not been forced upon them by the government. The Cherokees still remember the negroes as their former slaves and resent their sharing equally with them in tribal lands." At least the land provided for Cherokee freedmen under the treaty of 1866 enabled them to be somewhat independent of their former masters and allowed them a retreat from the violence so common in the outside world.[6]

Although the treaty of 1866 ostensibly combined the freedmen, Cherokee traditionalists, and highly acculturated former slaveholders into a unified Cherokee Nation, social and economic class distinctions and differing world views continued to separate the Cherokee people. Factionalism surfaced periodically after the Civil War particularly in the 1890s when the Dawes Commission decided to dissolve the Cherokee Nation, abolish communal ownership of property, and allot Cherokee land to individuals in fee simple. Progressive Cherokees who occupied the most valuable land favored the Commission's plan while conservatives who viewed the decision as another assault on traditional values opposed the plan so strongly that they refused to sign up for allotments and therefore lost what little they had. In recent years traditionalists have formed the Five Counties Movement or the Original Cherokee Community Organization to seek official recognition from the United States government. These Cherokees do not believe that the tribal council composed of highly acculturated Cherokees, such as William Keeler, chairman of the board of Phillips Petroleum, reflects their views or presents their needs to the Bureau of Indian Affairs.[7]

The institution of slavery helped shape the economic class structure and conflicting value systems which produced the persistent factionalism in the Cherokee Nation. One group of Cherokees clung to the traditional values which emphasized order, harmony, kinship, and economic equilibrium, and which scorned material wealth and political power, while another group gradually abandoned those beliefs and adopted European values. White traders introduced economic inequality and a value system which justified it, and the "civilization" program pursued by the United States government sanctioned the inequality, the adoption of capitalistic European values, and the introduction of African slave labor. At first the lingering influence of their noncapitalistic aboriginal culture tended to make Cherokees relatively lenient masters, but the perceptible differences between them and their white counterparts gradually diminished. While some Cherokees eagerly grasped the white man's "civilization," including slavery, the majority hoped to maintain their traditional way of life and these divergent goals gave rise to the factionalism. The removal crisis brought the conflict into the open with many highly acculturated slaveholders favoring migration to the West and most nonslaveholding conservatives vehemently opposing the move. The bitter feelings engendered by the controversy over the minority treaty of New Echota and the postremoval assassinations lay dormant until the Civil War allowed them once again to come to life. The issue of slavery had not been hotly contested in the Nation before the outbreak of war, but the institution immediately came to represent all that the traditionalists despised in the white man's "civilization." Despite a forced treaty with the Confederacy and active participation on that side by many Cherokee leaders, the conservative majority repudiated the alliance and the way of life that it symbolized and joined the Union cause. The treaty made with the United States after the war superficially reunited the

Nation but social and economic class distinctions and conflicting values continued to divide the Cherokees. This division, which exists today long after the dissolution of tribal government, has its roots in the institution of slavery and the economic inequality and cultural dichotomy that slavery produced.

Notes

Prologue

[1]The "New World" was not new, of course, to the Cherokees and other native Americans, but the term best conveys the European attitude toward the Western Hemisphere, which is one of the themes of the prologue, and will be used for that reason.

[2]Eric Williams discusses slavery in this context in *Capitalism and Slavery* (Chapel Hill, 1944).

[3]Laura Foner and Eugene Genovese present a broad spectrum of views on the comparison of British and Latin American slavery in *Slavery in the New World: A Reader in Comparative History* (Englewood Cliffs, N.J., 1969).

[4]Franklin W. Knight, *Slave Society in Cuba During the Nineteenth Century* (Madison, Wis., 1970), pp. 106–109, 192–94.

[5]Albert Memmi, *The Colonizer and the Colonized,* trans. Howard Greenfeld (Boston, 1965), p. 120.

[6]Ibid., p. 132.

Chapter 1

[1]Edward Gaylord Bourne, ed., *Narratives of the Career of Hernando de Soto,* 2 vols. (New York, 1922), 1:62, 65–72, 78. The chroniclers of the de Soto expedition provide the earliest sketches of the Cherokees. These accounts and others by European visitors are essential in an attempt to reconstruct precontact Cherokee culture. While archaeology may offer some assistance in revealing what the people ate and wore, the tools they used, how they constructed their houses, and their method of burial, a study of bondage and its place in Cherokee society must depend on reports by Europeans. Few historians have used these accounts to formulate an accurate picture of Cherokee

society before contact with whites. Two such examples are Henry T. Malone, *Cherokees of the Old South: A People in Transition* (Athens, 1956) and Grace Steele Woodward, *The Cherokees* (Norman, 1963). Malone's ethnocentric view of Cherokee culture is evident in the title of his first chapter, "Primitive Forest Children," and Woodward claims to trace the history of the tribe from "dark savagery into the sunlight of civilization" (p. 3).

[2]Samuel Cole Williams, ed., *Lieut. Henry Timberlake's Memoirs, 1756–1765* (Johnson City, Tenn., 1927), p. 94; John Brickell, *The Natural History of North Carolina* (Dublin, 1737), p. 320; John Haywood, *The Natural and Aboriginal History of Tennessee up to the First Settlements Therein by the White People in the Year 1768* (Jackson, Tenn., 1959; original ed., 1823), p. 222. Brickell's *Natural History* contains some original material but much of it is a plagiarism of John Lawson's earlier work, *A New Voyage to Carolina,* ed. by Hugh T. Lefler (Chapel Hill, 1967; original ed., 1709).

[3]Alexander Hewatt, *An Historical Account of the Rise and Progress of the Colonies of South Carolina and Georgia, 1779,* 2 vols. (London, 1779), 1:69; Samuel Cole Williams, ed., *Adair's History of the American Indians* (Johnson City, Tenn., 1930), pp. 417–18. *Adair's History* is an excellent source of information about southeastern Indians despite the author's theory that native Americans were the lost tribe of Israel.

[4]Samuel Cole Williams, *Adair's History,* pp. 418–19.

[5]The best work dealing with the role of vengeance and the importance of kinship in Cherokee society is John P. Reid, *A Law of Blood: Primitive Law of the Cherokee Nation* (New York, 1970).

[6]James Mooney, *Myths of the Cherokee and Sacred Formulas of the Cherokees* (19th and 7th Annual Reports, Bureau of American Ethnology; Reproduced, Nashville, 1972), p. 250.

[7]Samuel Cole Williams, *Adair's History,* pp. 408–10, 420.

[8]Newton D. Mereness, ed., *Travels in the American Colonies* (New York, 1916), p. 121.

[9]Brickell, *Natural History,* p. 320; Haywood, *Natural and Aboriginal History,* p. 229.

[10]Samuel Cole Williams, *Adair's History,* p. 172.

[11]Mereness, *Travels,* pp. 115–21.

[12]William L. McDowell, ed., *Journals of the Commissioners of the Indian Trade, Sept. 20, 1710–Aug. 29, 1718* (Columbia, S.C., 1955), pp. 333, 347, 391–401, 411–12.

[13]Quoted in Reid, *Law of Blood,* p. 191.

[14]Samuel Cole Williams, ed., *Early Travels in the Tennessee Country, 1540-1800* (Johnson City, Tenn., 1928), pp. 150–55.

[15]David Menzies, "A True Relation of the Unheard-of Sufferings of David Menzies, Surgeon, Among the Cherokees, and of His Surprising Deliverance," *Royal Magazine,* July 1761, p. 27.

[16]John Lawson, *Voyage,* p. 192; Mooney, *Myths,* pp. 203–204; Samuel Cole Williams, *Timberlake's Memoirs,* p. 94. Some Cherokees did practice polygamy, but monogamy was more common. However, marriages were usually "of a short continuance." Samuel Cole Williams, *Adair's History,* p. 153.

[17]Samuel Cole Williams, *Timberlake's Memoirs,* pp. 65–66, 82, 111.

[18]Reid, *Law of Blood,* pp. 192–93.

[19]Brickell, *Natural History,* p. 289; Samuel Cole Williams, *Adair's History,* pp. 462–63.

[20]Samuel Cole Williams, *Adair's History,* pp. 50, 462.

[21]Lawson, *Voyage,* p. 240.

[22]Ibid., pp. 204–206; Samuel Cole Williams, *Adair's History,* p. 406.

[23]Samuel Cole Williams, *Adair's History,* p. 462; Mark Van Doren, ed., *The Travels of William Bartram* (New York, 1940), p. 401; Lawson, *Voyage,* p. 184.

[24]Lawson, *Voyage,* pp. 216–18; Samuel Cole Williams, *Timberlake's Memoirs,* p. 111.

[25]Samuel Cole Williams, *Adair's History,* p. 435; Brickell, *Natural History,* pp. 326–27, 289, 363; Lawson, *Voyage,* p. 216.

[26]Mooney, *Myths,* pp. 242–48.

[27]Lawson, *Voyage,* p. 210.

[28]A series of polar oppositions characterized the Cherokees' belief system—the upper world opposed to the under world, east to west and north to south, summer to winter, plants to animals, agriculture to hunting, woman to man. The Cherokees responded to this world view by trying to keep everything in its proper place. A brief description of some aspects of the Cherokee world view can be found in Charles Hudson, "The Cherokee Concept of Natural Balance," *Indian Historian* 3 (1970):51–54. Also see Mooney, *Myths,* pp. 297–301.

[29]In *The Division of Labor in Society* (trans. George Simpson, Glencoe, Ill., 1933), Emile Durkheim cited crime as an example of deviancy which "brings together upright consciences and concentrates them" (p. 102). In *Wayward Puritans: A Study in the Sociology of Deviance* (New York, 1967), Kai T. Erikson applied Durkheim's

theory of deviance to the theological disputes in seventeenth-century New England and asserted that deviance "is not a simple kind of leakage which occurs when the machinery of society is in poor working order, but may be, in controlled quantities, an important condition for preserving the stability of social life. Deviant forms of behavior, by marking the outer edges of group life, give the inner structure its special character and thus supply the framework within which the people of the group develop an orderly sense of their own cultural identity" (p. 13). Winthrop D. Jordan in *White over Black: American Attitudes Toward the Negro, 1550–1812* (Chapel Hill, 1968) demonstrated that Europeans defined black Africans as the opposite of themselves and therefore deviant in an effort to establish their own identity and values: "From the first, Englishmen tended to set Negroes over against themselves, to stress what they conceived to be radically contrasting qualities of color, religion, and style of life, as well as animality and a peculiarly potent sexuality. . . . In fearfully hoping to escape the animal within himself the white man debased the Negro" (pp. 43, 582). Similarly, Roy Harvey Pearce in *The Savages of America: A Study of the Indian and the Idea of Civilization* (Baltimore, 1953) maintained that the Indian "became important for the English mind, not for what he was in and of himself, but for what he showed civilized men they were not and must not be" (p. 5). Since kinship was the most fundamental relationship in Cherokee society, it is certainly conceivable that the *atsi nahsa'i* were largely responsible for creating that "sense of mutuality among the people of a community by supplying a focus for group feeling" without which "social organization would be impossible." (Erikson, *Puritans,* p. 4.)

Chapter 2

[1]The major works dealing with Indian slavery—including Almon W. Lauber, *Indian Slavery in Colonial Times Within the Present Limits of the United States* (New York, 1913); Sanford Winston, "Indian Slavery in the Carolina Region," *Journal of Negro History* 19 (1934); and William R. Snell, "Indian Slavery in Colonial South Carolina" (Ph.D. diss., Univ. of Alabama, 1972)—ignore the effects of enslavement on the Indian tribes themselves.

[2]Clarence L. Ver Steeg, *Origins of a Southern Mosaic: Studies in Early Carolina and Georgia* (Athens, Ga., 1975), pp. 103–32; Gary B. Nash, *Red, White, and Black: The Peoples of Early America* (Engle-

wood Cliffs, N.J., 1974), pp. 111–13; Verner W. Crane, *The Southern Frontier, 1670–1732* (Durham, N.C., 1928), pp. 109–10. Crane adequately deals with the role of the Indian trade in the economy of South Carolina but generally neglects the economic changes within the tribes involved. A recent work which emphasizes this particular aspect of the Indian trade is John P. Reid, *A Better Kind of Hatchet: Law, Trade, and Diplomacy in the Cherokee Nation During the Early Years of European Contact* (University Park, Pa., 1976).

[3]Mary U. Rothrock, "Carolina Traders Among the Overhill Cherokees, 1690–1760," *East Tennessee Historical Society Publications* 1 (1929):4–5, 8; Crane, *Southern Frontier,* pp. 93, 110; John P. Brown, *Old Frontiers: The Story of the Cherokee Indians from the Earliest Times to the Date of Their Removal to the West, 1838* (Kingsport, Tenn., 1938), p. 44; Hewatt, *South Carolina and Georgia,* 2:7.

[4]One source described the Cherokees in 1708 as "being but ordinary hunters and less warriors." Crane, *Southern Frontier,* pp. 41, 112, 143.

[5]Chapman J. Milling, *Red Carolinians* (Chapel Hill, 1940), pp. 267–68; Crane, *Southern Frontier,* p. 62.

[6]Rothrock, "Carolina Traders," p. 6; McDowell, *Journals,* pp. 85–87, 120–21, 123, 154–55, 188, 325–29.

[7]Samuel Cole Williams, *Adair's History,* p. 440.

[8]Brickell, *Natural History,* p. 284.

[9]Mooney, *Myths,* p. 213; Crane, *Southern Frontier,* p. 116; Nancy O. Lurie, "Indian Cultural Adjustment to European Civilization," in *Seventeenth-Century America: Essays in Colonial History,* ed. James M. Smith (Chapel Hill, 1959), pp. 38–39; Hewatt, *South Carolina and Georgia,* 1:65–66.

[10]Hewatt, *South Carolina and Georgia,* 1:65–66.

[11]Samuel Cole Williams, *Adair's History,* p. 456.

[12]McDowell, *Journals,* pp. 236–37.

[13]Samuel Cole Williams, *Adair's History,* p. 407.

[14]McDowell, *Journals,* pp. 53–57, 140, 179.

[15]Crane, *Southern Frontier,* p. 20; Nash, *Red, White, and Black,* pp. 116–17; Lauber, *Indian Slavery,* pp. 144–45.

[16]Lauber, *Indian Slavery,* pp. 134–35.

[17]William L. Saunders, ed., *The Colonial Records of North Carolina,* 10 vols. (Raleigh, 1886–90), 1:900; Walter Clark, ed., *The State Records of North Carolina,* 15 vols. (Winston and Goldsboro, 1895–1905), 23:517.

[18]Hewatt, *South Carolina and Georgia,* 1:49, 156–57; Saunders,

Colonial Records, 2:52; Nash, *Red, White, and Black,* p. 146.

[19]Leonard Bloom, "The Acculturation of the Eastern Cherokees: Historical Aspects," *North Carolina Historical Review* 19 (1942): 334–35; Hewatt, *South Carolina and Georgia,* 1:202–203; Winston, "Indian Slavery," 433.

[20]McDowell, *Journals,* pp. 85–87, 129, 134, 186.

[21]Nash, *Red, White, and Black,* p. 113; Saunders, *Colonial Records,* 2:45; Crane, *Southern Frontier,* p. 112; Peter H. Wood, *Black Majority: Negroes in Colonial South Carolina from 1670 Through the Stono Rebellion* (New York, 1974), pp. 38–43.

[22]McDowell, *Journals,* pp. 198–99.

[23]Crane, *Southern Frontier,* p. 40; Hewatt, *South Carolina and Georgia,* 1:127, 2:229; Mereness, *Travels,* p. 95; McDowell, *Journals,* p. 49; Clark, *State Records,* 12:205, 13:204–205.

[24]Hewatt, *South Carolina and Georgia,* 1:241, 2:278; McDowell, *Journals,* pp. 127–28, 131.

[25]Samuel Cole Williams, *Adair's History,* pp. 407–409.

[26]Ibid., pp. 408, 410, 412–13; Samuel Cole Williams, *Timberlake's Memoirs,* p. 120; Hewatt, *South Carolina and Georgia,* 1:69.

[27]Samuel Cole Williams, *Adair's History,* pp. 413–14, 416.

[28]McDowell, *Journals,* p. 39.

[29]Samuel Cole Williams, *Timberlake's Memoirs,* p. 82.

[30]Samuel Cole Williams, *Adair's History,* p. 416.

[31]Lawson, *Voyage,* pp. 204–205.

[32]Samuel Cole Williams, *Adair's History,* pp. 459–60.

[33]Hewatt, *South Carolina and Georgia,* 2:4.

[34]This is the thesis of Frederick O. Gearing, *Priests and Warriors: Social Structures for Cherokee Politics in the 18th Century* (Menasha, Wis., 1962).

[35]Samuel Cole Williams, *Adair's History,* pp. 463, 443.

[36]Ibid., pp. 443–45; George Milligan-Johnston, "A Short Description of the Province of South Carolina," in *Colonial South Carolina: Two Contemporary Descriptions,* ed. Chapman J. Milling (Columbia, S.C., 1951), pp. 187–88.

[37]Hewatt, *South Carolina and Georgia,* 1:67.

[38]Bourne, *Narratives,* 1:221; Samuel Cole Williams, *Adair's History,* p. 443.

[39]Lawson, *Voyage,* p. 184.

[40]Samuel Cole Williams, *Adair's History,* p. 461; Brickell, *Natural History,* pp. 332, 344–45.

[41]Samuel Cole Williams, *Timberlake's Memoirs,* p. 111; Hewatt,

South Carolina and Georgia, 2:239; McDowell, *Journals,* p. 398; Samuel Cole Williams, *Early Travels,* pp. 151-52.

[42]McDowell, *Journals,* pp. 150-53.

[43]Francis Paul Prucha, *American Indian Policy in the Formative Years: The Indian Trade and Intercourse Acts, 1790-1834* (Lincoln, Neb., 1962), pp. 5-25.

CHAPTER 3

[1]R.R. Wright, "Negro Companions of the Spanish Explorers," *American Anthropologist* 4 (1902):217-28; Bourne, *Narratives,* 1:72; Herbert Aptheker, *American Negro Slave Revolts* (New York, 1943), p. 163; Woodbury Lowery, *The Spanish Settlements Within the Present Limits of the United States, 1513-1561* (New York and London, 1911), pp. 165-67; Michael Roethler, "Negro Slavery Among the Cherokee Indians, 1540-1866" (Ph.D. diss., Fordham Univ., 1964), p. 16; Lurie, "Indian Cultural Adjustment," pp. 35-36. Lurie notes that the natives of North America possessed no "sense of racial kinship."

[2]Following the Indian massacre of 1622, a pamphlet entitled "The Relation of the Barbarous Massacre in Time of Peace and League, Treacherously executed by the Native Infidels upon the English" pointed to a beneficial aspect of the disaster in that Indians who had previously been treated as friends could now be enslaved and forced to work for the Virginia colonists or exported to Bermuda. Lauber, *Indian Slavery,* p. 118. The first cargo of Africans to arrive in British North America preceded the massacre by only three years having come aboard a Dutch vessel in 1619. Kenneth M. Stampp, *The Peculiar Institution: Slavery in the Ante-Bellum South* (New York, 1956), p. 18.

[3]Winston, "Indian Slavery," pp. 437-38. Winston comments, "Unsteady, undependable workers, with a tendency to sicken, and a marked predilection for running away, the Indians, relatively few in numbers at best, were replaced by the more dependable Negro slaves."

[4]Brickell, *Natural History,* p. 282.

[5]Winston, "Indian Slavery," pp. 435-36, 440; Snell, "Slavery," p. 144. Snell found that in the years 1722 to 1730 the highest price commanded by the Indian men was £250 while from 1723 to 1730 African men brought as high as £330. Similarly Indian and African women sold for £155 and £280, respectively.

[6]Crane, *Southern Frontier,* pp. 113–14.

[7]Samuel Cole Williams, *Early Travels,* p. 154; Menzies, "Unheard-of Sufferings," p. 27; John Haywood, *The Civil and Political History of the State of Tennessee* (Knoxville, 1969; original ed., 1823), pp. 321–22.

[8]William L. McDowell, ed., *Documents Relating to Indian Affairs, May 21, 1750–Aug. 7, 1754* (Columbia, 1958), pp. 46, 83.

[9]Luther F. Addington, "Chief Benge's Last Raid," *Historical Society of Southwest Virginia* 2 (1966):124–33.

[10]Hewatt, *South Carolina and Georgia,* 2:8. Subsequent agreements and treaties carried similar provisions. In 1751, for example, Governor Glen of South Carolina and a delegation of Cherokees agreed that "if any Negro or Mullatto shall desert from his Master and shall fly to the Cherokee Country, the Indians shall do their utmost Endeavor to apprehend him, and shall deliver him to some of our Traders or bring him to Charles Town for which they shall have a reward." McDowell, *Documents, 1750–1754,* p. 190.

[11]Brickell, *Natural History,* p. 357; Wood, *Black Majority,* pp. 53, 262–63, 318.

[12]William S. Willis, Jr., "Divide and Rule: Red, White, and Black in the Southeast," in *Red, White, and Black: Symposium on Indians in the Old South,* ed. Charles M. Hudson (Athens, 1971), pp. 104, 106.

[13]Nash, *Red, White, and Black,* p. 295; Saunders, *Colonial Records,* 1:886, 10:118.

[14]Milligan-Johnston, "A Short Description," p. 136.

[15]McDowell, *Documents, 1750–1754,* p. 103. The slaves accurately assessed the racial composition of the population in South Carolina. In 1750, 25,000 whites lived in the state compared to 40,000 black slaves and 60,000 Indians. Nash remarks, "That white Carolinians were able to maintain a precarious hold on the situation is a testimony to their ability to play one Indian tribe against another and to their partial success in keeping Indians and Negroe slaves divided." Nash, *Red, White, and Black,* pp. 291–92.

[16]Kenneth W. Porter, "Negroes on the Southern Frontier, 1670–1763," *Journal of Negro History* 33 (1948): 56–58; Willis, "Divide and Rule," p. 106.

[17]In May 1751, for example, South Carolina enjoined traders from taking slaves or free blacks into Indian territory. In August of that year the colony imposed a £20 fine on violators and in December once again enacted a regulation prohibiting traders from employing "In-

dians, Negroes, or Slaves." McDowell, *Documents, 1750–1754,* pp. 88, 136, 199. John Richard Alden, *John Stuart and the Southern Colonial Frontier, 1754–1775: A Study of Indian Relations, War, Trade, and Land Problems in the Southern Wilderness, 1754–1775* (New York, 1944), pp. 19, 210; Rothrock, "Carolina Traders," p. 8.

[18]Mereness, *Travels,* pp. 138–39.

[19]Ibid., p. 150.

[20]William L. McDowell, ed., *Documents Relating to Indian Affairs, 1754–1765* (Columbia, 1970), pp. 426–27; Rothrock, "Carolina Traders," p. 8.

[21]Charles Hudson, *The Southeastern Indians* (Knoxville, 1976), pp. 317–50; Mooney, *Myths,* pp. 240, 251, 264, 270; John S. Mbiti, *African Religions and Philosophy* (New York, 1970), pp. 72, 80.

[22]Mbiti, *African Religions,* pp. 65–66; Mooney, *Myths,* pp. 239, 241. Many have debated whether Joel Chandler Harris's Uncle Remus stories are of Indian, African, or even European origin. See Mooney, *Myths,* pp. 233–34 and Adolph Gerber, "Uncle Remus Traced to the Old World," *Journal of American Folklore* 4 (1893):245–57. For a discussion of the similarities in the folklore of many cultures, see Alexander Haggerty Krappe, *The Science of Folklore* (London, 1930).

[23]Olaudah Equiano, *The Life of Olaudah Equiano or Gustavus Vassa, The African* (New York, 1969, original ed., 1837), p. 17. Osifekunde, an Ijebu boy whom pirates seized along the Nigerian coast, described the only somewhat more sophisticated division of labor and economy of his people: "The usual occupations of the Ijebu people are agriculture and gardening, using nothing but a hoe; raising herds of large and small cattle and domestic flocks; the fabrication of cotton textiles with very simple looms; gold mining, either by washing alluvium or in excavated mines; fishing with hook and line, nets, and even harpoons; and hunting with traps, but also with military weapons such as bows and arrows, lances, javelins, and even muskets. . . . There, where each family supplies its own labor for work too unskilled to require special training, it is hardly necessary to call on professional workmen. . . . What I have said about industry applies naturally to commerce as well: self-sufficient households rarely need to go shopping." P.C. Lloyd, ed., "Osifejunde of Ijebu" in *Africa Remembered: Narratives by West Africans from the Era of the Slave Trade,* ed. Philip D. Curtin (Madison, 1967), pp. 268–69.

[24]Basil Davidson, *The African Genus: An Introduction to African Cultural and Social History* (Boston and Toronto, 1969), pp. 33–36.

[25]Equiano, *Life,* pp. 12, 16, 18.

[26]Davidson, *African Genius*, pp. 57, 66; Hudson, "Cherokee Concept," pp. 51–54; Mooney, *Myths*, pp. 239–40.

[27]Mbiti, *African Religions*, pp. 135–38; John Grace, *Domestic Slavery in West Africa* (New York, 1975), p. 7.

[28]A. Norman Klein, "West African Unfree Labor Before and After the Rise of the Atlantic Slave Trade" in Foner and Genovese, eds., *Slavery in the New World*, pp. 89–91. Rattray in his classic work on the Ashantis identified these four categories of bondage as well as a fifth, the *domum*, or prisoners of war whom the Ashantis could execute at state ceremonies with the consent of the chief. R.S. Rattray, *Ashanti Law and Constitution* (London, 1956; original ed., 1929), pp. 34–46.

[29]Elizabeth Donnan, ed., *Documents Illustrative of the History of the Slave Trade to America*, 4 vols. (New York, 1969), 2:352. Equiano, *Life*, pp. 16, 20.

[30]Klein, "West African Unfree Labor," p. 90; Rick N. McKown, "The African Middle Man in the Transatlantic Slave Trade: A Study in Attitudes" (unpublished paper, 1967). McKown rather naïvely assumes that Africans would not have participated in the transatlantic slave trade if they had known the true nature of servitude in the western world.

[31]Klein, "West African Unfree Labor," p. 88; Davidson, *African Genius*, p. 75.

[32]Equiano, *Life*, p. 75.

[33]Donnan, *Slave Trade*, 2:351. Grace, *Domestic Slavery*, pp. 7–8, 220–55. Rodney claims that the distinction between domestic slaves and commercial slaves is a false one and that "there seems to be at least a *prima facie* case for the counter-assertion that many of the forms of slavery and subjection present in Africa in the nineteenth and twentieth centuries and considered indigenous to that continent were in reality engendered by the Atlantic slave trade." Walter Rodney, "African Slavery and Other Forms of Social Oppression on the Upper Guinea Coast in the Context of the Atlantic Slave Trade," *Journal of African History* 7 (1966):443.

[34]Samuel Cole Williams, *Adair's History*, p. 4. Robert Beverley gave a similar explanation for the color of the Indians' skin: "Their Colour, when they are grown up, is a Chestnut brown and tawny; but much clearer in their Infancy. Their Skin comes afterwards to harden and grow blacker, by greasing and Sunning themselves." Robert Beverley, *The History and Present State of Virginia*, ed. Louis B. Wright (Chapel Hill, 1947; original ed., 1705), p. 159. Works dealing with

European attitudes toward Indians include Pearce, *Savages of America;* Jordan, *White over Black,* pp. 89–91, 239–52; Gary B. Nash, "The Image of the Indian in the Southern Colonial Mind," *William and Mary Quarterly* 3d series, 29 (1972): 197–230; and James Axtell, "Through a Glass Darkly, Colonial Attitudes Toward the Native Americans," *American Indian Culture and Research Journal* 1 (1974): 17–28.

[35]Thomas Jefferson, *Notes on the State of Virginia* (Boston, 1832), pp. 6, 63, 143, 145. Ebenezer Newton, who visited the Cherokees in 1818, rejoiced that as a result of white missionary activity "the time was near, when these hitherto untutored tribes were enjoying the benefits to be derived from a virtuous and useful education, and that ere there will arise among them Philosophers, Poets, Orators, Civilians and Divines not inferior to those of any country." Charlotte Newton, ed., "Ebenezer Newton's 1818 Diary," *Georgia Historical Quarterly* 53 (1969):214.

[36]Helen T. Catterall, ed., *Judicial Cases Concerning American Slavery and the Negro,* 5 vols. (Washington, D.C., 1926–37), 2:416.

[37]Washburn may possibly have embellished his informant's account since it is found in the context of a comparison of Cherokee and Jewish cosmology. Cephas Washburn, *Reminiscences of the Indians* (Richmond, Va.), p. 192; *American State Papers,* Class 2: *Indian Affairs,* 2 vols. (Washington, D.C., 1832), 1:461.

[38]*Cherokee Phoenix and Indians' Advocate,* 21 Feb. 1828, 13 Apr. 1828.

CHAPTER 4

[1]Widows usually resumed use of their maiden names. The widow of James Vann, for example, is referred to as Peggy Scott, her maiden name, in the settlement of his estate in 1810. Cherokee Papers, Thomas Gilcrease Institute, Tulsa, Okla.

[2]Cherokee Nation, *Laws of the Cherokee Nation: Adopted by the Council at Various Times, Printed for the Benefit of the Nation,* vol. 5 of *The Constitutions and Laws of the American Indian Tribes* (Wilmington, Del., and London, 1973), p. 3. Although ownership of land seems to have passed from women to men, there is some indication that property descended from males but within the matrilineal clan. For example, Tayes Ke complained to Chief Ross in the hectic period

preceding removal that whites had seized a field that had been "left to him by his uncle the late Salegugee." Complaint, John Ross Papers, Thomas Gilcrease Institute. Women lost political as well as economic power in the process of "civilization." Adair had complained that the Cherokees "have been a considerable while under petticoat-government" and as late as 1785 the War Woman of Chota addressed the commissioners at the Hopewell treaty conference. When the Cherokees wrote a Constitution in 1827, however, they denied women a voice in the government. Samuel Cole Williams, *Adair's History,* p. 153; *American State Papers,* 1:41; Cherokee Nation, *Laws,* p. 121.

[3]William Bartram, "Observations on the Creek and Cherokee Indians, 1789," *Transactions of the American Ethnological Society* 3, part 1 (1854):66. The editor of the *Cherokee Advocate* later expressed pride that "in this respect the Cherokees have been considerably in advance of many of their white brethren, the rights of their women having been amply secured almost ever since they had written laws." *Cherokee Advocate,* 27 Feb. 1845.

[4]Joel R. Poinsett to Brigadier General Matthew Arbuckle, 17 Dec. 1838, John Ross to Joel R. Poinsett, 18 July 1839, Ross Papers.

[5]Mooney, *Myths,* pp. 242–48.

[6]Samuel Cole Williams, *Adair's History,* p. 147; Washburn, *Reminiscences,* pp. 206–207. Traditional Cherokees practiced this marriage ceremony at least as late as 1819, the year in which Washburn began his ministry among the Cherokees. The American Board missionary gave the following description of a Cherokee wedding: "The groom now receives from his mother a leg of venison and a blanket; the bride receives from her mother an ear of corn and a blanket. The groom and bride now commence stepping towards each other, and when they meet in the middle of the councilhouse the groom presents his venison, and the bride her corn, and the blankets are united. This ceremony put into words is a promise on the part of the man that he will provide meat for his family, and on the woman's part that she will furnish bread, and on the part of both that they will occupy the same bed."

[7]Malone, *Cherokees of the Old South,* p. 10; Woodward, *The Cherokees,* pp. 88–89; Mooney, *Myths,* p. 45.

[8]Benjamin Hawkins, *Letters of Benjamin Hawkins, 1796–1806,* vol. 9 of *Georgia Historical Society Collections* (Savannah, 1916), p. 23.

[9]George Washington to the Cherokee Nation, 1796, reprinted in the *Phoenix,* 20 Mar. 1828.

[10]Hawkins, *Letters,* p. 10.

[11]Ibid., pp. 21–24.

[12]Elias Boudinot, *An Address to the Whites* (Philadelphia, 1826), p. 8.

[13]Reid, *Law of Blood,* pp. 140–41.

[14]Ibid., p. 133; *Phoenix,* 6 May 1828, 21 May 1828.

[15]Samuel Cole Williams, *Adair's History,* pp. 459–60.

[16]Gearing, *Priests and Warriors.* Gearing fails to note the growing economic power of the warriors.

[17]Samuel Cole Williams, *Adair's History,* p. 462.

[18]Cherokee Nation, *Laws,* pp. 3–4, 28, 85–130; Census of the Eastern Cherokees, 1835, Record Group 75, National Archives, Washington, D.C.

[19]Census; *Phoenix,* 6 Mar. 1828.

[20]*Phoenix,* 10 Apr. 1828.

[21]Ibid., 24 Apr. 1828.

[22]For the purpose of comparison, see Stampp, *Peculiar Institution,* pp. 192–236.

[23]*Phoenix,* 10 Apr. 1828, 24 Apr. 1828.

[24]Ibid., 4 Nov. 1829, 11 Dec. 1830.

[25]Valuations of Property Owned by Cherokees in Various Counties in Georgia, Record Group 75, National Archives, Washington, D.C. Anyone owning more than ten slaves in 1835 was considered a large slaveholder among the Cherokees. Stampp considered the owners of more than twenty slaves to be members of the "planter class" among white southerners. In 1860 only 12 percent of white slaveholders qualified, and 72 percent owned less than ten slaves. Ten thousand or .026 percent of the 385,000 white slaveholders held more than fifty slaves while the three Cherokees who occupied this category comprised only .014 percent of the slaveholding Cherokees. Slightly over one fourth of white southern families owned slaves but less than 8 percent of Cherokee families had bondsmen. Stampp, *Peculiar Institution,* pp. 29–31.

[26]Valuations.

[27]Ibid. Assessors valued Ross's estate at $10,000, Vann's at $7,075.40, and Ridge's at $6,532.55. Census. The correlation was made with the Statistical Package for the Social Sciences on a Xerox 560 computer.

[28]Ibid.

[29]Census.

[30]Ibid.

[31]Bernard W. Sheehan, *Seeds of Extinction: Jeffersonian Philanthropy and the American Indian* (Chapel Hill, 1973), pp. 243–75. Sheehan describes both the philosophical framework of the early nineteenth-century philanthropists and their various programs for the "obliteration of savagery" and concludes that "removal made the best of a bad situation." An excellent study of the internal effects of Jefferson's Indian policy on the Cherokee Nation is William McLoughlin, "Thomas Jefferson and the Beginning of Cherokee Nationalism, 1806 to 1809," *William and Mary Quarterly* 3d series, 32 (1975): 547–80. Michael Rogin gives the following interpretation of Jackson's "civilizing" policy, which was based on Jefferson's: "It offered Indians not simply help, but a redefinition of their own identity. It defined them as children, which in fact they were not. It forced the tribes into childish dependence upon a white father." Michael Paul Rogin, *Fathers and Children: Andrew Jackson and the Subjugation of the American Indian* (New York, 1975), p. 208.

[32]Those Cherokees who chose to emigrate settled in communities which seem to have been clearly "progressive" or "conservative." In 1824 a missionary reported that in some villages everyone spoke English while in others no one understood the missionary's language. One settlement, Takautokaugh's Village, was so conservative that the chief actively opposed schools and churches. A. Finney to Jeremiah Evarts, 12 Aug. 1824, Records of the American Board of Commissioners for Foreign Missions, Houghton Library, Harvard University, Cambridge, Mass.

[33]Mooney, *Myths,* pp. 15, 239, 246–47; Hudson, *Southeastern Indians,* p. 132; Eugene L. Schwaab, *Travels in the Old South Selected from Periodicals of the Times,* 2 vols. (Lexington, Ky., 1974), 1: 224–25.

[34]Cherokee Nation, *Laws,* pp. 4–5, 136–37.

[35]Ronald E. Shaw, ed., *Andrew Jackson, 1767-1845: Chronology, Documents, Bibliographical Aids* (Dobbs Ferry, N.Y., 1969), pp. 26–27; Prucha, *American Indian Policy,* pp. 233–49; Prucha, "Andrew Jackson's Indian Policy: A Reassessment," *Journal of American History* 56 (1969):527–39. Prucha maintains that removal was the only "feasible alternative" to the "Indian problem" which Jackson faced. A less imperialistic and more accurate assessment of Jackson's overall Indian policy can be found in Ronald N. Satz, *American Indian Policy in the Jacksonian Era* (Lincoln, Neb., 1975). Satz assumes, however, that the ultimate goal of removal was the assimilation of the Indians and concludes that the policy failed because "American ethnocentrism and

the Indian desire to preserve their tribal identity combined to thwart the plans of those who wanted to transform them into Americans or at least to attach them closer to the 'protecting arm' of the federal government" (p. 294). In his psychoanalytical biography of Andrew Jackson, Rogin interprets Jackson's Indian policy as an attempt by the president whose "intensified loneliness, vengeful disappointment, and separation anxiety . . . prefigured in exaggerated form the problems of Jacksonian society" to relive his childhood while establishing himself as a dominant father figure: "Returning to childhood, in Indian war, Indian treaties, and Indian removal, Jackson mastered its regressive appeal. He infused American politics with regenerated paternal authority." Jackson insisted on infantilizing native Americans in order to affirm his paternal role. Removal from the corrupting influences of civilization would prolong infantilism and thereby prolong the necessity for Jackson's paternal supervision. Rogin, *Fathers and Children,* pp. 15, 209.

[36]Satz, *American Indian Policy,* pp. 1–63, 296–98; Grant Foreman, *Indian Removal: The Emigration of the Five Civilized Tribes of Indians* (Norman, Okla., 1932), pp. 229–312; Dale Van Every, *Disinherited: The Lost Birthright of the American Indian* (New York, 1966); Mooney, *Myths,* pp. 114–30; Malone, *Cherokees of the Old South,* pp. 171–84; Woodward, *The Cherokees,* pp. 157–91.

[37]*Worcester* v. *Georgia,* 6 Peters 515, 10 Curtis 214, 31 L. Ed. 501 (1832).

[38]John Ridge to Stand Watie, 6 Apr. 1832, Cherokee Nation Papers, University of Oklahoma Library, Norman, Okla.

[39]John Ridge to John Ross, Feb. 1833, Ross Papers.

[40]Complaints by Ayuque against Joel McCrary, 3 Apr. 1834, and Dianna against Richard Edmondson, 9 Apr. 1834, Ross Papers.

[41]Quoted in Sumner Lincoln Fairfield, "The Captivity of John Howard Payne," *North American Quarterly Magazine* 33 (1836):107–24.

[42]David Irwin (for Barron and Irwin) to John Ross, 1 Aug. 1834, Ross Papers.

[43]Evan Jones to John Ross, 29 Dec. 1837, Ross Papers.

[44]H.R. 425, 21st Cong., 1st sess. (1830); Sworn statement by Thomas Woodward, 16 Nov. 1840, Ross Papers.

[45]William Rogers to John Ross, 1 Feb. 1833, J. Peck to John Ross, 1 Feb. 1833, Ross Papers.

[46]For an outstanding work sympathetic to the Ridge family, see Thurman Wilkins, *Cherokee Tragedy: The Story of the Ridge Family and the Decimation of a People* (New York, 1970).

[47]George W. Paschal, "To the Public," n.p., n.d., Cherokee Nation Papers.

[48]Georgia's Governor's Letterbook, 1833, Georgia Department of Archives, Atlanta, Ga.

[49]Charles J. Kappler, ed., *Indian Affairs, Laws and Treaties,* 2 vols. (Washington, D.C., 1904), 2:439–47.

[50]Elizur Butler to David Greene, 5 Mar. 1845, Records of the American Board.

[51]H.R. 404, 25th Cong., 2d sess. (1838); H.R. 324, 25th Cong., 2d sess. (1838); H.R. 384, 25th Cong., 2d sess. (1838); John Ross to Samuel and John M. Truman, 3 May 1838, Ross Papers.

[52]Rebecca B. Spring to John Ross, 14 Mar. 1863, Ross Papers.

Chapter 5

[1]Requisition for Funds, 7 Nov. 1838, J.L. Hargett Collection, University of Oklahoma Library, Norman, Okla.; Grant Foreman, *Indian Removal,* p. 312.

[2]Indian-Pioneer History, 113 vols., Oklahoma Department of Archives, Oklahoma City, Okla., 43:407.

[3]"Number of Cherokees in Captain Geo. Hicks Detachment taken the 27th of Oct. 1838," Hargett Collection.

[4]John Ross to Captain John Page, 24 Aug. 1838, Thomas N. Clark to John Ross, 15 Nov. 1838, Ross Papers.

[5]Indian-Pioneer History, 50:117.

[6]Ibid., 107:453, 43:406. Elizabeth Ballard informed the interviewer that her "grandfather was a large slave owner and had brought his slaves with him. With the help of the negroes they erected comfortable log houses in which to live and house the negroes." 43:255. Henry Henderson, the son of Martin Vann and his slave Mollie, reported that when the household disembarked from the steamboat that had brought them to Indian country, Vann "had his slaves clear up land and make fence rails until he had several hundred acres under cultivation in corn and cotton." 28:395. Josiah Gregg, *Commerce of the Prairies,* ed. Max L. Moorhead (Norman, Okla., 1954), p. 400.

[7]Indian-Pioneer History, 63:366–67; *Advocate,* 26 Mar. 1846, 26 Feb. 1846, 7 Oct. 1847, 19 Feb. 1849, 1 Oct. 1850.

[8]Rennard Strickland, *Fire and the Spirits: Cherokee Law from Clan to Court* (Norman, Okla., 1975), pp. 67–69.

[9]Woodward, *The Cherokees,* pp. 223–34.

[10]A.B. Cunningham to Stand Watie, 10 Apr. 1846, John Rollin Ridge to Stand Watie, 10 Apr. 1846, Cherokee Nation Papers; *Advocate,* 7 May 1846.

[11]James Ross to John Ross, 26 Dec. 1839, Ross Papers; Sarah C. Watie to James M. Bell, 16 Apr. 1846, John Candy to Stand Watie, 10 Apr. 1846, Cherokee Nation Papers.

[12]*Advocate,* 17 June 1850; James Ross to John Ross, 26 Dec. 1839, Ross Papers; John Candy to Stand Watie, 10 Apr. 1846, Cherokee Nation Papers.

[13]*Advocate,* 1 May 1845, 27 Feb. 1845; Sarah C. Watie to James M. Bell, 16 Apr. 1846, Cherokee Nation Papers.

[14]*Advocate,* 26, Mar. 1846, 10 Dec. 1846. Similarly, Jane Love of Going Snake District placed an advertisement in the *Advocate* in which she offered $100 for the recovery of a fourteen-year-old boy who was "supposed to have been taken by some of the Cherokee outlaws and will be conveyed probably to Rusk County Texas or to the Cherokee village on the Brasos." *Advocate,* 26 Feb. 1846.

[15]Ibid., 19 Feb. 1849, 1 Oct. 1850.

[16]Ibid., 7 Oct. 1847.

[17]S.B.N. Ridge to Stand Watie, 22 Oct. 1844, Cherokee Nation Papers; *Advocate,* 26 Nov. 1846, 31 Dec. 1849.

[18]Ibid., 6 Jan. 1848, 5 June 1848, 2 Dec. 1847, 9 Dec. 1847. The *Advocate* carried another such account: "It is said that William Chisholm and Ann Pinder have been arrested on charges of aiding in the abduction of the negroes from the encampment at Fort Gibson some weeks since." *Advocate,* 6 Jan. 1848, 5 June 1848.

[19]Ibid., 17 Dec. 1846, 16 July 1849, 25 Mar. 1851. The Seminoles generally viewed the blacks among them as allies rather than slaves and vehemently protested the U.S. government's plan to place their tribe in the Creek Nation because they feared the enslavement of the blacks by the Creeks. The Seminole blacks, therefore, refused to leave the protection of federal troops at Fort Gibson, which was located on the boundary between the Creek and Cherokee nations. Foreman, *Indian Removal,* p. 370. In "Georgia Blacks During Secession and Civil War, 1859–1865" (Ph.D. diss., Univ. of Georgia, 1975), Clarence Mohr points out that the institution of slavery in Georgia broke down during a period of stress.

[20]*Advocate,* 23 Oct. 1845, 3 Sept. 1849. It is interesting that the reward for stolen slaves was usually larger than the reward for runaways.

[21]Indian-Pioneer History, 81:359–60.

[22]David Palmer to James Orr, 28 Sept. 1856, H.M. Hicks Collection, Thomas Gilcrease Institute, Tulsa, Okla.

[23]Indian-Pioneer History, 27:335.

[24]*Advocate,* 3 Aug. 1853, 5 June 1845.

[25]George P. Rawick, ed., *The American Slave: A Composite Autobiography,* 19 vols. (Westport, Conn., 1972), 7:267.

[26]Henry Bibb, "Narrative of the Life and Adventures of Henry Bibb, An American Slave" in *Puttin' on Ole Massa,* ed. Gilbert Osofsky (New York, 1969), pp. 140–62; David Palmer to James Orr, 28 Sept. 1856, H.M. Hicks Collection.

[27]An account of the unique alliance between Seminoles and blacks can be found in Lawrence Foster, *Negro-Indian Relationships in the Southeast* (Philadelphia, 1935) and in David F. Littlefield, Jr., *Africans and Seminoles: From Removal to Emancipation* (Westport, Conn., 1977).

[28]*Advocate,* 26 Feb. 1846, 18 Sept. 1852, 7 May 1849, 3 Sept. 1849, 6 Jan. 1852. Betty Robertson noted the linguistic affiliation of her mother and husband: "My mammy was a Cherokee slave, and talked it good. My husband was a Cherokee born negro, too, and when he got mad he forgit all the English he knowed." The lack of fluency in English certainly made escape more difficult if not impossible for people like those described by Robertson. Rawick, *American Slave,* 7:266.

[29]*Advocate,* 25 Dec. 1945, 16 Apr. 1846, 17 Dec. 1846, 24 July 1848.

[30]Cherokee Nation, *Laws,* pp. 62–63; John Ross to the National Committee and Council, 17 Nov. 1842, Ross Papers. It is possible that a major revolt by Cherokee bondsmen preceded the one by Vann's slaves. The *St. Louis Argus* published an account of an insurrection among slaves in Indian Territory in the summer of 1841. The *Argus* had obtained information about the revolt from "a gentleman from Fort Leavenworth." The unidentified gentleman reported that a group of runaways from the Cherokee and Choctaw nations and the state of Arkansas joined some Seminole blacks and together made their way toward the Rio Grande, where the fugitives believed they would find a town of refuge. The runaways, whose number totaled six hundred, constructed a log fort on the Red River and repelled an attack by three companies of U.S. dragoons sent from Fort Gibson. A company of infantry with cannons reinforced the dragoons and in the subsequent attack "the bravery and number of refugees availed nothing against the irresistible charge of the dragoons." The soldiers hanged some of the

rebels and they whipped others before returning them to their masters. The account of the rebellion published in the *Argus* is the only one available, as official correspondence makes no mention of it. The National Council did pass an act authorizing the appointment of patrol companies for the purpose of controlling the activities of slaves and an act which prohibited the teaching of blacks to read and write in the fall of 1841. These acts could have been in response to a slave revolt, but no direct correlation can be established. It is reasonable to assume, therefore, that the account in the *Argus* was based on rumor and that no wide-scale insurrection occurred in 1841. Alvin Rucker, "The Story of a Slave Uprising in Oklahoma," *Daily Oklahoman,* 30 Oct. 1932; Cherokee Nation, *Laws,* pp. 53–55.

[31]Rawick, *American Slave,* 7:267–68.

[32]H.L. Smith to Stand Watie, 4 Apr. 1846, Cherokee Nation Papers.

[33]*Advocate,* 13 Feb. 1845, 1 May 1845, 25 Sept. 1845, 24 July 1848.

[34]Cherokee Nation, *Laws,* p. 7. The Old Settlers had passed the following slave code in 1833: "Resolved by the National Committee and Council that six months from and after this date no Slave or Slaves shall have the right to own any kind of property whatever, and all Slaves now holding property, shall be required to sell off their property within the above specified time, and in case any Slave should fail to sell his or her property by the above time then the Light Horse shall proceed to sell his or her property to the highest bidder for the benefit of the owner of the Slave." In 1835 the council had supplemented the code with the following provision: "The Chiefs add to the foregoing that slaves shall not gamble, nor drink ardent spirits.—Add, that if any slave is caught playing cards or drinking ardent spirits he shall receive 25 lashes by the Light Horse. Further resolved that if any slave shall abuse a free person he shall receive sixty lashes to be inflicted by the Light Horse." Resolutions of the Western Cherokees, 2 Dec. 1833, 26 Oct. 1835, Ross Papers.

[35]Cherokee Nation, *Laws,* p. 19; *Phoenix,* 24 Apr. 1848.

[36]Captain Shoe Boots to the National Council, 20 Oct. 1824 (Certified copy from the Book of Record, 1837), Cherokee Nation Papers; Census of 1835.

[37]*Advocate,* 19 Feb. 1849, 17 June 1847; Rawick, *American Slave,* 7:344–47; Indian-Pioneer History, 75:33; Daniel Butrick to David Greene, 1 Jan. 1845, Records of the American Board.

[38]Cherokee Nation, *Laws,* pp. 44, 71.

[39]Ibid., pp. 44, 212; Samuel Worcester to David Greene, 17 Jan.

1835, Daniel Butrick to David Greene, 1 Jan. 1845, Records of the American Board.

[40]Cherokee Nation, *Laws,* pp. 53–54.

[41]*Advocate,* 3 Aug. 1853.

[42]Cherokee Nation, *Laws,* p. 55.

[43]American Board of Commissioners for Foreign Missions, *First Ten Annual Reports of the American Board of Commissioners for Foreign Missions, with Other Documents of the Board* (Boston, 1834), pp. 86, 193, 287; Journal of the Cherokee Mission, 17 Aug. 1818, 27 Dec. 1818, Records of the American Board.

[44]*Phoenix,* 17 Mar. 1832; Journal of the Cherokee Mission, 17 Oct. 1820, Cephas Washburn and A. Finney to Jeremiah Evarts, 27 July 1822, Laura Potter to Daniel Greene, 30 Aug. 1833, Records of the American Board.

[45]Cherokee Nation, *Laws,* p. 173; Indian-Pioneer History, 106:445; *African Repository* 29 (Mar. 1853); Daniel Butrick to David Greene, 1 Jan. 1845, Elizur Butler to David Greene, 5 Mar. 1845, Samuel Worcester to S.B. Treat, 17 Aug. 1849, Records of the American Board.

[46]*Phoenix,* 6 Mar. 1828, 17 Sept. 1828.

[47]*Advocate,* 16 Nov. 1844, 2 Jan. 1845, 9 Jan. 1845, 26 June 1845. By the 1850s a movement was well under way in the white South to reopen the African slave trade, but apparently it attracted no followers among the Cherokees. For a description of the movement see Ronald T. Takaki, *A Pro-Slavery Crusade: The Agitation to Reopen the African Slave Trade* (New York, 1971).

[48]*Phoenix,* 6 Mar. 1828, 28 Jan. 1828, 13 Nov. 1830.

[49]*Advocate,* 16 Jan. 1845, 3 July 1845, 9 Jan. 1845.

[50]*Advocate,* 28 Aug. 1845; William Shorey Coody to John Ross, 17 May 1838, Ross Papers. The theory that slavery was a positive good developed in the period 1820–35 and reached its height in the years 1835–60. Cherokees seem to have considered slavery to be a necessary evil and not a positive good. For a discussion of the "positive good" theory see William Sumner Jenkins, *Pro-Slavery Thought in the Old South* (Chapel Hill, 1935), pp. 65–106.

[51]*Advocate,* 21 Nov. 1844, 12 June 1845.

[52]Thomas L. M'Kenney, *Memoirs, Official and Personal,* 2 vols. (New York, 1846), 1:39.

[53]*Phoenix,* 6 Mar. 1828, 25 Feb. 1829, 25 Mar. 1829, 28 Sept. 1828, 8 Oct. 1828, 21 July 1828, 28 Jan. 1829. For a history of the American Colonization Society see P.J. Staudenraus, *The African Colonization Movement, 1816–1865* (New York, 1961).

[54]William Chamberlain to R.R. Gurley, 19 Mar. 1830, 7 June 1831, Records of the American Colonization Society, Library of Congress, Washington, D.C.

[55]*Advocate,* 21 Nov. 1844, 19 Dec. 1844, 6 Feb. 1845, 8 May 1845.

[56]*African Repository* 29 (Mar. 1853); *Advocate,* 16 Mar. 1853.

Chapter 6

[1]M'Kenney, *Memoirs,* 1:37; Gold Letter, 8 Dec. 1829, Cherokee Letters Collection, Georgia Department of Archives, Atlanta, Ga.

[2]In 1835 there were approximately 12 Cherokees for every slave belonging to a Cherokee in Georgia, 5 Cherokees per slave in Alabama and Tennessee, and 99 Cherokees per slave in North Carolina. Census of 1835; M'Kenney, *Memoirs,* 1:37; Moravian Diaries, 9 Oct. 1800, Moravian Archives, Winston-Salem, N.C.

[3]M'Kenney, *Memoirs,* 1:37; Gold Letter, 8 Dec. 1829, George M. Waters to the National Council, 14 Feb. 1831, Cherokee Letters Collection; Moravian Diaries, 9 Oct. 1800.

[4]Francis R. Goulding, *Sapelo; or, Child-Life on the Tide-Water* (New York, 1870), p. 68.

[5]Edwin James, comp., *Account of an Expedition from Pittsburgh to the Rocky Mountains Performed in the Years 1819 and '20* (Philadelphia, 1823), cited in Kay M. Teall, ed., *Black History in Oklahoma: A Resource Book* (Oklahoma City, 1971), p. 14; Samuel Worcester to David Greene, 17 Jan. 1835, Daniel Butrick to David Greene, 1 Jan. 1845, Records of the American Board.

[6]Adelaide L. Fries, ed., *Records of the Moravians in North Carolina,* 7 vols. (Raleigh, 1947), 6:2799; Edmund Schwarze, *History of the Moravian Mission Among Southern Indian Tribes of the United States* (Bethlehem, Pa., 1923), pp. 63, 70–71, 79, 81; Clemens de Baillou, "The Diaries of the Moravian Brotherhood at the Cherokee Mission in Springplace, Georgia, for the Years 1800–1804," *Georgia Historical Quarterly* 54 (1970):573.

[7]*Phoenix,* 31 Dec. 1831, 4 Feb. 1832; Bibb, "Narrative," p. 162.

[8]Indian-Pioneer History, 5:54, 43:407, 106:442, 107:460.

[9]*Advocate,* 10 Feb. 1852; R.G. Meigs to John Ross, n.d., Ross Papers; Rawick, *American Slave,* 7:288.

[10]Indian-Pioneer History, 107:453–54.

[11]Ibid., 43:407, 93:150, 106:442, 107:460–63; Rawick, *American Slave,* 7:258, 287.

[12]Rawick, *American Slave,* 7:266, 285, 345; Grant Foreman, ed., *A Traveler in Indian Territory: The Journal of Ethan Allen Hitchcock, Later Major General in the United States Army* (Cedar Rapids, Iowa, 1930), pp. 44–45. The superior education Ross's daughter received in the East is in accord with the Cherokees' belief that women should be as well-educated as men. In 1846 the National Council appropriated money for the construction of two institutions of higher education, one for men and the other for women. The Cherokees used Mount Holyoke as a model for their Female Seminary, which was staffed by highly recommended graduates of that pioneer institution in equal education for women. An excellent account of antebellum days at the Cherokee Female Seminary by a young teacher sent from Mount Holyoke can be found in *The Journal of Ellen Whitmore,* ed. Lola Garrett Bowers and Kathleen Garrett (Tahlequah, Okla., 1953).

[13]Grant Foreman, *Journal of Ethan Allen Hitchcock,* p. 45; Indian-Pioneer History, 61:390.

[14]Indian-Pioneer History, 43:406–407, 107:453, 460. For a description of river transportation on the Mississippi and other western rivers by a contemporary of Vann see "Steamboating in the Southwest" in *Travels in the Old South,* ed. Schwaab, pp. 397–406. Muriel H. Wright deals with boating in Indian Territory in her article, "Early Navigation and Commerce Along the Arkansas and Red Rivers in Oklahoma," *Chronicles of Oklahoma* 8 (1930):65–88.

[15]Rawick, *American Slave,* 7:267–68; *Advocate,* 16 Nov. 1844; Grant Foreman, ed., "Reminiscences of Mr. R.P. Vann, East of Webbers Falls, Oklahoma, September 28, 1932," *Chronicles of Oklahoma* 11 (1933):838–44. The explosion of the *Lucy Walker* did not discourage other members of the Vann family from investing in steamboats. The *Advocate* of 24 Apr. 1845 published a notice that James S. Vann had purchased the steamboat "Franklin" and intended to operate it on the Arkansas River.

[16]*Advocate,* 27 Mar. 1845.

[17]C. Runyan to John Ross, 2 Aug. 1839, 20 Aug. 1839, 28 Jan. 1840, J.H. Lynch to John Ross, 18 June 1840, Ross Papers.

[18]Gregg, *Commerce,* p. 351; Cherokee Nation, *Laws,* pp. 58–59, 177–78; Grant Foreman, "Salt Works in Early Oklahoma," *Chronicles of Oklahoma* 10 (1932): 474–500.

[19]Indian-Pioneer History, 61:386–87.

[20]Grant Foreman, "Salt Works," p. 480.

[21]Indian-Pioneer History, 54:30–31, 83:441, 98:220, 24:497. "Butterfly root" also called "pleurisy root" is from a milkweed (*Asclepias*

tuberosa) which has bright reddish-orange flowers; "horsemint" (*Monarda punctata*) is also known as "wild bergamont"; "polecat bush" (*Rhus aromatica*) is a member of the cashew family.

[22]Ibid., 108:213; Charles Lanman, *Adventures in the Wilds of the United States and British American Provinces* (Philadelphia, 1856), pp. 417–20.

[23]James, *Account of an Expedition,* and Charles Joseph Latrobe, *The Rambler in North America* (London, 1836), cited in Teall, *Black History in Oklahoma,* pp. 14–15; Indian-Pioneer History, 112:179; Journal of the Cherokee Mission, 23 Apr. 1818, William Chamberlain's Journal, 12 Mar. 1825, Records of the American Board.

[24]John Rollin Ridge to Stand Watie, 2 July 1849, J.W. Washbourne to Stand Watie, 1 Dec. 1849, Cherokee Nation Papers.

[25]Catterall, *Judicial Cases,* 5:250; J.W. Washbourne to Stand Watie, 23 Dec. 1857, Cherokee Nation Papers.

[26]Grant Foreman, ed., "Notes of a Missionary Among the Cherokees," *Chronicles of Oklahoma* 16 (1938):177; Daniel Butrick's Journal, 11 Apr. 1826, Cephas Washburn to Jeremiah Evarts, 27 Oct. 1828, Records of the American Board.

[27]Catterall, *Judicial Cases,* 5:250; Stand Watie to Andrew Adair, 10 Apr. 1849, Bill of Sale, Jacob and Sebrina Croft to Stand Watie, June 1856, Cherokee Nation Papers; Bill of Sale, Sally Factor to W. Smith, 15 June 1840, Sally Factor to Richard Field, 4 Aug. 1840, John Drew Papers, Thomas Gilcrease Institute, Tulsa, Okla.; Indian-Pioneer History, 61:386, 107:455; Rawick, *American Slave,* 7:290–91.

[28]*Advocate,* 3 Nov. 1852, 20 Apr. 1853; John Staples to John Drew, July 1859, Drew Papers.

[29]Rawick, *American Slave,* 7:289–90.

[30]Sarah Paschal to Stand Watie, 22 June 1852, Cherokee Nation Papers.

[31]*African Repository* 29 (Mar. 1853); Indian-Pioneer History, 8: 513.

[32]Bill of Sale, John Drew to Charlotte Drew, 7 Apr. 1857, Drew Papers. One particular exception was the awarding of slaves in the estate of Andrew Adair to John Drew in satisfaction of a debt: "You are hereby commanded to proceed and place the Negroes Parler and Kate and her increase [four children] in peaceable possession of Jno. Drew in accordance with a decision of this Court made on the 18th day of Nov. 1857." The list of Adair's assets at the time of his death clearly names Kate as Parler's wife and the children as theirs.

[33]Sarah Paschal to Stand Watie, 25 Sept. 1852, Cherokee Nation Pa-

pers; Indian-Pioneer History, 48:89, 106:443–44; Rawick, *American Slave*, 7:266, 285, 345. The sale of slaves to pay legal fees or the exchange of slaves to lawyers for their services seems to have been a fairly common practice. Statements by A. McCoy and W.J. Howard, 31 July 1837, Cherokee Nation Papers; Statement by Jonathan Mulkey, 21 Oct. 1840, Bill of Sale, William Dutch to John Drew, 5 Nov. 1847, Drew Papers.

[34]J.C. Ellsworth of David Greene, 24 July 1833, Records of the American Board.

[35]Indian-Pioneer History, 106:443; Rawick, *American Slave*, 7:258.

[36]Indian-Pioneer History, 48:95, 106:443.

[37]Ibid., 1:51; Rawick, *American Slave*, 7:268–69, 293, 351; Daniel Butrick to David Greene, 1 Jan. 1845, Records of the American Board.

[38]Indian-Pioneer History, 1:53. Betting apparently was an indigenous practice among southeastern Indians and, unlike many of their vices, was not acquired from whites. In 1775 James Adair wrote: "The Indians are much addicted to gaming, and will often stake everything they possess." Williams, *Adair's History*, p. 428.

[39]Indian-Pioneer History, 1:461–62; James Mooney, "The Cherokee Ball Play," *American Anthropologist* 3 (1890):105–36; Williams, *Adair's History*, pp. 119–20, 428–30. Originally the ball game was far more than a sport; it was an acceptable way to release aggression and settle disagreements. Feuding clans resolved disputes through the ball game, and different tribes occasionally met to compete on the ball ground rather than the battlefield.

[40]Indian-Pioneer History, 10:253; John R. Swanton, "The Green Corn Dance," *Chronicles of Oklahoma* 10 (1932): 170–95. The Green Corn Ceremony also originally had far more significance than merely a harvest festival, for it marked the end of the old and the beginning of the new in personal relationships as well as fire and provisions.

[41]Indian-Pioneer History, 14:38; Rawick, *American Slave*, 7:285–87.

[42]Indian-Pioneer History, 106:443, 107:464; Rawick, *American Slave*, 7:258, 286–87, 347–50.

[43]Indian-Pioneer History, 8:513, 61:390; Rawick, *American Slave*, 7:345–47.

[44]Indian-Pioneer History, 43:407, 106:442; Rawick, *American Slave*, 7:258, 266, 286, 348–49.

[45]Rawick, *American Slave*, 7:258, 285, 345.

[46]Ibid., 266–67, 349; Indian-Pioneer History, 14:39, 43:407.

[47]Indian-Pioneer History, 14:39, 43:408, 107:462; Rawick, *American Slave*, 7:287, 351.

[48]Indian-Pioneer History, 14:39, 106:442, 107:464; Rawick, *American Slave,* 7:266, 285–86, 346, 351.

[49]Indian-Pioneer History, 61:392; Rawick, *American Slave,* 7:261, 267, 289, 345–47.

[50]Indian-Pioneer History, 61:392; Rawick, *American Slave,* 7:346.

CHAPTER 7

[1]*Advocate,* 18 Mar. 1850, 8 Apr. 1850, 15 Apr. 1850, 20 May 1850, 28 Oct. 1851.

[2]Cephas Washburn to Jeremiah Evarts, 27 Oct. 1828, J.C. Ellsworth to David Greene, 24 July 1833, Records of the American Board. For a general work on missionary activities among native Americans see Robert F. Berkhofer, Jr., *Salvation and the Savage: An Analysis of Protestant Missions and American Indian Response* (Lexington, Ky., 1965). Competent works dealing with the ministry of the American Board of Commissioners for Foreign Missions include William Ellsworth Strong, *The Story of the American Board* (New York, 1969); Robert Sparks Walker, *Torchlights to the Cherokees: The Brainerd Mission* (New York, 1931); and Althea Bass, *Cherokee Messenger: A Life of Samuel Austin Worcester* (Norman, Okla., 1936).

[3]An excellent discussion of the conflict between the missionaries in the field and the Prudential Committee can be found in Robert Lewit, "Indian Missions and Antislavery Sentiments: A Conflict of Evangelical and Humanitarian Ideals," *Mississippi Valley Historical Review* 50 (1963–64):39–55.

[4]*Advocate,* 23 Oct. 1848. The missionaries apparently continued hiring slaves on occasion because in 1855 Charles Cutler Torrey, who had just arrived in Indian Territory, wrote in his journal that his colleagues hired slaves if they "wished extra help." In addition to hiring slaves, Worcester signed as a witness a bill of sale by which Sophia was sold but the right to her children retained and seemed to have no pangs of conscience as a result of his act. Grant Foreman, "Notes of a Missionary," p. 177; Bill of Sale, Lydia Hoyt to Abijah Hicks, 10 May 1853, H.M. Hicks Collection.

[5]*Advocate,* 30 Oct. 1848.

[6]William S. Robertson to his parents, 24 Apr. 1854, H.M. Hicks Collection.

[7]*Advocate,* 28 May 1849.

[8]Samuel Worcester to S.B. Treat, 8 Aug. 1853, Records of the

American Board; E.C. Routh, "Early Missionaries to the Cherokees," *Chronicles of Oklahoma* 15 (1937):449–65; Woodward, *The Cherokees,* pp. 258–59.

[9]Vinson Lackey, "New Springplace," *Chronicles of Oklahoma* 17 (1939): 182.

[10]David Palmer to James Orr, 28 Sept. 1856, H.M. Hicks Collection.

[11]Ibid.; Grant Foreman, "Notes of a Missionary," p. 177; Indian-Pioneer History, 73:213; Samuel Worcester to S.B. Treat, 27 Aug. 1855, Records of the American Board.

[12]Charles K. Whipple, *Relation of the American Board of Commissioners for Foreign Missions to Slavery* (Boston, 1861), pp. 3–5.

[13]The asking price for the 800,000-acre tract was $500,000 plus interest from 1835, when the Cherokees received title and immediately began having trouble with the whites who settled there. The United States agreed to pay the $500,000 but balked at paying the interest while the Confederacy agreed to pay both principal and interest. The United States ultimately received the land after the Civil War when the Cherokees were forced to cede the tract to the government, which was supposed to hold the land "in trust" until it could be disposed of. In light of the financial problems the Cherokees were having with the United States, Pike was an excellent choice as Confederate commissioner to the five "civilized" tribes. An Arkansas lawyer, Pike had achieved a reputation of fair dealing with the Indians and had only recently successfully represented the Choctaws in a suit against the United States in which they had been awarded almost $3,000,000. Woodward, *The Cherokees,* pp. 259–60.

[14]Henry M. Rector to John Ross, 29 Jan. 1861, Ross Papers.

[15]John Ross to Henry M. Rector, 22 Feb. 1861, John Ross to Lt. Col. J.R. Kannady, 17 May 1861, Ross Papers; U.S., War Department, *The War of the Rebellion: A Compilation of the Official Records of the Union and Confederate Armies,* Series 1, 3:596–97.

[16]John Ross, Address to the National Council, n.d., Ross Papers.

[17]Ibid., John Ross to Albert Pike, 1 July 1861, Ross Papers.

[18]Henry M. Rector to John Ross, 29 Jan. 1861, John Ross to Henry M. Rector, 22 Feb. 1861, Ross Papers; John Ross to William P. Ross, 15 Feb. 1861, Cherokee Nation Papers.

[19]John Ross and Joseph Vann to John Drew, 2 July 1861, Ross Papers; Minutes of the Executive Council, 21 July 1861, Cherokee Nation Papers.

[20]John Ross, Address to the National Council, n.d., Ross Papers.

[21]W.P. Adair to Stand Watie, 29 Aug. 1861, Cherokee Nation Pa-

pers. Most Cherokees seemed to realize that the factionalism which developed over the issue of removal merely surfaced again in 1861. Annie Eliza Hendrix told a WPA interviewer that the Civil War "afforded an opportunity for this old feud to burst forth in all its fury." Indian-Pioneer History, 92:376.

[22]W.P. Adair to Stand Watie, 29 Aug. 1861, J.W. Washbourne and A.M. Wilson to Stand Watie, 18 May 1861, Cherokee Nation Papers.

[23]J.P. Evarts to John Ross, 2 July 1861, John Ross and Joseph Vann to John Drew, 2 July 1861, Ross Papers.

[24]Indian-Pioneer History, 11:284.

[25]U.S., War Department, *The War of the Rebellion,* Series 1, 3:580, 587.

[26]Although a slave state, Missouri did not secede and Confederate strategists planned an invasion of the state through the Cherokee Nation. Fearing that such a move would prompt Ross to request protection from the Union, General McCulloch vetoed the idea. U.S., War Department, *The War of the Rebellion,* Series 1, 3:594–96, 691–92; Evan Jones to W.P. Dole, 21 Jan. 1862, Ross Papers.

[27]U.S., War Department, *The War of the Rebellion,* Series 1, 8:5–25; unaddressed letter from William P. Ross, 9 Dec. 1861, Ross Papers.

[28]Rawick, *American Slave,* 7:257, 259, 288–89.

[29]Hannah Hicks, "The Diary of Hannah Hicks," *American Scene* 13 (1972):10.

[30]Ibid., p. 8.

[31]Sworn statement of Sarah Stapler, 1878, Hargett Collection. After the death of his first wife during removal, Ross married Mary Bryan Stapler, a Quaker from Philadelphia, whose sister Sarah came to live with the Rosses in Indian Territory and fled with them to Kansas in 1862. Ross spent most of the war with his wife's relatives in Philadelphia.

[32]Hicks, "Diary," pp. 7–8. Hicks's diary consists primarily of accounts of abuses by one side or the other and of attempts to hide Union sympathizers from Watie's men. She also documents the gradual exodus from the Nation as Unionists departed with every federal force that invaded. Other sources indicate the great lengths to which some Cherokees went to avoid conscription. Emma Price Roach told a WPA interviewer that her father was an only child in his teens when Watie's government passed the law and, in order to protect her son, the boys' mother disguised him as a girl for the remainder of the war. Indian-Pioneer History, 8:403.

[33]Original copies of these acts can be found in Box 53 of the Cherokee Nation Papers. It is interesting that John Jones, the abolitionist Baptist missionary, acted as clerk to the council.

[34]Indian-Pioneer History, 43:255; Rawick, *American Slave,* 7:290, 350–51. For an account of the difficulties encountered by Cherokees who fled to Texas and the Choctaw Nation see Angie Debo, "Southern Refugees of the Cherokee Nation," *Southwestern Historical Quarterly* 35 (1932):255–66.

[35]Teall, *Black History in Oklahoma,* pp. 54–67; fragment of a letter in the Ross Papers contained in the Hargett Collection.

[36]Nancy Lynch to James M. Bell, 28 Jan. 1866, Stand Watie to Saladin Ridge Watie, 16 May 1866, Cherokee Nation Papers.

EPILOGUE

[1]Details of reconstruction in the Cherokee Nation can be found in M. Thomas Bailey, *Reconstruction In Indian Territory: A Story of Avarice, Discrimination, and Opportunism* (Port Washington, N.Y., and London, 1972), pp. 1–82, 159–91; and Hannah R. Warren, "Reconstruction in the Cherokee Nation," *Chronicles of Oklahoma* 45 (1967–68): 180–89.

[2]J.W. Washbourne to J.A. Scales, 20 June 1866, Cherokee Nation Papers.

[3]Elias Cornelius Boudinot to W.P. Boudinot, 2 July 1866, J.W. Washbourne to J.A. Scales, 1 June 1866, Cherokee Nation Papers.

[4]Kappler, *Treaties,* 2: 942–50.

[5]Elias Cornelius Boudinot to Stand Watie, 23 July 1866, Cherokee Nation Papers.

[6]J.W. Deupree to James M. Bell, 17 June 1868, Cherokee Nation Papers; *Bartlesville Enterprise,* 10 Feb. 1905. The black population was concentrated in the conservative districts of Cooweescowee, Tahlequah, Illinois. "Summary of the Census of the Cherokee Nation" (Washington, D.C., 1881).

[7]Robert K. Thomas, "The Redbird Smith Movement," in *Symposium on Cherokee and Iroquois Culture,* ed. William N. Fenton and John Gulick (Washington, D.C., 1961); Peter Collier, *When Shall They Rest?* (New York, 1973), pp. 144–47.

Bibliographical Essay

Historians have traditionally regarded European imperialism in North America in terms of military encounters, diplomatic intrigues, and political machinations. Although these factors certainly contributed to the extermination of native American cultures, there was a far more destructive force in Western Civilization than militarism or political cleverness. Not content with destroying or subjugating the Indians, the invaders of this continent combined ethnocentrism with a particularly intense missionary zeal and considered it their duty to supplant indigenous cultures with their own brand of "civilization." Slavery characterized the society which Europeans established in what is now the southern United States and that institution was a major aspect of the "civilization" which whites imparted to the natives they found there. The Cherokees and other North American Indians responded to the "civilizing" efforts of Europeans by selectively adopting and transforming aspects of Western culture and by altering indigenous methods and institutions in an effort to survive. Some Cherokees, particularly those with white ancestry, accepted "civilization" and the institution of slavery more rapidly than others, and the result was the development of an economic, social, and political inequality alien to aboriginal Cherokee culture.

A study of the changes within Cherokee society generated by the acceptance of the "civilization" characterized by plantation slavery requires an examination and understanding of both cultures involved. Unfortunately historians have generally neglected Indian cultures, their modification in response to European demands, and their effect upon white institutions that were accepted. Leonard Bloom's article, "The Acculturation of the Eastern Cherokees: Historical Aspects," demonstrates the ineptness with which most historians have investigated cultural transmission and adjustment. They have preferred to relegate such matters to the sociologist or anthropologist and to continue writing within the narrow framework of white values and European cultural patterns and ignoring the highly developed and complex native cultures.

Most general studies of the Cherokees by historians are written totally from the white perspective and emphasize the political history of white-red relations. These include Charles C. Royce, *The Cherokee Nation of Indians*; Emmett Starr, *History of the Cherokee Indians*; John P. Brown, *Old Frontiers: The Story of the Cherokee Indians from the Earliest Times to the Date of Their Removal to the West, 1838*; Marion L. Starkey, *The Cherokee Nation*; and Morris L. Wardell, *A Political History of the Cherokee Nation, 1838–1907*. Two works that offer some social history, Henry T. Malone's *Cherokees of the Old South: A People in Transition* and Grace Steele Woodward's *The Cherokees,* paternalistically describe the Cherokees. (See chap. 1, n. 1.) Even sympathetic studies of removal, such as Grant Foreman's *Indian Removal* and Dale Van Every's *Disinherited: The Lost Birthright of the American Indian,* ignore the cultural implications of the crisis.

In order to gain a deeper understanding of Cherokee culture, the historian is forced to cross disciplinary boundaries and peruse anthropological studies. Charles Hudson's *The Southeastern Indians* blends anthropology, archeology, and history to produce an ethnohistory of the Southeast, a cultural complex of which the Cherokees were a part. In *Myths of the Cherokees* James Mooney reveals the Cherokees' world view and the intricacies of their belief system. William H. Gilbert, Jr., describes the matrilineal kinship system of the Cherokees and its pervasive influence on their society in *The Eastern Cherokees.* John P. Reid in *A Law of Blood: Primitive Law of the Cherokee Nation* points out the importance of kinship and vengeance in Cherokee culture, and Frederick O. Gearing in *Priests and Warriors: Social Structures for Cherokee Politics in the 18th Century* examines gradual changes in the Cherokee political system. These works are indispensible to the study of the institution of slavery because the belief system shaped attitudes toward the slave, the kinship system determined his place in society, and the legal and judicial systems enforced it. Historians must follow the example of works like these if they are to correct traditional narrowness and retrieve native Americans from the cloak of anonymity with which they have been concealed.

The first problem encountered in taking this approach for an inquiry into the institution of slavery among the Cherokees is the dearth of useful material on Cherokees before European contact. The historian must, therefore, judiciously employ descriptions by Europeans in reconstructing precontact Cherokee society. The chroniclers of the de Soto expedition have provided the earliest sketches of the Cherokees and Edward Gaylord Bourne has collected these in *Narratives of the Career of Hernando de Soto.* Three compilations of accounts by various Europeans, some of whom had experiences among the Cherokees, are Alexander S. Salley, *Narratives of Early Carolina, 1650–1708;* Newton D. Mereness, *Travels in the American Colonies*; and Samuel Cole Williams, *Early Travels in the Tennessee Country, 1540–1800.* The journals of Colonel George Chicken, the South Carolina Indian commissioner, and Antoine Bonnefoy, a Frenchman whom the Cherokees captured and adopted, are particularly important. "A True Relation of the Unheard-of Sufferings of David Menzies, Surgeon, Among the Cherokees, and of His Surprising Deliverance" gives a less pleasant version of Indian captivity. There are also numerous references to the Cherokees in *The Shaftesbury Papers and Other Papers Relating to Carolina and the First Settlement on Ashley River Prior to the Year 1676,* edited by Langdon Cheeves; *Colonial South Carolina: Two Contemporary Descriptions,* edited by Chapman J. Milling; and *Historical Collection of South Carolina,* edited by B.R. Carroll.

The Indian traders who followed these early sojourners among the Cherokees did much to hasten the destruction of Indian culture. It is ironic that one of the traders has provided us with an unusually perceptive account of Indian life. James Adair lived among southeastern Indians from 1735 to 1768, married an Indian woman, and adopted many Indian customs. *Adair's History of the American Indians* contains valuable information in spite of the author's theory that native Americans were the lost tribes of Israel.

Other important sources for material concerning Cherokee life in the eighteenth century are *Lieut. Henry Timberlake's Memoirs, 1756–1765, The Travels of William Bartram,* and Bartram's "Observations on the Creek and Cherokee Indians, 1789." Timberlake, a British soldier who conducted a delegation of Cherokees to London in 1761, was an admirer of and a friend to the Nation. The naturalist William Bartram traveled extensively in the southeastern United States from 1773 to 1777 and recorded his observations of Indian culture with the same precision as he did the flora and fauna.

Early historians also provide clues that help unravel the mysteries of Cherokee life. The best known and most useful is John Lawson's *A New Voyage to Carolina.* John Brickell's *The Natural History of North Carolina* contains some original information, but much of it is a plagiarism of Lawson's earlier work. Alexander Hewatt's *An Historical Account of the Rise and Progress of the Colonies of South Carolina and Georgia, 1779,* John Haywood's *The Natural and Aboriginal History of Tennessee up to the First Settlements Therein by the White People in the Year 1768,* and John H. Logan's *A History of the Upper Country of South Carolina from the Earliest Periods to the War of Independence* frequently refer to the Cherokees.

The traders were the earliest bearers of white "civilization" to the "savages," and their activities have been related in Verner W. Crane, *The Southern Frontier, 1670–1732*; Mary U. Rothrock, "Carolina Traders Among the Overhill Cherokees, 1690–1760"; and Franklin W. Neil, "Virginia and the Cherokee Indian Trade, 1673–1752" and "Virginia and the Cherokee Indian Trade, 1753–1775." In *A Better Kind of Hatchet: Law, Trade and Diplomacy in the Cherokee Nation During the Early Years of European Contact,* John P. Reid points out that Europeans had to alter their customary trading practices and regulations in order to cope with cultural differences and concludes that aboriginal Cherokee law actually changed far less than European law. Since South Carolina controlled most of the trade with the Cherokees, that colony's records provide the best source of information. William L. McDowell has edited three volumes of those records—*Journals of the Commissioners of the Indian Trade: Sept. 20, 1710–Aug. 29, 1718*; *Documents Relating to Indian Affairs: May 21, 1750–Aug. 7, 1754*; and *Documents Relating to Indian Affairs, 1754–1765.*

The "civilization" program embarked upon by the United States government at the turn of the nineteenth century resulted in additional changes in aboriginal Cherokee culture. In *Seeds of Extinction: Jeffersonian Philanthropy and the American Indian,* Bernard Sheehan credits the government's policy and individual philanthropy inspired by the policy with undermining Indian culture and insists that cultural destruction was inevitable. Benjamin Hawkins who served as Indian agent from 1796 to 1801 began implementation of the "civilization" program among the Cherokees and his correspondence, which has been published in *Letters of Benjamin Hawkins, 1796–1806,* plots the progress of the Cherokees toward "civilization." Other works which give insight into the transformation of Cherokee culture are *American State Papers,* Class II: *Indian Affairs*; William L. Saunders, ed., *The Colonial Records of North Carolina*; and Walter Clark, ed., *The State Records of North Carolina.*

The role played by white missionaries in the destruction of Cherokee culture cannot be overemphasized. In *Salvation and the Savage: An Analysis of Protestant Missions and American Indian Response,* Robert F. Berkhofer points out that the Indian who converted to Christianity also had to adopt the white man's clothing, language, and technology as well as his God, prayers, and church services. The accounts of missionaries—including those found in Daniel S. Butrick's *Journal,* Selected Papers Relating to the Removal of the Cherokee Indians from Georgia, *Records of the Moravians in North Carolina,* edited by Adelaide L. Fries, and *First Ten Annual Reports of the American Board of Commissioners for Foreign Missions, With Other Documents of the Board*—are valuable for documenting the changes in Cherokee culture which took place.

Missionaries, government agents, and traders often carried their black slaves with them to the Cherokee Nation, but this was not the first contact between Africans and Cherokees. Blacks accompanied de Soto and other conquistadors on expeditions into the hinterland of the North American continent according to R.R. Wright in his article, "Negro Companions of the Spanish Explorers." Some Cherokees came to share the fate of many Africans when the enslavement and sale of Indian war captives became big business in the English colonies, particularly in South Carolina. Crane's *Southern Frontier,* Almon W. Lauber's *Indian Slavery in Colonial Times Within the Present Limits of the United States,* William R. Snell's "Indian Slavery in Colonial South Carolina," and Sanford Winston's "Indian Slavery in the Carolina Region" explore this subject. Irving A. Hallowell in "American Indians, White and Black: The Phenomenon of Transculturation" points out that "black" and "slave" were not synonymous in the Indian mind, for many blacks entered into the Indian "web of social relationships" (p. 523). Intermarriage occurred but not so frequently among the Cherokees as some other tribes according to James Johnston in "Documentary Evidence of the Relations of Negroes and Indians."

Relations between Indians and blacks were not always so cordial however. Kenneth W. Porter in "Negroes on the Southern Frontier, 1670–1763" and "Relations Between Indians and Negroes Within the Present Limits of the United States" relates the use of black soldiers by English colonists in their wars with the Indians. In *Black Majority: Negroes in Colonial South Carolina from 1670 Through the Stono Rebellion,* Peter Wood describes how whites employed Indians in the capture of fugitive slaves and the suppression of the Stono Rebellion. William S. Willis interprets this as a conscious effort on the part of whites to arouse hatred between these two oppressed and therefore potentially allied peoples in "Divide and Rule: Red, White and Black in the Southeast," which is included in Charles M. Hudson, ed. *Red, White, and Black: Symposium on Indians in the Old South.*

The reactions of Africans and Indians upon first meeting one another are unknown. Certainly blacks found in the indigenous Cherokee culture some elements reminiscent of their own native cultures. The diversity of the peoples of Africa makes it difficult to generalize about cultural characteristics, but three works—Basil Davidson, *The African Genius: An Introduction to African Cultural and Social History,* John S. Mbiti, *African Religions and Philosophies,* and A.R. Radcliffe-Browne and Daryll Forde, eds., *African Systems of Kinship and Marriage*—describe African culture as being based economically on subsistence agriculture and socially on kinship. These factors determined the nature of the African bondage described in *The Life of Olaudah Equiano or Gustavus Vassa, the African,* Phillip D. Curtin's *Africa Remembered: Narratives by West Africans from the Era of the Slave Trade,* and Elizabeth Donnan's *Documents Illustrative of the History of the Slave Trade to America.* These accounts and works, such as A. Norman Klein, "West African Unfree Labor Before and After the Rise of the Atlantic Slave Trade" (from *Slavery in the New World: A Reader in Comparative History,* edited by Laura Foner and Eugene D. Genovese), Rick N. McKown, "The African Middleman in the Transatlantic Slave Trade: A Study in Attitudes," R.S. Rattray, *Ashanti Law and Constitution,* and John Grace, *Domestic Slavery in West Africa,* portray a system of slavery that has a parallel in Cherokee society. Such insights into African bondage are essential to an understanding of the enslavement of blacks by Cherokees because although the tribe adopted much from white society, their own cultural traditions as well as those of enslaved Africans remained strong.

The interviews with former slaves conducted by the WPA in the 1930s afford the most comprehensive view of the everyday lives of African slaves owned by Cherokees. George P. Rawick includes some of these interviews in *The American Slave: A Composite Autobiography.* The Indian-Pioneer History located in the Oklahoma Department of Archives, Oklahoma City, contains the typescripts of many additional interviews.

The Indian-Pioneer History also includes interviews with Cherokee conservatives and former slaveholders. Other sources for antebellum Cherokee history are the manuscript collections at the University of Oklahoma in Norman and the Thomas Gilcrease Institute in Tulsa. In general the material at the University of Oklahoma reflects the views of the highly acculturated slaveholders who forced a Confederate alliance in the Civil War while the Gilcrease collection contains the papers of John Ross, John Drew, and other leaders who represented the traditionalists and ultimately sided with the Union. An indication of the extent to which some Cherokees accepted plantation slavery and white attitudes towards black bondsmen and other Cherokees resisted "white civilization" can be found in these collections and in the laws of the Cherokee Nation, the records and journals of missionaries and travelers to Indian Territory, the United States records relating to Indian Affairs located in the National Archives, and the Nation's two newspapers, *The Cherokee Phoenix and Indians' Advocate* and *The Cherokee Advocate.*

Some previous work has been done on the subject of slavery among the Cherokees. Annie Heloise Abel's three volume work *Slaveholding Indians* is dated in its perspective and primarily concerns relations between the slaveholding tribes and the governments of the United States and the Confederacy and Indian participation in the Civil War. J.B. Davis in "Slavery in the Cherokee Nation" and Rudi Halliburton in "Black Slave Control in the Cherokee Nation" and "Origin of Black Slavery Among the Cherokees" merely discuss the legal aspects of slavery. In his dissertation "Negro Slavery Among the Cherokee Indians, 1540–1866" Michael Roethler hails slavery as the vehicle of "civilization." In *Red Over Black* Rudi Halliburton echoes this theme and attempts, primarily through an explication of Cherokee laws, to prove that Cherokees were as harsh masters as whites. A brief but more accurate study of slavery among the Cherokees and Choctaws is William G. McLoughlin, "Red Indians, Black Slavery and White Racism: America's Slaveholding Indians," but McLoughlin fails to analyze the effects of slavery on Indian society and culture.

Many historians have examined the institution of slavery among whites in the antebellum South. These studies provide the knowledge which is essential for understanding the modifications imposed on the white antebellum slave system by Cherokee culture. Kenneth Stampp's pioneer institutional study of slavery, *The Peculiar Institution: Slavery in the Ante-Bellum South,* provides an excellent point of reference from which to compare Cherokee and white slaveholding. While Robert William Fogel and Stanley E. Engerman perhaps paint a far more pleasant picture of slavery in *Time on the Cross: The Economics of American Negro Slavery* than their sources justify, their assessment of slavery as a capitalistic economic institution applies to slavery among the Cherokees as well as whites. John Blassingame vividly describes the daily lives of slaves in *The Slave Community in the Ante-Bellum South* as does Eugene D. Genovese in *Roll, Jordan, Roll: The World the Slaves Made.*

The methodology employed in a study of comparative slavery, such as this one, has been developed primarily by historians interested in Latin American history. Frank Tannenbaum in *Slave and Citizen: The Negro in the Americas* and Stanley Elkins in *Slavery: A Problem in American Institutional and Intellectual Life* suggest that cultural, religious, and legal differences tended to make slavery more lenient in Latin America than in the southern United States. In contrast David Brion Davis in *The Problem of Slavery in Western Culture* insists that all European systems of bondage were basically the same. Franklin K. Knight, however, concludes in *Slave Society in Cuba During the Nineteenth Century* that differences existed but the level of economic development rather than the church or the metropolitan government dictated the nature of slavery and that leniency declined in Cuba with the advent of a capitalistic plantation economy. An investigation of slavery among the Cherokees generally supports Knight's conclusions. As Cherokee planters became increasingly concerned with maximizing profits, they abandoned the traditional Cherokee values which had tended to ameliorate the harsher aspects of plantation slavery.

Bibliography

I. Primary Sources

A. *Manuscripts*

Atlanta, Ga. Georgia Department of Archives. Cherokee Letters Collection.

______. Georgia Governor's Letterbook, 1833.

Austin, Texas. University of Texas Library. Stand Watie Papers. Microfilm copy, University of Oklahoma.

Cambridge, Mass. Houghton Library. Harvard University. Records of the American Board of Commissioners for Foreign Missions.

Cullowhee, N.C. Western Carolina University Library. William Holland Thomas Papers.

Norman, Okla. University of Oklahoma Library. Cherokee Miscellany.

______. Cherokee Nation Papers.

______. J.L. Hargett Collection.

______. Papers of Na Na Ha Nee Tee, Pathkiller, Major Ridge, Thomas Pegg, Lewis Downing, and George Lowry.

______. Uncatalogued Cherokee Papers.

Oklahoma City, Okla. Oklahoma Historical Society. Indian-Pioneer History.

Tulsa, Okla. Thomas Gilcrease Institute. Cherokee Papers.

______. John Drew Papers.

______. H.M. Hicks Collection.

______. Dwight Hitchcock's Diaries, 1852–63.

______. John Howard Payne Papers.

______. John Ross Papers.

Washington, D.C. Library of Congress. Records of the American Colonization Society, 1792–1866. Microfilm copy, University of Georgia.

______. National Archives. Indian Affairs. Record Group 75. Microfilm copy, Western Carolina University.

Winston-Salem, N.C. Moravian Archives. Moravian Diaries. Microfilm copy, University of Georgia.

B. *Published Primary Sources*

American Board of Commissioners for Foreign Missions. *Committee on Anti-Slavery Memorials Report . . . September, 1845, with a Historical Statement of Previous Proceedings.* Boston, 1845.

______. *First Ten Annual Reports of the American Board of Commissioners for Foreign Missions, with Other Documents of the Board.* Boston, 1834.

Anderson, Rufus, ed. *Memoir of Catherine Brown, A Christian Indian of the Cherokee Nation.* Philadelphia, 1831.

Bartram, William. "Observations on the Creek and Cherokee Indians, 1789." *Transactions of the American Ethnological Society* 3, pt. 1 (1853):1–81.

Baynton, Benjamin. *Authentic Memoirs of William Augustus Bowles, Esquire, Ambassador from the United Nations of Creeks and Cherokees to the Court of London.* London, 1791.

Beverley, Robert. *The History and Present State of Virginia.* Edited by Louis B. Wright. Chapel Hill, 1947; original ed., 1705.

Bibb, Henry. "Narrative of the Life and Adventures of Henry Bibb, An American Slave," in *Puttin' on Ole Massa.* Edited by Gilbert Osofsky. New York, 1969.

Boudinot, Elias. *An Address to the Whites.* Philadelphia, 1826.

Bourne, Edward Gaylord, ed. *Narratives of the Career of Hernando de Soto.* 2 vols. New York, 1922.

Brickell, John. *The Natural History of North Carolina.* Dublin, 1737.

Carroll, B.R., ed. *Historical Collection of South Carolina.* New York, 1836.

Catterall, Helen T., ed. *Judicial Cases Concerning American Slavery and the Negro.* 5 vols. Washington, D.C., 1926–37.

Cheeves, Langdon, ed. *The Shaftesbury Papers and Other Papers Relating to Carolina and the First Settlements on Ashley River Prior to the Year 1676.* 5 vols. of *South Carolina Historical Society Collections.* Richmond, Va., 1897.

Cherokee Nation. *Laws of the Cherokee Nation: Adopted by the Council at Various Times, Reprinted for the Benefit of the Nation.* Vol. 5 of *The Constitutions and Laws of the American Indian Tribes.* Wilmington, Del., and London, 1973.

______. *Laws of the Cherokee Nation, Passed During the Years 1839–1867*. Vol. 6 of *The Constitutions and Laws of the American Indian Tribes*. Wilmington, Del., and London, 1973.

Clark, Walter, ed. *The State Records of North Carolina*. 15 vols. Winston, N.C., and Goldsboro, N.C., 1895–1905.

Curtin, Phillip D., ed. *Africa Remembered: Narratives by West Africans from the Era of the Slave Trade*. Madison, Wis., 1967.

Dale, Edward Everett, ed. "Letters of the Two Boudinots." *Chronicles of Oklahoma* 6 (1928):328–47.

______. "Some Letters of General Stand Watie." *Chronicles of Oklahoma* 1 (1921):30–59; 131–49.

Dale, Edward Everett, and Litton, Gaston, eds. *Cherokee Cavaliers*. Norman, Okla., 1940.

Donnan, Elizabeth, ed. *Documents Illustrative of the History of the Slave Trade to America*. 4 vols. New York, 1969.

Emerson, Ralph Waldo. "A Letter to the President Concerning the Removal of the Cherokee Indians from Georgia." *American Indian* 5 (1950):28–31.

Equiano, Olaudah. *The Life of Olaudah Equiano or Gustavus Vassa, The African*. New York, 1969, original ed., 1837.

Featherstonhaugh, G.W. *A Canoe Voyage up the Minnay Sotor; with an Account of the Lead and Copper Deposits in Wisconsin; of the Gold Region in the Cherokee Country; and Sketches of Popular Manners*. 2 vols. London, 1847.

Folmsbee, Stanley J., and Lewis, Madeline Kneberg, eds. Wade, Gerald W., trans. "Journals of the Juan Pardo Expeditions, 1566–1567." *East Tennessee Historical Society Publications* 35 (1965):106–21.

Foreman, Carolyn Thomas, ed. "Journal of a Tour in the Indian Territory." *Chronicles of Oklahoma* 10 (1932):219–56.

Foreman, Grant, ed. "The Journal of Elijah Hicks." *Chronicles of Oklahoma* 13 (1935):68–99.

______. "Missionaries of the Latter Day Saints Church in Indian Territory." *Chronicles of Oklahoma* 13 (1935):196–213.

______. "The Murder of Elias Boudinot." *Chronicles of Oklahoma* 12 (1934):19–24.

______. "Notes of a Missionary Among the Cherokees." *Chronicles of Oklahoma* 16 (1938):171–89.

______. "Reminiscences of Mr. R.P. Vann, East of Webbers Falls, Oklahoma, September 28, 1932." *Chronicles of Oklahoma* 11 (1933):838–44.

———. *A Traveler in Indian Territory: The Journal of Ethan Allen Hitchcock, Later Major General in the United States Army*. Cedar Rapids, Iowa, 1930.

Fries, Adelaide L., ed. *Records of the Moravians in North Carolina*. 7 vols. Raleigh, 1947.

Goulding, Francis R. *Sapelo; or, Child-Life on the Tide-Water*. New York, 1870.

Gregg, Josiah. *Commerce of the Prairies*. Edited by Max L. Moorhead. Norman, Okla., 1954.

Hagy, James W. and Folmsbee, Stanley J., eds. "The Lost Archives of the Cherokee Nation." *East Tennessee Historical Society Publications* 43 (1971):112–22; 44 (1972):114–25; 45 (1973):88–98.

Hawkins, Benjamin. *Letters of Benjamin Hawkins, 1796–1806*. Vol. 9 of *Georgia Historical Society Collections*. Savannah, 1916.

Haywood, John. *The Civil and Political History of the State of Tennessee*. Knoxville, 1969; original ed., 1823.

———. *The Natural and Aboriginal History of Tennessee up to the First Settlements Therein by the White People in the Year 1768*. Jackson, Tenn., 1959; original ed., 1823.

Hewatt, Alexander. *An Historical Account of the Rise and Progress of the Colonies of South Carolina and Georgia, 1779*. 2 vols. London, 1779.

Hicks, Hannah. "The Diary of Hannah Hicks." *American Scene* 13 (1972).

James, Edwin, comp. *Account of an Expedition from Pittsburgh to the Rocky Mountains Performed in the Years 1819 and '20*. Philadelphia, 1823.

Jefferson, Thomas. *Notes on the State of Virginia*. Boston, 1832.

Kilpatrick, Jack Frederick, and Kilpatrick, Anna Gritts, eds. *New Echota Letters: Contributions of Samuel A. Worcester to the Cherokee Phoenix*. Dallas, 1968.

Lanman, Charles. *Adventures in the Wilds of the United States and British American Provinces*. Philadelphia, 1856.

Latrobe, Charles Joseph. *The Rambler in North America*. London, 1836.

Lawson, John. *A New Voyage to Carolina*. Edited by Hugh T. Lefler. Chapel Hill, 1967.

Lloyd, P.C., ed. "Osifejunde of Ijebu" in *Africa Remembered: Narratives of West Africa from the Era of the Slave Trade*. Edited by Phillip D. Curtin. Madison, 1967.

Logan, John H. *A History of the Upper Country of South Carolina from the Earliest Periods to the War of Independence.* Charleston and Columbia, S.C., 1859.

Lumpkin, Wilson. *The Removal of the Cherokee Indians from Georgia.* New York, 1969.

McDowell, William L., ed. *Documents Relating to Indian Affairs, May 21, 1750–Aug. 7, 1754.* Columbia, S.C., 1958.

______. *Documents Relating to Indian Affairs, 1754–1765.* Columbia, S.C., 1970.

______. *Journals of the Commissioners of the Indian Trade, Sept. 20, 1710–Aug. 29, 1718.* Columbia, S.C., 1955.

M'Kenney, Thomas L. *Memoirs, Official and Personal.* 2 vols. New York, 1846.

Menzies, David. "A True Relation of the Unheard-of Sufferings of David Menzies, Surgeon, Among the Cherokees, and of His Surprising Deliverance." *Royal Magazine,* July 1761, pp. 27–29.

Mereness, Newton D., ed. *Travels in the American Colonies.* New York, 1916.

Meserve, John Bartlett, ed. "The Indian Removal Message of President Jackson." *Chronicles of Oklahoma* 13 (1935):63–67.

Milligan-Johnston, George. "A Short Description of the Province of South Carolina" in *Colonial South Carolina: Two Contemporary Descriptions.* Edited by Chapman J. Milling. Columbia, S.C., 1951.

Milling, Chapman J., ed. *Colonial South Carolina: Two Contemporary Descriptions.* Columbia, S.C., 1951.

Morse, Jedidiah. *A Report to the Secretary of War on Indian Affairs, 1822.* Reprint ed., New York, 1970.

Newton, Charlotte, ed. "Ebenezer Newton's 1818 Diary." *Georgia Historical Quarterly* 53 (1969):205–19.

Nuttall, Thomas. *A Journal of Travels into the Arkansas Territory During the Year 1819.* Vol. 13 of *Early Western Travels, 1748–1846.* Edited by Reuben Gold Thwaites. New York, 1966.

Oliphant, James Orin. *Through the South and West with Jeremiah Evarts in 1826.* Lewisburg, Pa., 1956.

Payne, John Howard. *John Howard Payne to His Countrymen.* Athens, Ga., 1961.

Rawick, George P., ed. *The American Slave: A Composite Autobiography.* 19 vols. Westport, Conn., 1972.

Ross, Mrs. William P., ed. *The Life and Times of Honorable William P. Ross of the Cherokee Nation.* Ft. Smith, Ark., 1893.

Salley, Alexander S., ed. *Narratives of Early Carolina 1650–1708.* New York, 1911.

Saunders, William L., ed. *The Colonial Records of North Carolina.* 10 vols. Raleigh, 1886–90.

Schwaab, Eugene L., ed. *Travels in the Old South Selected from Periodicals of the Times.* 2 vols. Lexington, Ky., 1974.

Shaw, Ronald E., ed. *Andrew Jackson, 1767–1845: Chronology, Documents, Bibliographical Aids.* Dobbs Ferry, N.Y., 1969.

Teall, Kay M., ed. *Black History in Oklahoma: A Resource Book.* Oklahoma City, 1971.

Tuttle, Sarah. *Letters and Conversations on the Cherokee Mission.* Boston, 1830.

Van Doren, Mark, ed. *The Travels of William Bartram.* New York, 1940.

Washburn, Cephas. *Reminiscences of the Indians.* Richmond, Va., 1869.

Whipple, Charles K. *Relations of the American Board of Commissioners for Foreign Missions to Slavery.* Boston, 1861.

Whitmore, Ellen. *The Journal of Ellen Whitmore.* Edited by Lola Garrett Bowers and Kathleen Garrett. Tahlequah, Okla., 1953.

Williams, Samuel Cole., ed. *Adair's History of the American Indians.* Johnson City, Tenn., 1930.

______. *Early Travels in the Tennessee Country, 1540–1800.* Johnson City,Tenn., 1928.

______. *Lieut. Henry Timberlake's Memoirs, 1756–1765.* Johnson City, Tenn., 1927.

C. *Newspapers and Periodicals*

African Repository, 1825–66.

The Cherokee Advocate, 1844–53.

The Cherokee Messenger, 1844–46.

The Cherokee Phoenix and Indians' Advocate, 1828–34.

Niles National Register, 1811–49.

D. *United States Government Documents*

American State Papers. Class 2: *Indian Affairs.* 2 vols. Washington, D.C., 1832.

Congress. House. H.R. 384. 25th Cong., 2d sess., 1838.

______. H.R. 324. 25th Cong., 2d sess., 1838.

______. H.R. 404. 25th Cong., 2d sess., 1838.

Kappler, Charles J., ed. *Indian Affairs, Laws and Treaties.* 2 vols. Washington, D.C., 1904.

Summary of the Census of the Cherokee Nation. Washington, D.C., 1881.

Supreme Court. *Worcester* v. *Georgia.* 6 Peters 515, 10 Curtis 214, 31 L. Ed. 501 (1832).

War Department. *The War of the Rebellion: A Compilation of the Official Records of the Union and Confederate Armies.* Series 1, Vols. 1, 3, 8, 13.

II. Secondary Works

A. *Books*

Abel, Annie Heloise. *Slaveholding Indians.* 3 vols. Cleveland, 1915–25.

Ajayi, J.F. Ade, and Crowder, Michael, eds. *History of West Africa.* 2 vols. New York, 1972.

Alden, John Richard. *John Stuart and the Southern Colonial Frontier, 1754–1775: A Study of Indian Relations, War, Trade, and Land Problems in the Southern Wilderness, 1754–1775.* New York, 1944.

Anderson, Mabel Washbourne. *Life of General Stand Watie.* Pryor, Okla., 1915.

Aptheker, Herbert. *American Negro Slave Revolts.* New York, 1943.

Arnow, Harriette Simpson. *Seedtime on the Cumberland.* New York, 1960.

Bailey, M. Thomas. *Reconstruction in Indian Territory: A Story of Avarice, Discrimination and Opportunism.* Port Washington, N.Y., and London, 1972.

Bass, Althea. *Cherokee Messenger: A Life of Samuel Austin Worcester.* Norman, Okla., 1936.

Berkhofer, Robert F., Jr. *Salvation and the Savage: An Analysis of Protestant Missions and American Indian Response.* Lexington, Ky., 1965.

Blassingame, John W. *The Slave Community in the Ante-Bellum South.* New York, 1972.

Britton, Wiley. *The Union Indian Brigade in the Civil War.* Kansas City, Mo., 1922.

Brown, John P. *Old Frontiers: The Story of the Cherokee Indians from the Earliest Times to the Date of Their Removal to the West, 1838.* Kingsport, Tenn., 1938.

Collier, Peter. *When Shall They Rest?* New York, 1973.

Conrad, Alfred H., and Meyer, John R. *The Economics of Slavery.* Chicago, 1964.
Corkran, David H. *The Cherokee Frontier: Conflict and Survival, 1740–62.* Norman, Okla., 1962.
Cotterill, R. Spencer. *The Southern Indians: The Story of the Civilized Tribes before Removal.* Norman, Okla., 1954.
Crane, Verner W. *The Southern Frontier, 1670–1732.* Durham, N.C., 1928.
Cunningham, Frank. *General Stand Watie's Confederate Indians.* San Antonio, 1959.
Davidson, Basil. *The African Genius: An Introduction to African Cultural and Social History.* Boston and Toronto, 1969.
______. *Black Mother: The Years of the African Slave Trade.* Boston, 1961.
Davis, David Brion. *The Problem of Slavery in Western Culture.* Ithaca, N.Y., 1966.
Eaton, Rachel Caroline. *John Ross and the Cherokee Indians.* Menasha, Wis., 1914.
Elkins, Stanley M. *Slavery: A Problem in American Institutional and Intellectual Life.* Chicago, 1968.
Fenton, William N., and Gulick, John, eds. *Symposium on Cherokee and Iroquois Culture.* Washington, D.C., 1961.
Foner, Laura, and Genovese, Eugene, eds. *Slavery in the New World: A Reader in Comparative History.* Englewood Cliffs, N.J., 1969.
Fogel, Robert William, and Engerman, Stanley E. *Time on the Cross: The Economics of American Negro Slavery.* 2 vols. Boston, 1974.
Foreman, Grant. *Indian Removal: The Emigration of the Five Civilized Tribes of Indians.* Norman, Okla., 1932.
Foster, Lawrence. *Negro-Indian Relationships in the Southeast.* Philadelphia, 1935.
Gabriel, Ralph Henry. *Elias Boudinot, Cherokee, and His America.* Norman, Okla., 1941.
Gearing, Frederick O. *Priests and Warriors: Social Structures for Cherokee Politics in the 18th Century.* Menasha, Wis., 1962.
Genovese, Eugene D. *Roll, Jordan, Roll: The World the Slaves Made.* New York, 1974.
Gilbert, William, H., Jr. *The Eastern Cherokees.* Washington, D.C., 1943.
Grace, John. *Domestic Slavery in West Africa.* New York, 1975.
Gray, Lewis C. *History of Agriculture in the Southern United States to 1860.* 2 vols. New York, 1933, 1941.

Halliburton, R., Jr. *Red Over Black: Black Slavery among the Cherokee Indians.* Westport, Conn., 1977.

Hudson, Charles M. *The Southeastern Indians.* Knoxville, 1976.

______, ed. *Four Centuries of Southern Indians.* Athens, Ga., 1975.

______. *Red, White, and Black: Symposium on Indians in the Old South.* Athens, Ga., 1971.

James, James Alton. *English Institutions and the American Indian.* Baltimore, 1894.

Jenkins, William Sumner. *Pro-Slavery Thought in the Old South.* Chapel Hill, 1935.

Jordan, Winthrop D. *White over Black: American Attitudes Toward the Negro, 1550–1812.* Chapel Hill, 1968.

Knight, Franklin W. *Slave Society in Cuba During the Nineteenth Century.* Madison, Wis., 1970.

Lauber, Almon W. *Indian Slavery in Colonial Times Within the Present Limits of the United States.* New York, 1913.

Littlefield, David F., Jr. *Africans and Seminoles: From Removal to Emancipation.* Westport, Conn., 1977.

Lowery, Woodbury. *The Spanish Settlements Within the Present Limits of the United States, 1513–1561.* New York and London, 1911.

Malone, Henry Thompson. *Cherokees of the Old South: A People in Transition.* Athens, Ga., 1956.

Mbiti, John S. *African Religions and Philosophy.* New York, 1970.

Memmi, Albert. *The Colonizer and the Colonized.* Trans. Howard Greenfeld. Boston, 1965.

Meriwether, Robert Lee. *The Expansion of South Carolina, 1729–1765.* Kingsport, Tenn., 1940.

Milling, Chapman J. *Red Carolinians.* Chapel Hill, 1940.

Mooney, James. *Myths of the Cherokee and Sacred Formulas of the Cherokees.* 19th and 7th Annual Reports, *Bureau of American Ethnology.* Reproduced Nashville, 1972.

Moulton, Gary E. *John Ross: Cherokee Chief.* Athens, Ga., 1977.

Nash, Gary B. *Red, White, and Black: The Peoples of Early America.* Englewood Cliffs, N.J., 1974.

Pearce, Roy Harvey. *The Savages of America: A Study of the Indian and the Idea of Civilization.* Baltimore, 1953.

Pound, Merritt B. *Benjamin Hawkins—Indian Agent.* Athens, Ga., 1951.

Prucha, Francis Paul. *American Indian Policy in the Formative Years: The Indian Trade and Intercourse Acts, 1790–1834.* Lincoln, Neb., 1962.

Radcliffe-Brown, A.R., and Forde, Daryll, eds. *African Systems of Kinship and Marriage*. London, New York, Toronto, 1950.

Rattray, R.S. *Ashanti Law and Constitution*. London, 1956; original ed., 1929.

Reid, John P. *A Better Kind of Hatchet: Law, Trade and Diplomacy in the Cherokee Nation During the Early Years of European Contact*. University Park, Pa., 1976.

______. *A Law of Blood: Primitive Law of the Cherokee Nation*. New York, 1970.

Rogin, Michael Paul. *Fathers and Children: Andrew Jackson and the Subjugation of the American Indian*. New York, 1975.

Royce, C.C. *The Cherokee Nation of Indians*. Washington, D.C., 1887.

Satz, Ronald N. *American Indian Policy in the Jacksonian Era*. Lincoln, Neb., 1975.

Schwarze, Edmund. *History of the Moravian Missions among Southern Indian Tribes of the United States*. Bethlehem, Pa., 1923.

Sheehan, Bernard W. *Seeds of Extinction: Jeffersonian Philanthropy and the American Indian*. Chapel Hill, 1973.

Spoehr, Alexander. *Changing Kinship Systems: A Study in the Acculturation of the Creeks, Cherokee, and Choctaw*. Chicago, 1947.

Stampp, Kenneth M. *The Peculiar Institution: Slavery in the Ante-Bellum South*. New York, 1956.

Starkey, Marion L. *The Cherokee Nation*. New York, 1946.

Starr, Emmett. *History of the Cherokee Indians*. Oklahoma City, 1921.

Staudenraus, P.J. *The African Colonization Movement, 1816–1865*. New York, 1961.

Strickland, Rennard. *Fire and the Spirits: Cherokee Law from Clan to Court*. Norman, Okla., 1975.

Strong, William Ellsworth. *The Story of the American Board*. New York, 1969.

Swanton, John R. *The Indians of the Southeastern United States*. Washington, D.C., 1946.

Takaki, Ronald T. *A Pro-Slavery Crusade: The Agitation to Reopen the African Slave Trade*. New York, 1971.

Tannenbaum, Frank. *Slave and Citizen: The Negro in the Americas*. New York, 1946.

Tolson, Arthur L. *The Black Oklahomans: A History, 1541–1972*. New Orleans, 1974.

Ver Steeg, Clarence L. *Origins of a Southern Mosaic: Studies in Early Carolina and Georgia*. Athens, Ga., 1975.

Van Every, Dale. *Disinherited: The Lost Birthright of the American Indian.* New York, 1966.
Walker, Robert Sparks. *Torchlights to the Cherokees: The Brainerd Mission.* New York, 1931.
Wardell, Morris L. *A Political History of the Cherokee Nation, 1838-1907.* Norman, Okla., 1938.
Wilkins, Thurman. *Cherokee Tragedy: The Story of the Ridge Family and the Decimation of a People.* New York, 1970.
Williams, Eric. *Capitalism and Slavery.* Chapel Hill, 1944.
Williams, Samuel Cole. *Dawn of Tennessee Valley and Tennessee History.* Johnson City, Tenn., 1937.
______. *History of the Lost State of Franklin.* Johnson City, Tenn., 1924.
Wood, Peter H. *Black Majority: Negroes in Colonial South Carolina from 1670 Through the Stono Rebellion.* New York, 1974.
Woodward, Grace Steele. *The Cherokees.* Norman, Okla., 1963.
Wright, Muriel H. *Springplace, Moravian Mission, Cherokee Nation.* Guthrie, Okla., 1940.

B. *Articles*

Addington, Luther F. "Chief Benge's Last Raid." *Historical Society of Southwest Virginia* 2 (1966):124–33.
Anderson, Mabel Washbourne. "General Stand Watie." *Chronicles of Oklahoma* 10 (1932):540–48.
Andrews, Thomas F. "Freedmen in Indian Territory: A Post-Civil War Dilemma." *Journal of the West* 4 (1965):367–76.
Axtell, James. "Through a Glass Darkly, Colonial Attitudes Toward the Native Americans." *American Indian Culture and Research Journal* 1 (1974):17–28.
Banks, Dean. "Civil War Refugees from Indian Territory in the North, 1861–1864." *Chronicles of Oklahoma* 41 (1963–64):286–98.
Bass, Dorothy C. "Gideon Blackburn's Mission to the Cherokees: Christianization and Civilization." *Journal of Presbyterian History* 52 (Fall, 1974).
Bearss, Edwin C. "The Civil War Comes to Indian Territory, 1861: The Flight of Opothleyoholo." *Journal of the West* 11 (1972):9–42.
Beeson, Leola Selma. "Homes of Distinguished Cherokee Indians." *Chronicles of Oklahoma* 11 (1933):927–41.
Berkhofer, Robert F., Jr. "Protestants, Pagans, and Sequences Among the North American Indians, 1760–1860." *Ethnohistory* 10 (1963):201–33.

Bloom, Leonard. "The Acculturation of the Eastern Cherokees: Historical Aspects." *North Carolina Historical Review* 19 (1942):323–58.

Busia, K.A. "The Ashanti of the Gold Coast" in *African Worlds: Studies in the Cosmological Ideas and Social Values of African Peoples.* Edited by Daryll Forde. London, 1954.

Collins, Linton McGee. "The Activities of the Missionaries Among the Cherokees." *Georgia Historical Quarterly* 7 (1922):285–322.

Corkran, David H. "Cherokee Pre-History." *North Carolina Historical Review* 34 (1957):455, 458–59.

Dale, Edward Everett. "The Cherokees in the Confederacy." *Journal of Southern History* 13 (1947):159–85.

Davis, J.B. "Slavery in the Cherokee Nation." *Chronicles of Oklahoma* 11 (1933):1056–72.

de Baillou, Clemens. "The Chief Vann House, the Vanns, Tavern and Ferry." *Early Georgia* 2 (1957):3–11.

______. "The Diaries of the Moravian Brotherhood at the Cherokee Mission in Spring Place, Georgia, for the Years 1800–1804." *Georgia Historical Quarterly* 54 (1970):571–76.

Debo, Angie. "Southern Refugees of the Cherokee Nation." *Southwestern Historical Quarterly* 35 (1932):255–66.

Delly, Lillian. "Episode at Cornwall." *Chronicles of Oklahoma* 51 (1973):444–50.

Duncan, James. "The Keetoowah Society." *Chronicles of Oklahoma* 4 (1926):251–55.

Fairfield, Sumner Lincoln. "The Captivity of John Howard Payne." *North American Quarterly Magazine* 33 (1836):107–24.

Fischer, LeRoy H. "The Civil War Era in Indian Territory." *Journal of the West* 12 (1973):345–55.

Foreman, Grant. "Dwight Mission." *Chronicles of Oklahoma* 12 (1934):42–51.

______. "Salt Works in Early Oklahoma." *Chronicles of Oklahoma* 10 (1932):474–500.

Franks, Kenny A. "Political Intrigue in the Cherokee Nation, 1839." *Journal of the West* 13 (1974):17–25.

Gearing, Fred. "The Structural Poses of 18th Century Cherokee Villages." *American Anthropologist* 60 (1958):1148–57.

Halliburton, Rudi, Jr. "Black Slave Control in the Cherokee Nation." *Journal of Ethnic Studies* 3 (1975):23–36.

______. "Origins of Black Slavery Among the Cherokees." *Chronicles of Oklahoma* 52 (1974–75):483–96.

Hallowell, A. Irving. "American Indians, White and Black: The Phenomenon of Transculturalization." *Current Anthropology* 4 (1963): 519–31.

Hammond, Peter B. "Afro-American Indians, and Afro-Asians: Cultural Contacts Between Africa and the Peoples of Asia and Aboriginal America" in *Expanding Horizons in African Studies*. Edited by Gwendolan M. Carter and Ann Paden. Evanston, Ill., 1969.

Heath, Gary N. "The First Federal Invasion of Indian Territory." *Chronicles of Oklahoma* 44 (1966–67):409–19.

Hudson, Charles. "The Cherokee Concept of Natural Balance." *Indian Historian* 3 (1970):51–54.

Johnston, James H. "Documentary Evidence of the Relations of Negroes and Indians." *Journal of Negro History* 14 (1929):21–23.

Klein, A. Norman. "West African Unfree Labor Before and After the Rise of the Atlantic Slave Trade" in *Slavery in the New World: A Reader in Comparative History*. Edited by Laura Foner and Eugene D. Genovese. Englewood Cliffs, N.J., 1966.

Knight, Oliver. "History of the Cherokees, 1830–1846." *Chronicles of Oklahoma* 34 (1956–57):159–82.

Lackey, Vinson. "New Springplace." *Chronicles of Oklahoma* 17 (1939):178–83.

Lambert, Paul F. "The Cherokee Reconstruction Treaty of 1866." *Journal of the West* 12 (1973):471–89.

Lewit, Robert. "Indian Missions and Antislavery Sentiments: A Conflict of Evangelical and Humanitarian Ideals." *Mississippi Valley Historical Review* 50 (1963–64):39–55.

Littlefield, Daniel F., Jr., and Underhill, Lonnie E. "Slave 'Revolt' in the Cherokee Nation, 1842." *American Indian Quarterly* 3 (1977):121–31.

Lofton, John M., Jr. "White, Indian, and Negro Contacts in Colonial South Carolina." *Southern Indian Studies* 1 (1949):3–12.

Lurie, Nancy O. "Indian Cultural Adjustment to European Civilization" in *Seventeenth-Century America: Essays in Colonial History*. Edited by James M. Smith. Chapel Hill, 1959.

Lystad, Robert A. "Marriage and Kinship Among the Ashanti and Azni: A Study in Differential Acculturation" in *Continuity and Change in African Cultures*. Edited by William Bascom and Melville Herskovits. Chicago, 1959.

McLoughlin, William G. "Red Indians, Black Slavery and White Racism: America's Slaveholding Indians." *American Quarterly* 26 (1974):367–85.

______. "Thomas Jefferson and the Beginning of the Cherokee Nationalism, 1806–1809." *William and Mary Quarterly* 3d series, 32 (1975):547–80.

Malone, Henry T. "The Cherokees Become a Civilized Tribe." *Early Georgia* 2 (1957):12–15.

Martin, Robert G. "The Cherokee Phoenix: Pioneer of Indian Journalism." *Chronicles of Oklahoma* 25 (1947–48):102–18.

Meserve, John Bartlett. "Chief John Ross." *Chronicles of Oklahoma* 13 (1935):421–37.

Mooney, James. "The Cherokee Ball Play." *American Anthropologist* 3 (1890):105–32.

Morton, Ohland. "Confederate Government Relations with the Five Civilized Tribes." *Chronicles of Oklahoma* 31 (1953–54):189–204, 299–322.

Moulton, Gary E. "John Ross and W.P. Dole: A Case Study of Lincoln's Indian Policy." *Journal of the West* 12 (1973):414–23.

Nash, Gary. "The Image of the Indian in the Southern Colonial Mind." *William and Mary Quarterly* 3d series, 29 (1972):197–230.

Neil, Franklin W. "Virginia and the Cherokee Indian Trade, 1673–1752." *East Tennessee Historical Society Publications* 4 (1932):3–21.

______. "Virginia and the Cherokee Indian Trade, 1753–1775." *East Tennessee Historical Society Publications* 5 (1933):22–38.

Porter, Kenneth W. "Negroes on the Southern Frontier, 1670–1763." *Journal of Negro History* 33 (1948):53–78.

______. "Relations between Negroes and Indians Within the Present Limits of the United States." *Journal of Negro History* 17 (1932):287–367.

Pound, Merrit B. "Benjamin Hawkins, Indian Agent." *Georgia Historical Quarterly* 13 (1929):392–409.

Price, Edward T. "A Geographic Analysis of White-Negro-Indian Racial Mixtures in Eastern United States." *Annals of the Association of American Geographers* 43 (1953):138–56.

Prucha, Francis Paul. "Andrew Jackson's Indian Policy: A Reassessment." *Journal of American History* 56 (1969):527–39.

Puckett, James M., Jr. *Georgia Genealogical Society Quarterly* 3, Series 3 (March, 1967).

Ramage, B.J. "Georgia and the Cherokees." *American Historical Magazine and Tennessee Historical Society Quarterly* 7 (1902):199–208.

Rampp, Lary. "Negro Troop Activity in Indian Territory, 1863–1865." *Chronicles of Oklahoma* 47 (1969):531–59.

Rodney, Walter. "African Slavery and Other Forms of Social Oppression on the Upper Guinea Coast in the Context of the Atlantic Slave Trade." *Journal of African History* 7 (1966):431–43.

Rothrock, Mary U. "Carolina Traders among the Overhill Cherokees, 1690–1760." *East Tennessee Historical Society Publications* 1 (1929):3–18.

Routh, E.C. "Early Missionaries to the Cherokees." *Chronicles of Oklahoma* 15 (1937):449–65.

Rucker, Alvin. "The Story of Slave Uprising in Oklahoma." *Daily Oklahoman,* 30 Oct. 1932.

Rutland, Robert A. "Political Background of the Cherokee Treaty of New Echota." *Chronicles of Oklahoma* 27 (1949–50):389–406.

Strickland, Rennard. "Christian Gotlieb Priber: Utopian Precursor of the Cherokee Government." *Chronicles of Oklahoma* 48 (1970):264–79.

Swanton, John R. "The Green Corn Dance." *Chronicles of Oklahoma* 10 (1932):170–95.

Thomas, Robert K. "The Redbird Smith Movement" in *Symposium on Cherokee and Iroquois Culture.* Edited by William N. Fenton and John Gulick. Washington, D.C., 1961.

Warren, Hanna R. "Reconstruction in the Cherokee Nation." *Chronicles of Oklahoma* 45 (1967–68):180–89.

Willey, William J. "The Second Federal Invasion of Indian Territory." *Chronicles of Oklahoma* 44 (1966–67):420–30.

William, Samuel Cole. "Christian Mission to the Overhill Cherokees." *Chronicles of Oklahoma* 12 (1934):66–73.

Willis, William S., Jr. "Divide and Rule: Red, White, and Black in the Old South" in *Red, White, and Black: Symposium on Indians in the Old South.* Edited by Charles M. Hudson. Athens, Ga. 1971.

Willson, Walt. "Freedmen in the Indian Territory During Reconstruction." *Chronicles of Oklahoma* 49 (1971):230–44.

Wilms, Douglas C. "Georgia Land Lottery of 1832." *Chronicles of Oklahoma* 52 (1974):52–60.

Winston, Sanford. "Indian Slavery in the Carolina Region." *Journal of Negro History* 19 (1934):431–40.

Wright, Muriel H. "Early Navigation and Commerce Along the Arkansas and Red Rivers in Oklahoma." *Chronicles of Oklahoma* 8 (1930):65–88.

______. "Notes on Colonel Elias C. Boudinot." *Chronicles of Oklahoma* 41 (1963–64):382–407.

______. "Samuel Austin Worcester: A Dedication." *Chronicles of Oklahoma* 37 (1959–60):2–21.

Wright, R.R. "Negro Companions of the Spanish Explorers." *American Anthropologist* 4 (1902):217–28.

C. *Unpublished Works*

Bahoc, Charles Lee. "John Ross: Unionist or Secessionist in 1861." M.A. thesis, Univ. of Tulsa, 1968.

Holland, Cullen Joe. "The Cherokee Indian Newspapers, 1828–1906." Ph.D. diss., Univ. of Minnesota, 1956.

McKown, Rick N. "The African Middle Man in the Transatlantic Slave Trade: A Study in Attitudes." Unpublished paper, 1967.

Persico, Victor Richard. "Cherokee Social Structure in the Early Nineteenth Century." M.A. thesis, Univ. of Georgia, 1974.

Reed, Gerard Alexander. "The Ross-Watie Conflict: Factionalism in the Cherokee Nation, 1839–1865." Ph.D. diss., Univ. of Oklahoma, 1967.

Roethler, Michael. "Negro Slavery among the Cherokee Indians, 1540–1866." Ph.D. diss., Fordham Univ., 1964.

Snell, William R. "Indian Slavery in Colonial South Carolina." Ph.D. diss., Univ. of Alabama, 1972.

Taylor, Celia B. "Cherokee and Creek Folklore Elements in the Uncle Remus Stories." M.A. thesis, Auburn Univ., 1959.

Tyner, Howard T. "The Keetoowah Society in Cherokee History." M.A. thesis, Univ. of Tulsa, 1949.

Index

Abolitionism, 81, 91, 120, 124, 128
Abram (slave), 42
Adair, Edward, 59
Adair, G.W., 74
Adair, James, 5, 7, 12–14, 21–23, 32–33, 46–47
Adair, William Penn, 111
An Address to the Whites (Elias Boudinot), 54–55
African: agriculture, 43; belief systems, 42; economies, 43, 154 n.23; kinship systems, 43–44; myths, 42, 154 n.22; slavery, 43–46, 155 n.33; warfare, 44–45
African Repository, 90
Agriculture: aboriginal Cherokee, 14–15, 52; Cherokee plantation, 50, 54–55, 58–60, 96–97, 99; European, in the Americas, xi. *See also* Cotton; Grain; Livestock
Aiky (free black), 76–77, 85
Alberty, Bluford, 74–75
Alcohol, 57, 75, 88, 98–99
Allotment, 143
American Board of Commissioners for Foreign Missions. *See* Missionaries
American Colonization Society, 93–94
American Revolution, 11, 29
Appalachees, 26
Arbuckle, Matthew, 73
Arkansas: Cherokees in, 48, 61, 72–73, 98, 106, 153 n.32; pressures Cherokee Nation to secede, 126; slaves purchased in, 72, 109; stolen slaves sold in, 77. *See also* Old Settlers
Arkansas River, 83, 102, 104
Arthur, Gabriel, 20
Ashanti, 44–45
Atsi nahsa'i: as anomalies, 17; as deviants, 17–18; labor of, 13–15
Attakullakulla, 34
Attitudes: of Cherokees toward blacks, 48–49; of Cherokees regarding slavery, 90–95; of Europeans toward Africans, 46–47, 148–49 n.29; of Europeans toward Indians, 5, 46–47, 148–49 n.29, 155–56 n.34. *See also* Ethnocentrism; Race
Ayllón, Lucas Vázquez de, 36

Baldridge, Green Fox, 59
Ball game, 113, 169 n.39
Ballard, Elizabeth, 161 n.6
Baptist. *See* Missionaries
Barnwell, Colonel John, 28–29
Bartram, William, 14, 51
Battiest, Jane (slave), 114
Bean, Mrs. William, 11
Bell, James M., 140, 143
Bell, John A., 74
Benge, Chief, 38–39
Benin, 43

Benn, Samuel, 41–42
Betsy (free black), 85
Bibb, Henry (slave), 81, 99, 113
Black Dog, 12
Black Fox, 62
Blount, William, 48
Bonnefoy, Antoine, 8–9, 34, 37
Boudinot, Elias: assassinated, 73; delivers address, 54–55; signs removal treaty, 66–67
Boudinot, Elias Cornelius, 142
Bowl, Chief, 38
Brainerd Mission, 88, 108
Brickell, John, 22, 37
Brown, David, 92–93
Bull Run, Battle of, 131
Butler, Elizur, 67, 120
Butler, George, 123, 130
Butrick, Daniel, 98, 108

Cabin Creek, Battle of, 139
California: controversy over Statehood of, 119; as destination of fugitive slaves, 80–81
Campbell, Archibald, 76
Campbell, Colonel Arthur, 39
Camp metings, 112–13
Canaan (Moravian Mission), 124
Capital, investment of, 60, 71–72
Captives: adoption of, 8–9, 11–12; blacks held as, 37–38; bounties for, 25; as diplomatic tools, 7; impurity of, 5; ownership of, 34; release of, 7, 11; return of, 6, 29; sale of, 8, 25–26, 30, 55; seizure of, 4–5; treatment of, 5–9, 12. *See also Atsi nahsa'i*; European captives; Indian slaves
Catawbas, 25, 29
Census of 1835, 56, 58–60, 85
Cesar, 29, 34
Chamberlain, William, 93–94
Charite Hagey, 34
Charleston, as base for traders, 20, 23, 26, 29
Cherokee, aboriginal: belief system, xii, 16–17, 42, 61–62, 75, 143–44, 148 n.28; economy, 12–15, 32–33, 35; kinship, 9, 11–12, 16–18, 51; myths, 5–6, 16–17, 42, 52; political organization, 13–14, 17–18, 31–32, 55–56; towns, 21, 32. *See also* Agriculture; *Atsi nahsa'i*; Captives; Chiefs; Scalping; Torture; Warfare; Warriors; Women, Cherokee
Cherokee Advocate: articles concerning slavery in, 83–84, 87–88, 90–95; on the Civil War, 119; crimes reported in, 74–79; office of, ransacked, 136; supports missionaries, 122. *See also* Fugitive slaves
Cherokee Female Seminary, 167 n.12
Cherokee language, 60, 82, 159 n.32, 163 n.28
Cherokee Nation: Constitution of (1827), 48, 56, 84, 156–57 n.2; Constitution of (1839), 73, 84; council of, 51, 56, 62, 84–85, 97, 127, 129, 137–38, 167 n.12; dissolution of, 143; factionalism in, 66–69, 72–74, 119, 129–31, 141, 143–44, 171–72 n.21; laws of, 48, 51–52, 55–58, 62, 73, 104–105, 137–38. *See also* Free blacks; Slave code
Cherokee neutral lands, 126, 142, 171 n.13
Cherokee Phoenix, 58; articles regarding slavery in, 90–95. *See also* Fugitive slaves
Cherokee War, 29, 34, 41–42
Chestowe (Yuchi town), 23–24
Chickamaugans, 38–39
Chickasaws, 20, 29; Confederates seek refuge with, 138; slavery among, 72
Chicken, George, 6, 41
Chiefs, Cherokee, 3, 30–32, 55–56

Choctaws, 20; Confederates seek refuge with, 138; slavery among, 72
Churches, 112–13
"Civilization": European beliefs about, 46–47, 156 n.35; U.S. program for, of Indians, 50–51, 53–54, 60–61, 159 n.31
Civil War (U.S.), 109, 125, 131–39
Clans. *See* Cherokee, aboriginal: kinship
Class structure in Cherokee society, 32–35, 70–72, 96–97, 129, 144–45
Cofitachequi, Lady of, 3, 36
Colonization: of the Americas by Europeans, xi–xiv; of blacks in Africa, 92–94. *See also* American Colonization Society; France; Great Britain; Liberia; Moore, Abraham; Spain
The Colonizer and the Colonized (Albert Memmi), xiii
Color. *See* Race
Compact of 1802, 60–62, 66
Confederate States of America, 126, 128, 137. *See also* Civil War (U.S.); Hubbard, David; McCulloch, Benjamin; Pike, Albert
Congarees (trading factory), 21
Congarees (tribe), 29
Conjuror. *See* Charite Hagey
Conspiracies, between Indians and blacks, 40–41
Coody, William Shorey, 92, 100, 108, 110
Cooper, Douglas, 134–35
Cotton, 54, 97, 99, 100–101, 161 n.6
Cotton gins, 99, 101
Cowee, 21
Creeks, 7, 29; Confederates seek refuge with, 138; flee to Kansas, 134; slavery among, 72, 79, 162 n.19; in War of 1812, 62
Crime: in aboriginal Cherokee society, 33–34; in Cherokee Nation, 74–78
Cuming, Sir Alexander, 20, 32

Dahomey, 45
Dawes Commission, 143
Dearborn, Henry, 61
Deerskins, 15, 20, 53, 55. *See also* Trade
Demere, Raymond, 7–8, 34
De Soto, Hernando, 3, 33, 36
Doherty, Cornelius, 41–42
Dole, W.P., 134
Drew, John, 82–83, 109, 127–28, 131, 134
Dwight Mission, 89, 108

Eastern Cherokees after removal. *See* Qualla Cherokees
Ellsworth, J.C., 111
England. *See* Great Britain
English language, 60, 106–107
Enslavement: of Africans by Africans, 43–44; of Africans by Europeans, xi, 36–37; of Indians by Europeans, xi, 3, 25–26, 28, 36–37. *See also* Captives; Slavery, defense of; Slave trade
Equiano, Olaudah, 43–45
Ethnocentrism: of Europeans, 3–5, 32; of historians, 146–47 n.1
Euchee. *See* Yuchis
European captives, 7, 8–9, 11, 29–30, 34
European rivalries, 7–8, 20, 25, 29–30, 34, 55. *See also* Great Britain; France; Spain
Evarts, Jeremiah, 88

Ferries, 59–60, 97–98
Five Counties Movement. *See* Original Cherokee Community Organization
Fort Gibson, 73, 83, 102, 162 n.19

Fort Loudoun, 7–8, 34, 42
Fort Prince George, 42
Fort Smith, 141
Foster, Tom, 105
France, xi, 7–8, 20
Free blacks: assaults on, 74–75; colonization of, 94; kidnapping of, 72, 76–78; laws governing, 48–49, 84–85, 87; in removal, 71
Freedmen, 142–43, 173 n.6
French and Indian War, 11, 31
French John, 7, 34
Fugitive slaves, 37–38, 78–82; advertisements for, 79–80, 82, 99; aid to, 80, 91; Cherokee capture of, 39–40, 153 n.10; crimes of, 82; rewards for, 79–80

Georgia: in the Indian trade, 41; and removal, 60–67; slave code of, 89; slaves purchased in, 72
Georgia Guard, 64, 65, 89
Glen, James, 31
Grain, 33, 54–56, 60, 97, 99–102, 125, 161 n.6
Grant, James, 41
Great Britain, xi, xii, 7, 20, 35
Green Corn Ceremony, 13, 113, 169 n.40
Gregg, Josiah, 72, 104
Grover, Hanna, 80–81
Groves, Tom, 106
Guales, 26
Guerrin, Mat, 76–77

Hastings, Theophilus, 26, 28
Hatton, William, 41
Hawkins, Benjamin, 53–54
Henderson, Henry (slave), 161 n.6
Henderson Purchase. *See* Transylvania Company
Henderson roll. *See* Census of 1835
Hendrix, Annie Eliza, 171–72 n.21
Hicks, George, 71
Hicks, Hannah, 136, 172 n.32
Hitchcock, Ethan Allen, 101–102
Honey Springs, Battle of, 139
Horse racing, 113
Horseshoe Bend, Battle of, 62
Hubbard, David, 126
Hughes, Mary, 11
Hunting, 15, 52–53, 61
Hunting grounds, 33, 53

Illinois River, 102
Indian policy. *See* United States, Indian policy of
Indian Removal Act, 63
Indian slaves, 152 n.2, 3; emancipation of, 28–29, 47; export of, 26, 28–29; importation of, forbidden, 37; sale of, 20, 29; treatment of, 28. *See also* Captives
Inlow, Philip, 71
Intermarriage. *See* Marriage; Miscegenation
Irving, Washington, 106–107

Jackson, Andrew, 62, 159–60 n.35
Jefferson, Thomas: and race, 47; and removal, 60–61
Johnson, Andrew, 141
Johnson, Ben, 115, 117–18, 139
Johnson, Ned, 85
Jones, Cadwallader, 20–21
Jones, Evan, 65, 123–25, 134
Jones, John, 123–25

Kah-lan-to-li-ka, 78
"Kana'ti and Selu: The Origin of Game and Corn" (James Mooney), 52
Kannady, J.R., 127
Kansas: fugitive slaves in, 81, 139; strike in, 124; Unionists flee to, 134–35, 137
Keeler, William, 144
Keetowahs, 123, 125, 130–31, 135–36, 139–40
Keowee, 21, 40

Kinship. *See* Cherokee, aboriginal
Knights of the Golden Circle. *See* Southern Rights Party

Labor: demand for, xi, 13, 18, 19, 35, 50, 71–72; division of, 15, 52–53
Land cession, 53. *See also* Treaty
Landrum, Benjamin Franklin, 89
Latrobe, Charles Joseph, 106–107
Lawson, John, 11, 13–14, 16, 31–32
Liberia, 93–94, 110
Lighthorse Guard, 56
Literacy, 60. *See also* Cherokee language; English language
Little Carpenter. *See* Attakullakulla
Little Turkey, 48
Livestock, 54–55, 71, 87, 97–99, 101, 114, 125
Livingston, Elizabeth, 39
Livingston, Susanna, 39
London, Cherokee visit, 20
Long, Alexander, 23, 25
Long, Stephen H., 106
Lonian, Moses (slave), 115
Lowery, John, 113–14
"Lucy Walker," 103
Lumpkin, Wilson, 66–67
Lyttleton, Henry, 8

McCulloch, Benjamin, 127, 131, 134, 172 n.26
McIntosh, Johnson, 77
McNair, Chaney (slave), 89, 111–12, 117
Mankiller, 7–8
Marriage: aboriginal Cherokee, 9, 11, 148 n.16, 157 n.6; between Indians and blacks, 36, 57–58, 76, 84–85, 98; between Indians and whites, 11, 50–51, 60. *See also* Miscegenation
Marshall, John, 63
Mays, Samuel, 59
Meigs, Return J., 56, 61
Meigs, R.R., 107
Memmi, Albert, xiii
Menzies, David, 9, 38
Methodists. *See* Missionaries
Mills, 54, 59–60, 105
Miscegenation, 57–58, 84–85, 114, 161 n.6
Missionaries, 85; American Board of Commissioners for Foreign Missions, 63, 88–89, 93, 98, 108, 111, 120–22; Baptist, 65, 123–24; Colonization Society organized by, 93; emancipation of slaves by, 120; flee to Kansas, 125; employ slaves, 98–99, 108, 120, 170 n.4; imprisonment of, 63, 66; instruction of blacks by, 88–89; Methodist, 122–23; Moravian, 98–99, 124; oppose removal, 68; oppose slavery, 91, 111, 119–25; slaves used as translators by, 106. *See also* Butler, Elizur; Butrick, Daniel; Chamberlain, William; Ellsworth, J.C.; Evarts, Jeremiah; Jones, Evan; Jones, John; Sawyer, Sophia; Torrey, Charles Cutler
Mississippi River, 83, 97
Mooney, James, 5, 52
Moore, Abraham, and family (free blacks), 89, 94, 110
Moore, James, 25
Moravians. *See* Missionaries
Moytoy, 32

Nannie (free black), 76–77
National Party, 66, 69, 72, 78, 129
Nave, Andrew, 109
Needham, James, 20
Newton, Ebenezer, 106, 156 n.35
North Carolina: fear of red-black conspiracies in, 40; in the Cherokee War, 25
North Carolina Cherokees. *See* Qualla Cherokees

Ohio River, 83, 103–104
Old Hop, 7–8, 34
Old Settlers, 72–74, 104–105, 164 n.34
Opothleyohola (Creek), 134
Original Cherokee Community Organization, 143–44
Overseers, 97, 99–100, 102

Pacification. *See* Warfare, termination of
Pack, Elizabeth, 76
Pardo, Juan, 36
Park Hill, 80, 102, 124, 137
Partridge, 34
Paschal, George, 66
Paschal, Sarah (née Ridge), 110
Payne, John Howard, 64–65
Pegg, Thomas, 137, 139
Phillips, Martha (slave), 80
Pike, Albert, 126, 128, 131
Pins. *See* Keetowahs
Pollock, Thomas, 26
Proclamation of 1763, 35
Property: descent of, 13, 50–51, 156–57 n.2; protection of, 51, 55–56; seizure of, by Georgians, 63–65. *See also* Slaves, black, property owned by
Property, chattel: disposal of, 13; interment of, with dead, 13; ownership of, 34; removal of, 70–71
Property, real: ownership of, 9, 11, 14, 33, 51–52, 55, 71–72, 156–57 n.2
Property, slaves as, 58

Qualla Cherokees, 106
Quanasse, 21–22
Queen Anne's War, 20

Race, 36–37, 46–49
Railroads, 141–42
Ratcliff, Dick, 111, 114
Rector, Henry M., 126, 128
Red River, 138–39
Removal: Cherokee opposition to, 61–62; of 1808–1810, 61–62; of 1817–1819, 61; Jackson advocates, 62; proposed, 60–61; psychological impact of, 75–76, 78–79; white opposition to, 67–68. *See also* Treaty, of New Echota
Richardson, Chaney (slave), 111, 114, 117, 135
Ridge, John: assassination of, 73; estate of, 59; reaction of, to *Worcester* v. *Georgia,* 63; signs removal treaty, 66–67
Ridge, Major: assassination of, 73; signs removal treaty, 66–67; slaves of, 107
Roach, Emma Price, 172 n.32
Robertson, Betty, 83, 111, 163 n.28
Robertson, William S., 122–23
Robinson, Ella Coody, 100, 114
Ross, John, 51–52; authority of, restored, 139; captured by federal troops, 137; estate of, 59; imprisonment of, 64–65; marriage of, 172 n.31; opposes division of the Nation, 141; opposes removal, 63–68; opposes Watie, 134; removal of, 71; slaves of, 71, 99–100; steamboat of, 104; unifies Nation, 72–73; urges neutrality in Civil War, 126–29
Ross, Lewis, 72, 83, 96–97, 102, 105, 115
Ross, Dr. R.D., 81
Ross, William P., 75
Runaway slaves. *See* Fugitive slaves

Salina, 102
Salines, 104–105
Savannahs, 25, 29. *See also* Shawnees
Savannah Town, 21
Sawyer, Sophia, 89
Scales, Joseph, 116–18
Scalping, 4–5, 74

Seminoles, slavery among, 72, 79, 81–82, 162 n.19
Seven Years' War. *See* French and Indian War
Sexual roles. *See* Women, Cherokee
Sharp, John, 41
Shawnees, 12. *See also* Savannahs
Sheppard, Joe, 100, 109, 115
Sheppard, Morris, 100–101, 108–10, 114, 116–17, 135–36, 138
Shoe Boots, 84–85
Slave code, 57–58, 84–89, 164 n.34
Slaveholders: as church members, 120, 123; estates of, 58–59, 96–98, 100–102, 158 n.27; literacy of, 60; number of, 57, 158 n.25; participation in government by, 56–57, 59–60; removal of, 70–71; wealth of, 58–60
Slave patrol, 57, 87–88
Slave revolts, 36–37, 57, 82–83, 163–64 n.30
Slavery, defense of, 91–92, 165 n.50
Slaves, black: children of, 84–85, 114–16; clothing of, 117; during Civil War, 138–39; emancipation of, 67, 85, 91, 111, 138; families of, 80, 82, 110–14, 168 n.32; food of, 115–16; hiring of, 107–108, 139; houses of, 116; instruction of, 88–89, 98; join Union army, 139; labor of, 71–72, 97–98, 100–103, 105–107, 114–15, 117; legal status of, xii; marriage among, 98; medical treatment by, 106; medical treatment of, 116–17; names of, 111–12; number of, 166 n.2; old age of, 115; as overseers, 100; passes required of, 87, 112, 114; permitted to find their own masters, 110; prices of, 37, 107, 152 n.5; property owned by, 57, 87, 98; punishment of, 81, 98–100, 117–18; purchase freedom, 110; removal of, 70–71; resistance by, 80–81; sale of, 58, 72, 81, 108–12, 168–69 n.33; theft by, 87, 115–16; theft of, 38–39, 65, 72, 74, 76, 162 n.14, 162 n.18; as translators, 106–107. *See also* Enslavement; Fugitive slaves; Slave code; Slave revolts; Slave trade
Slaves, Indian. *See* Indian slaves
Slave trade: on the frontier, 38; in Indian Territory, 72, 77–78, 109–10; international, 90–91, 155 n.30, 165 n.47; in West Africa, 45–46
Slave Woman, 7
Smith, Archilla, 74
Smith, Richard, 40
Snelgrave, William, 44–45
South Carolina: fear of red-black conspiracy in, 40; in the Indian trade, 19–23, 25, 41; population of (1708), 28; population of (1750), 153 n.15; theft of slaves in, 38; uses black militiamen, 41
Southern Rights Party, 129–30
Spain, xi, 3, 20, 25, 34, 36
Spinning, 54, 101, 114
Spotswood, Alexander, 40
Springplace: old, 98–99; new, 124
Starr, Creek, 76
Starr, James, 74–75, 77
Starr, Tom, 74
Starr gang, 74, 77. *See also* Guerrin, Mat; Starr, Creek; Starr, James; Starr, Tom
Steamboats, 70, 83, 102–104, 167 n.15
Stephens, John, 29
Stono War, 25
Stuart, John, 34, 40

Ta-Ke-e-tuh, 48
Tahlequah, 81, 137
Takattokah council (1839), 73
Tanneries, 105
Taverns, 97

Taylor, Richard, 89, 111
Te-Kah-se-na-ky, 71
Tellico, 21–22
Tennessee, slave trade in, 72, 109
Tennessee River, 97
Terrapin, 54
Texas: Confederates flee to, 138; stolen slaves sold in, 77
Timberlake, Henry, 4, 11, 30–31
Torrey, Charles Cutler, 80, 108, 124–25, 170 n.4
Torture, 5, 11, 31
Trade, 96; regulation of, 21–23, 25–26, 28, 41–42, 153–54 n.17. *See also* Captives; Deerskins; Enslavement; Slave trade; Trade goods; Traders
Trade goods, 21–22, 30, 34; Cherokee dependence on, 22–23, 26, 31
Traders: conduct of, 33; incite warfare, 23, 25; location and licensing of, 21; purchase captives, 26, 28; slaves of, 41–42; wealth of, 33
Transylvania Company, 53
Treaty: with the British (1730), 20, 39; at the conclusion of the Cherokee War (1760), 29; with the Confederacy, 131, 134, 137–38; of New Echota, 66, 73, 78; obligations of the United States under, 126–28; for removal of Arkansas Cherokees (1828), 73; with the United States (1866), 142–43. *See also* Land cession
Treaty Party, 66–67, 70, 72–74, 78
Tugaloo, 21
Tunesee, 21–22
Tuscaroras, 4, 26, 28

Uktena, 16–17, 42
United States: Cherokee support for, in Civil War, 134–35, 137–38; Indian policy of, 50, 53–54, 60–63, 159–60 n.35; invades Indian Territory, 136–38. *See also* "Civilization"; Civil War (U.S.); Removal
United States Congress, 65
United States Supreme Court, 63

Vann, Avery, 105
Vann, David, 59, 77
Vann, Gilbert, 111
Vann, James (d. 1809), 97–99
Vann, Joseph (d. 1844): boats of, 83, 102–103; estate of, 58, 97–98; removal of, 70; slaves of, 58, 70, 82–83
Vann, Joseph (Assistant Principal Chief): edits *Advocate,* 99; favors neutrality in the Civil War, 127–28
Vann, R.P., 103
Vann, Sam, 112
Vaught, Catherine, 51–52
Vaught, James, 51–52
"Victoria," 104
Virginia: in the Indian trade, 20; fear of red-black conspiracies in, 40; theft of slaves in, 39

Walker, Agnes, 85
Ward, Nancy, 11
Warfare: Cherokees as victims of, 29; frequency of, 4; increase in, 23; motivation for, 4, 23, 25–26, 29–31; preparation for, 6; return from, 5, 7; termination of, 46, 50, 53. *See also* Captives; Chiefs, War party; Warriors
War of 1812, 62
War party, 6, 30–31
Warriors: own captives, 8, 30, 34; political power of, 31–33, 55–56; purity of, 6; torture of, 5
War Women, 11, 156–57 n.2
Washburn, Cephas, 48, 156 n.37
Washington, George, 53–54
Waters, George M., 58–59 n.97

Watie, 59
Watie, Sarah, 75
Watie, Stand: in the Civil War, 129–31, 134, 137, 139–42; during removal, 66–67, 74, 119; slaves of, 108
Watts, Elizabeth, 130–31
Weaving, 101
Webbers Falls, 102, 130
Wellborn, Isaac, 51–52
Western Cherokee. *See* Old Settlers
Westoes, 25
Whitemire, Johnson, 76
Wiggen, Eleazer, 23, 25
Wills Valley African Benevolent Society, 93–94
Wilson, Sarah (slave), 85, 101, 111, 114–18, 131, 139
Women, Cherokee, 50–53; adopt captives, 9, 11; economic role of, 9, 11, 14, 52–54; rights of, 3, 51–52, 156 n.1, 156–57 n.2, 157 n.3; torture by, 5; treatment of, when captured, 6–7. *See also* War Women
Woodward, Dr. Henry, 20
Woodward, Thomas, 71
Woolenwaugh, 8
Worcester, Samuel Austin, 63, 98, 120, 123–25, 170 n.4
Worcester v. *Georgia,* 63
Works Project Administration, 80. *See also* Ballard, Elizabeth; Battiest, Jane; Foster, Tom; Grover, Hanna; Henderson, Henry; Hendrix, Annie Eliza; Lonian, Moses; McNair, Chaney; Meigs, R.R.; Phillips, Martha; Richardson, Chaney; Robertson, Betty; Robinson, Ella Coody; Roach, Emma Price; Scales, Joseph; Sheppard, Morris; Vann, Gilbert; Vann, R.P.; Vann, Sam; Walker, Agnes; Watts, Elizabeth; Wilson, Sarah

Xuala, 36

Yamassee War, 30, 37
Yonaguska, 106
Yuchis, 23, 26

Slavery and the Evolution of Cherokee Society, 1540–1866 has been composed on the Compugraphic phototypesetter in 11-point Garamond with 1-point spacing between the lines. The display type is Garamond as well. The book was designed by Jim Billingsley, typeset by Metricomp, Inc., printed offset by Thomson-Shore, Inc., and bound by John H. Dekker & Sons.

THE UNIVERSITY OF TENNESSEE PRESS : KNOXVILLE